We live in a culture of immediacy which ... pace of Google rather than a garden. Th[e] ... takes time, patience, relationships, forgiveness, and fellow gardeners. If you're looking for this book to give you all the answers, the author quickly reveals that ministry is never that simple. However, if you need encouragement from a friend who is also tilling the soil, planting seeds, weeding, and finding joy in the simple harvest, enjoy reading as Reverend Schmidtke points you to Christ who has always been in the gardening business and has asked you to grab a shovel and dig in.

Sarah Salzberg, M.Th.
Theology Teacher, Orange Lutheran High School
Speaker, *WordDelivered.com*

Pastor John Schmidtke brings hope in abundance for Christian workers and leaders in urban ministry. He gives us the blessing of a narrative theology of the God who cares, who heals, and who empowers, chapter by chapter. The result is not only a sense of what God has done in St. Louis, but also what God does wherever the seed of His Word is planted with love. Pastor Schmidtke's wisdom and discernment, hard-won on the streets, resonate with me and will do so with any who want to take up their cross and follow Jesus in the city!

Rev. Dr. David H. Benke, Pastor
St. Peter's Evangelical Lutheran Church
Brooklyn, New York

Commitment, faithfulness, perseverance, empowerment, and trust in the God who loves all people with an everlasting love. These are the "facts of faith" you'll find in this book. If you want to read a book about how God changes lives, as well as a book on urban ministry from the ground up, this book is for you. At times in urban ministry, one is faced with the truth that "all you've got is Jesus." When you read this book from Pastor John Schmidtke, you'll realize why "He's all you need."

Rev. Dr. Gregory P. Seltz
Executive Director, Lutheran Center for Religious Liberty, Washington D.C.
Speaker Emeritus, *The Lutheran Hour*

This is not a narrow focus or only for ministry in unsafe, low-income, broken neighborhoods. John Schmidtke shows how the raw stuff of brutal city life can be met with Jesus' love in a welcoming congregation. Where do you live? Some socio-economic situations make it easier to hide raw emotions, but they're there. This book offers countless insights for ministry wherever God has placed you.

Dr. Dale Meyer, President
Concordia Seminary
St. Louis, Missouri

For decades, John Schmidtke has been a pastor in one of the most forgotten places in St Louis. What you hold in your hands is not academic research or a consultant's strategy. These essays are what happens when a prophet goes to Nineveh, and God gets glory in the city.

Rev. Jeff Cloeter, Senior Pastor
Christ Memorial Lutheran Church, St. Louis, Missouri
Author of *Loved & Sent*

A wise person once said, "If you want to go fast, walk alone. If you want to go far, walk together." John Schmidtke has walked far—together with the Lord's people in the city through three decades—and is still walking. Let this book be a traveling companion for your journey in ministry. John's words are a cup of cool water. Take them slowly, a sip or two a day. They will take you far.

Rev. Dr. Michael Zeigler
Speaker, *The Lutheran Hour*, Lutheran Hour Ministries

Pastor John Schmidtke is a theologian's theologian, a preacher's preacher, and a pastor's pastor. He is unique in our Lutheran context because he is also a practitioner. We served together in Saint Louis as pastors fresh out of the seminary experience. I can remember sitting in his office, as he was surrounded by homiletic materials, seeking a way to speak the truth in love to an aging, established Lutheran community located in a volatile and changing bi-racial, multiethnic context. Now 30-plus years later, Pastor has blessed us with the fruit of his sacrifice, service, learning, and most important, his experience. What you hold in your hands is a love letter that originates in the heart of God and has been formed through John over many years. What you hold in your hands is a clear testimony to how love for God unites people in service, despite socio-economic and ethnic obstacles. What you hold in your hands is a service manual and ministry guide that will support young ministers, and guide tenured ones, in their formation. What you hold in your hands is a strategy for ministry expansion through educating and empowering the people of God. What you hold in your hands is a gift from John's heart to be read, marked, and inwardly digested multiple times. It will not disappoint and will lead the reader to a level of introspection and self-revelation that will help the shepherd be a blessing to all those being led.

Dr. Victor Belton
Mission Facilitator, Florida Georgia District, LCMS

Pastor Schmidtke's heart-touching stories offer wisdom and practical lessons from a lifetime of frontline, multi-cultural ministry. Need inspiration and knowledge to embolden your work in Christian urban ministry? Look no further. As you walk through Pastor John's joys and struggles, you will be well equipped to serve others with a humble and loving heart.

Dr. Susan Hewitt, Ed.D.
Advisor for Christian Organizational Leadership

A PLACE
NOT
FORGOTTEN

Inspiration and Encouragement
for Those Who Care about the City

JOHN R. SCHMIDTKE

TENTH
POWER

TENTHPOWERPUBLISHING

www.tenthpowerpublishing.com

Design by Inkwell Creative

Softcover ISBN: 978-1-938840-35-7
e-book ISBN: 978-1-938840-36-4

10 9 8 7 6 5 4 3 2 1

With gratitude to the Lord for the gifts He has given me.

With honor to my wife, Sharon, for her unending love for me.

FIGHT FOR ME

FIGHT FOR ME BEFORE
My life really gets going
And foolish unGodly patterns in me start showing.

FIGHT FOR ME BEFORE
I've closed my ears or my mind
To wisdom that others' experiences could help me to find.

FIGHT FOR ME BEFORE
While I am a branch that is still tender
Movable, Correctable, with RIGHT things to remember.

FIGHT FOR ME BEFORE,
I have much worldly exposure
And it's powerful controlling voices try to take me over.

FIGHT FOR ME BEFORE!

FIGHT FOR ME BEFORE
By spending time with me
Investing in me a vision of who GOD wants me to be.

FIGHT FOR ME BEFORE
You introduce me to the Savior Jesus, who loves me and died for me,
You show me how to come to our Heavenly Father who will be there for me,
You bring me to the Holy Spirit who promises to fill me and comes to calm me.

FIGHT FOR ME BEFORE
This world tries to show me who to be,
You make clear to me my true identity
That I'm a child of Him who gave His Son for me, at Calvary,
Promises never to leave me
Ever since the powerful water was poured upon me!

FIGHT FOR ME BEFORE
Self-centeredness starts to live,
Show me how to love, how to serve, and how to forgive!

FIGHT FOR ME BEFORE
Tutor me in how to pray
Show me how to start each day the right way
With hearing from the Lord who will never lead me astray
Put your life with God on display
That I may see
How opening God's Word is what every person needs.

FIGHT FOR ME BEFORE

FIGHT FOR ME BEFORE
I go to school
By pouring into me
My A,B,C's   My 1,2,3's   My do-re-mi's   and respect for authority
Don't put me behind because you didn't spend the time to begin developing
my mind!

FIGHT FOR ME BEFORE

FIGHT FOR ME BEFORE
I go to my first job
Teach me how to be honest, to work hard, and receive criticism without
"going off!"

FIGHT FOR ME BEFORE
I start to live thinking everything's owed to me,
Show me a content and grateful spirit trusting the Lord to bless me.

FIGHT FOR ME BEFORE

FIGHT FOR ME BEFORE
Focus me to search for solutions
And not just scream about what's wrong.
Expose me to how talk is fine, but action is better,
What we DO with our life is the real measure,
Of being what the Lord wants us to be,
His Hands, His Voice, His LOVE, for others to see, through you and me.

FIGHT FOR ME BEFORE

FIGHT FOR ME BEFORE
I grow up and I have a family
So that through me,
God's love may again be duplicated accurately.

FIGHT FOR ME BEFORE

by John R. Schmidtke
2020

ACKNOWLEDGMENTS

Throughout this book, I have referred to many individuals who made an important mark on my life. I want to also give thanks to God for a few others.

First, I thank the Lord for three men who have been pastors to me on my journey:

Rev. Quentin Poulson, "my Bishop," for your listening ear, wise counsel, incredible wit, and timely encouragement.

Rev. Gerard Bolling, my partner in ministry at Bethlehem, for your support and refreshing visions of ministry, especially to young adults. Pastor Bolling is the most gifted young pastor I have *ever* known.

Dr. David Schmidtke, though not ordained, you have been a pastor to me in so many ways and for such a long time. You always cheered me on to not quit and to get up when I have fallen down.

I also want to say thanks...

To my other two brothers, Dr. James Schmidtke and Mr. Thomas Schmidtke, who for years have given me their listening ear and support and have looked after my personal financial affairs and the investment affairs of our ministry with great expertise and loving dedication.

To my creative musical sister, Annette Silver-Betts, part of our family who has been by our side in this ministry, working with us and encouraging us for decades.

To my musical brothers, Daryl Lester and Dywanne "P. Kee" Harris. I am grateful for how the Holy Spirit has knit our minds and hearts together in creativity for the sake of bringing the name of the Savior to more and more people.

To my "ATL" spiritual sister and listening ear, Yolanda Spivey, you are a blessing to me and my family.

To the incredible group of pastor "brothers" of our Bethlehem sister churches—without your continual support, this story would not be such a magnification of the greatness of our God.

To Rev. Jeff Cloeter, who has pushed me for years to write this book. He is one of the great pastoral leaders of our church body today and an incredible friend and colleague!

To Dr. Tony Evans and The Urban Alternative ministry—through the many years of your Church Development Conferences, your ministry gave our church a pattern to dynamically bring the Word of God to people in the inner-city. The imprint of you and your ministry is abundant on what the Lord has done in this place over the past 30 years.

To Bishop Kenneth Ulmer, thanks for personal time to encourage me as a young pastor and for your ministry example that there are no limits on what the Lord can do.

To Mrs. Ida Odom—you are the urban ministry trailblazer who put before me the concept of growing a church through ministry with children and youth. And you showed the world how to do it from a simple parsonage backyard in Chicago's South Side.

TABLE OF CONTENTS

A LETTER OF INTRODUCTION   **19**

1. MY 30th CHRISTMAS EVE... A Night with a Lesson   **21**

2. MINISTRY IN TANGLED LIFE WEBS   **24**

3. THE "T" WORD   **27**

4. MANY POLES IN THE WATER   **31**

5. ~~WE CAN'T~~   **35**

6. THE KEY TO GREAT MINISTRY PARTNERSHIPS   **38**

7. TIME MANAGEMENT   **41**

8. GROWING SOMETHING "URBAN STYLE"   **46**

9. "GIFTED" IS NOT ENOUGH   **52**

10. THE VALUE OF "100"   **54**

11. YOU NEED A CONSISTENT DIVERSION   **57**

12. SIFTING IS NECESSARY   **59**

13. INVITING PEOPLE TO WHAT?   **61**

14. DEAR PASSIONATE PEOPLE LIKE ME...   **64**

15. THE LAZY WAY, THE INEFFECTIVE WAY, NOT JESUS' WAY   **67**

16. THERE ARE GOING TO BE SOME LOW DAYS   **72**

17. STUDYING PEOPLE or SERVING PEOPLE or BOTH   **74**

18. REMEMBER WHAT'S REALLY AT WORK   **78**

19. A STREAM OF NEW VISITORS   **81**

20. PUTTING FAMILY BACK INTO URBAN AREAS   **83**

21. A MUST FOR YOUR MINISTRY DESKTOP   **93**

22. I NEED MY WEEKLY FAMILY MEETING   **97**

23. WHEN BAR-JESUS SHOWS UP   **100**

24. A SPIRITUAL PACEMAKER   **103**

25. HOW TO EAT PRIME RIB 106

26. CAN WE "SING A NEW SONG"? 108

27. STOP & SMELL THE ROSES, ESPECIALLY NOTICE 112
JUST THE BUDS

28. A MINISTRY OF TODAY 114

29. PARTNERSHIPS ARE GOLD! 117

30. "I'M LOOKING FOR SOME ASSISTANCE" 123

31. A WORD ABOUT COMPENSATION 127

32. REACH THE CHILDREN, REACH THE FAMILY 133

33. A PLACE WHERE RECOVERY IS NOT A CLICHÉ 139

34. 10,080 144

35. DIFFICULT PEOPLE 147

36. THE VITALITY OF BIBLICAL AUTHORITY 152

37. A VARIATION ON 1 PETER 4:8 156

38. THE GROWTH PROGRESSION 158

39. PLEASE DON'T TEASE 166

40. AN ENTREPRENEURIAL SPIRIT 168

41. PRODUCING TOMORROW 179

42. IT TAKES A TEAM 182

43. THE NECESSITY OF REINVENTION 190

44. THE DECEPTION OF "ITRT" 193

45. YOU NEVER GET USED TO IT 195

46. START NEW or TRANSFORM THE OLD? 199

47. FUNDING MINISTRY 210

48. FUNDING TAKES TIME 212

49. STORYTELLING 214

50. LONGEVITY 218

51. "YOU SHOULD" follows "I AM"   **221**

52. IF YOU CAN, INVOLVE YOUR DONORS IN THE STORY   **222**

53. BE SURE TO SAY "THANK YOU"   **224**

54. KEEP WORKING TO EXPAND YOUR PRESENT
     DONOR BASE   **226**

55. KEEP GROWING IN YOUR UNDERSTANDING
     OF PEOPLE   **228**

56. GREAT, BUT COMPLEX   **230**

57. PEOPLE FIRES   **234**

58. THE JOHN 6:26–27 PEOPLE PROBLEM   **237**

59. SOLIDIFY & MAGNIFY   **239**

60. THE DOCTRINE OF CHIPS   **243**

61. ACCOUNTABILITY IS A FRIEND, NOT AN ENEMY   **246**

62. THE 3–4 THINGS   **250**

63. SHEPHERDING PEOPLE   **252**

64. WHAT YOU CAN CONTROL vs. WHAT YOU CAN'T   **258**

65. BE CAREFUL WHEN YOU WORK IN THE MUD   **260**

66. A RIDDLE ABOUT RAISING KIDS & URBAN MINISTRY   **264**

67. KEEP TRYING FOR THE WIN!   **270**

68. URBAN   **272**

69. SHARON'S YEARLY CALENDARS   **276**

70. HELP FROM ABOVE   **278**

71. TELL THE TRUTH MOMENTS   **280**

72. ENABLE ME TO REST   **284**

73. A FEW WORDS ABOUT PREACHING   **286**

74. PREACHING "BEEFS"   **295**

75. THE COURAGE TO FOCUS ON JESUS   **297**

76. PLAN... PREP... PERSEVERE   **303**

77. SOMETIMES YOU HAVE TO BE THE CHRISTIAN PARENT   **308**

78. THE OTHER SIDE OF VISION   **312**

79. THE OTHER SIDE OF VISION, Part 2: The Hard Part   **315**

80. ESPECIALLY   **320**

81. BE A FOUNTAIN, NOT A DRAIN   **324**

82. NEXT   **326**

83. WHAT'S GREAT ABOUT MINISTERING IN AN URBAN PLACE   **329**

84. CHURCH or BUSINESS, WHICH ONE IS IT?   **333**

85. RAISING UP 21ST CENTURY URBAN MINISTRY   **340**
    WORKERS—A FOLLOW UP TO "CHURCH or BUSINESS,
    WHICH ONE IS IT?"

86. THE BETHLEHEM EMPLOYMENT AGENCY   **344**

87. INJUSTICE   **348**

88. INCARNATION   **356**

89. STRONG ROCK or TRANSPARENT HUMAN? BOTH   **362**

90. MOMENTS OF AWE   **364**

91. GRATEFUL & THIRSTING   **366**

92. MVP   **369**

93. F-A-M-I-L-Y   **371**

Epilogue   **379**

Scripture Index   **381**

Topical Index   **387**

A LETTER OF INTRODUCTION

Dear Friend,

Let me admit in advance: this is a LONG BOOK. I think it became long because of what I envisioned it to be.

Is it an inspirational book? Sure, it's like that.

Is it a textbook for urban ministry? Yes, sort of like that too.

Is it a devotional book? That would also be somewhat true. I've tried to ground every essay in God's power for our lives—His Word. I don't want you to believe what I say, but what God says.

Here's what I think is the best description for the book—this is a JOURNEY BOOK. My first objective in writing it is to walk alongside someone who decides to follow the call to work in an urban ministry. That has even influenced me to write in more of an oral style where you hear my voice, rather than sounding like a didactic textbook.

I hope these essays encourage you to know that you're not on the urban path alone. I want to give you a little insight about urban ministry, challenge you to think about some things in a fresh way, and also remind you that this important work God has called you to do is THE BEST!

Even those who don't work in an urban ministry, but are familiar with an urban ministry like Bethlehem Lutheran Church, might find this collection of essays interesting and enlightening about what the journey of my life and ministry has been like at 2153 Salisbury Street in St. Louis, Missouri.

Please note: there is much Scripture in this book. That's where the power for life and ministry are found. However, I am intentionally not writing out each Scripture passage. I want to encourage you to have your Bible by your side as you read and OPEN your Bible to search the Word of God for yourself. God the Holy Spirit may show you something beyond what I have pointed to in the essays.

As a journey book, my best advice is not to read it in one sitting, but to read an essay or two a day and then chew on it.

Let God the Holy Spirit speak to you through it.

John

1

MY 30th CHRISTMAS EVE... A Night with a Lesson

You would have thought that by my 30th Christmas Eve at Bethlehem in 2018, things would have been different, but that was far from the case. Over the years, our congregation traditionally worshipped the birth of Christ on the Sunday before Christmas, not on Christmas Eve or Christmas Day. Initially, that concept was really new to me. I came from a home church tradition at Immanuel Lutheran Church in Sheboygan, Wisconsin, during the 1960s and 1970s when Christmas Eve was "the night"! The church would be packed for all the worship services. Of course, not only would the regular Sunday crowd be there, but on Christmas Eve even the "two-to-three times a year people" would come!

I'm told it was like that at Bethlehem back in its heyday. But the church I came to pastor in 1989 had dwindled down to about a dozen people who would gather for Christmas Day worship. Of course, as some would tell me back then, "No way! We would never have Christmas Eve worship. At night? It's not safe." As the years passed, however, we transitioned to a Christmas Eve worship service of about 40–50 people. It was a quiet, intimate, nice gathering—even though the Sunday before Christmas was still really THE DAY for Christmas worship at Bethlehem. The year when our adult Christmas play was cancelled on the Sunday before Christmas (because of weather) and was rescheduled for Christmas Eve, we even made it to over 120 people! I thought then maybe a new Christmas Eve tradition was developing, but the rise in attendance only lasted that one year.

By December 24, 2018, our church had grown to about 140 people in worship on Sunday mornings, and even more during the whole month of December. We had also just completed a three-day presentation of our Christmas play that drew 420 people! Still, I expected attendance at Christmas Eve worship might remain only in the mid- to low-40s. We had been such a busy church over the past five days the week prior, but I never could have imagined how small that night would turn out to be!

When the service started at 6:15 on Christmas Eve, there were eight of us gathered (and four of the eight were Schmidtke family members). I kept looking for "the crowd" to come in the door a few minutes late, but they never came. Then three other people straggled in as the service went on. None of my deacons came. None of them called to tell me they weren't going to make the service. No one even called afterward to see how the Christmas Eve service went. Only two out of 20 of our church board members showed up. Of our six part-time staff members, only one was there.

The enemy really was working on my heart and soul that night. I remember thinking, "Really? After 30 years being at the same ministry, this is it—11 people on Christmas Eve?" I grew up watching pastors leading Christmas worship with hundreds of people packing the church! But this is how things look after being at a place for 30 years? Frustrated, angry, and discouraged, I began worship. Yes, I know. I forgot who was to have our full attention this night. It wasn't my night, but His, and yet my flesh was wounded! Then, in the midst of worship and just before I got up to preach, I HEARD God's voice in the manner of our Minister of Music, Annette Silver-Betts. She sang a beautiful arrangement of "Mary Did You Know?"—a song we had never heard before at our church. She had prepared it especially for this night. God was actually using her not only to encourage those gathered, but also to strategically target me. I looked at the small group of 11 who had come to be encouraged in the Savior, especially my wife, daughter, and granddaughter (our boys were out of town at their in-laws for this Christmas). That's when I SAW God's presence among our small group celebrating His wonderful news that Christ has come.

Maybe you've faced hard moments like this in ministry. Here was the lesson I was reminded of:

You have to be in this ministry for the Lord, not for yourself, or you'll never stay in it.

An urban place is so up and down—the highest spiritual highs on one day, and the lowest spiritual lows on the next day.

Even longevity and hard work in a ministry won't make you immune from the enemy trying to pull you down into dark places of frustration where you want to quit and put the focus of your heart on yourself, not on the Lord.

So what do you do? Listen for God's voice (which I heard that Christmas Eve in Annette's song), watch for God's presence (which I saw in family and faithful friends who were there with me to worship), and cling to God's promises (which always remind me that God loves me and that it is CHRIST who is to be in the spotlight, not me and my feelings).

Do I have some work to do with our congregation to encourage them to put the worship of Christ during Christmas ahead of their cooking, their socializing, their shopping, or whatever else they were doing that night? Yes. Even church leaders need that reminder. While I work on that, instead of giving up and looking for a call to a new church (always a real temptation from the enemy in urban churches), I need to keep my heart focused on what is solid and true: God loves us and sent His Son for us. Just as Joshua said to God's people, Israel, right before he died, so it is true for you and me: "Not one word of all the good words which the Lord your God spoke concerning you has failed; all have been fulfilled for you, not one of them has failed." The Lord can be trusted! He will be faithful!

2

MINISTRY IN TANGLED LIFE WEBS

*T*iana got pregnant in high school. She dropped out by her sophomore
year. She started having babies, and now at 23, she has four kids. She has
worked on and off in fast food but has lost many jobs because of unreliable
childcare. Could her mama help with taking care of her kids? Nope, her
mama is still fighting a cocaine addiction, and her daddy has never been
part of her life. She survived on welfare checks and living with several "baby
daddys" until each of those relationships went south and dissolved.

She originally came to Bethlehem through a friend. She is excited about
the strength that the Lord has brought to her life since that first day. Her
kids got involved in church programs, and her oldest son began attending
our charter school and Bethlehem After School (BAS) program. The kids
attended programs at Bethlehem three nights each week, and church had
become their "second home." They were learning about Jesus and becoming
happy kids because of all the love they received in the BLC family. Tiana's
outlook on life also turned around in the past two-and-a-half years. She
felt as if there was hope that possibly she could make a change in her
life, one issue at a time. Among many brothers and sisters in similar life
circumstances, Tiana is the only person in her family who knows Christ
and is in church.

But now, the run-down apartment house that Tiana was staying in has
been closed down by the city. There are so many violations on the property,
and the slum landlord doesn't want to fix it and spend the little rent money
that he had been getting inconsistently from Tiana and three other families
who lived at the address. The good news is that Tiana and her kids have
found a place where they can move. The bad news is that it is on the deep
southside of St. Louis, about 30 minutes away from Bethlehem and at least
a solid hour one-way on the Bi-State Bus.

What will happen to Tiana? She wants to do right. She wants to walk with the Lord, but the distance between us and where she is now living (the only place she could find to stay), will very likely disconnect her from the Bethlehem family and all of the growth she was experiencing.

This is the common ministry picture of so many people that churches like Bethlehem minister to. Maybe you've faced something similar at your church. It's a tough situation. Honestly, some churches will ignore the "Tianas," because she and her family don't fit the demographic they're trying to reach. They're seeking to become a large ministry with great facilities and wonderful programs. Even though it's unsaid among churches located "in the hood," if the truth were told, those churches would say, "We don't want to mess with 'Tianas.' They're too much trouble... too many issues. And there won't be much return on them. She's got no tithes and offerings... she doesn't have manpower to help us in our programs. She needs more from us than she can give to us... we're struggling ourselves at our church just to keep the doors open!" In the end, the "Tianas" just drift away until the next crisis and then reach out when help is needed.

I put this in front of you NOT to lay a guilt trip on anybody, but rather to put forth a real life ministry picture of what so many people our small urban churches have before them. Many of those we deal with come with a "tangled web" of issues.

Consider Tiana's situation:

- She has lots of kids to parent.

- She is unemployed, which creates a financial issue that affects where she can live. Having kids also changes things. She can't just skip meals or stay in a place where she can "rough it" with no heat in the wintertime, etc. (Remember, if she gets government money and the government finds out that her kids are in that kind of unsafe environment, she'll get her kids taken away)

- She has no dependable transportation, which will make her connection to Bethlehem harder.

- As her connection to the Savior via Bethlehem becomes more inconsistent, it will then affect her spirit and may push her into depression and possible drug use. Sometimes people get to a place where they are so overwhelmed and say, "The heck with this—I'm going to get two hours of relief and escape."

- Because Tiana didn't finish high school, she is probably very unemployable as far as job skills.

- Tiana has such an overwhelming wealth of issues facing her at 23 that her outlook on the future is very likely "hopeless."

So what do we, as the church, do? First, let's recognize that what we do will not be simple or easy. We pray for God to lead us and show us His pathway for ministry. Honestly, I've been guilty of not beginning with enough prayer. Second, let's notice that our ministry to the "Tianas" will have similar pathways, but it will never be exactly the same, even with the "next Tiana." Different people will need different approaches—that's what our government often doesn't understand in its efforts to help people. We will continue to hold up the Good News of God's love in Jesus Christ to Tiana. Unless we can find a church that will love Tiana deeply in her new neighborhood (this is often the problem since such churches in urban areas are hard to find), we need to keep Tiana connected to the people of God at Bethlehem, even with the longer distance.

In addition, while we can't solve all of Tiana's life issues, there is a moment of opportunity to engage a larger team of sister churches to help. When a small urban church has a network of sister churches with the time and resources they lack, there is so much more help to go around. Resources, beds, furniture, sometimes babysitting help, and so on—when closely connected with worship, Bible study, and prayer at the outreach urban church—can be "gifts of the Savior's love" that the Holy Spirit can use in powerful ways. This is a labor-intensive, long term ministry journey for Tiana and her family.

Are you feeling this already? You, the pastor or individual church leader, can be a part of this work, but you can't carry the whole ministry to Tiana yourself long term! While you may have initiated the work with Tiana, you have to connect other brothers and sisters in Christ to Tiana. That's how you serve in this tangled web, as well as in all of the tangled webs you will face.

If you do not do this, you will burn yourself out, Tiana won't be effectively served, and you won't be able to be there for the 20 other "Tianas" who are also looking for help.

Here are some lessons I've learned:

- **Ministry to many in the city is a tangled web, but God hasn't called us to look away and do nothing.**
- **We can't fix every problem every person has. And God hasn't called us to do this.**
- **Our capacity to help grows when we involve others beyond ourselves and beyond our church to help the "Tianas."**
- **While the "Tianas" have so many concerns, fixing only their housing, employment, childcare, and monetary and emotional needs still doesn't stop Tiana from eternal separation from the Lord in hell. We need to help Tiana and her family stay trusting Jesus their Savior!**

3

THE "T" WORD

The "T" word that every worker in the inner-city knows about is "TRANSIENCY." We're not the only church context facing challenges with transiency among people. However, since many urban ministries usually have a small numerical base of people in their churches, new people who come, and then go, might affect our churches more than others. Just to be crystal clear about what transiency is, notice this definition from the Merriam-Webster Dictionary: "passing especially quickly into and out of existence, passing through or by a place with only a brief stay." The emphasis is on the word "passing," as opposed to "staying." That's the hard part. There is an excitement when new people come to our churches in the inner-city. Anyone who comes from another church with "developed" ministry skills creates a special joy at our church because people think, "Maybe there is a little help for the load for our ministry." When those same new people then pass through and leave, there is depression because the jobs they were doing and the help they were giving must now, again, be re-absorbed by the usually small group of people in that urban church. Sadly, during the short time that a "developed" ministry person has served in our ministries, their replacement has often neither been identified nor trained.

There is also great joy that comes to a congregation when a person attends our church who is just coming to know Christ. It's exciting for someone's life to be changed through the Gospel. In our church tradition, I spend a number of weeks taking a new Christian through the basic Christian doctrine curriculum we call "confirmation." It is a wonderful time of getting to know that person, their family, and their giftedness from the Lord! It's great to see them growing and serving in the church. That new person and their family then really get into the flow of the congregation's life.

BUT THEN... the "T" word. Stuff happens, many times stuff that is out of our control. They have to move from where they were living. Or their job shift changes to Sunday mornings or other times that keep them from participating in the life of the church. If they were recovering from some devastating addictions, often one of their "old crowd" shows up in their life and a relapse occurs for a variety of reasons. They may get pulled over in a traffic stop, and then their past trouble with the law catches up with them and they get locked up. Before you know it, that new person starts to miss worship and ministry events, their cell phone number no longer works, they can rarely be reached by knocking on their door, and shortly afterwards, they disappear completely.

The REALITY of transiency is that it is a definite component of most inner-city mission fields, and there are other realities that accompany it. Personally, it hurts. It is painful when someone you had so many hopes and dreams for as a fellow worker in the ministry leaves. It is also discouraging when you invest so much time, energy, and resources in them, and then they leave before it seems you have seen much ministry return on your investment. Yes, I know my investment into that person was an investment of the Gospel into both their spiritual life and the Kingdom at large. I know... but it is still a little frustrating.

Here's another hard reality of transiency—it often affects funding. Let me explain. Most urban small congregations cannot exist off of what comes in through the offering plate. We are constantly searching for donations and writing grant applications. Many funders are results-driven. When donors see progress and make the remark, "Last year you had 100 people in your ministry," they want to know why this year your numbers "lowered" to only 80 people. Why? It's transiency—people come, people go. Transiency is unpredictable. It does affect outside funding! Those effects often result in resource losses, which then often affect ministry potential and certainly affect the emotional health of those working in the trenches of the inner-city ministry. It is just the way it is. Transiency is a big contributing factor as to why many urban ministry and community workers themselves don't stay in inner-city contexts for the long term.

To be sure, especially in urban churches, you can see how transiency stems from outside factors beyond our control. However, at the same time, individual churches do bear some responsibility for it. **Sometimes people come and then pass through quickly because our congregations can't—or choose not to—try to meet the needs of the new people who have come.**

No church can be everything to everyone. Most inner-city small churches don't have the resources to provide the smorgasbord of ministry offerings that large suburban churches offer. But when a small urban church is self-focused and not trying to share the Gospel with its community, that is noted quickly by new people, and they are just as quickly out the door. When a small urban church allows their traditions to rule above the authority of God's Word, many new people are here today and gone tomorrow. Especially among the younger generations of new Christians today and especially in our technology age, people will quickly sense a church's unwillingness to keep the message of God's love while transmitting it in new ways that speak to new contexts of people. If young adults sense rigidness about a ministry, they WILL LEAVE. To assume as some do that they will "educate these young people into the right ways to do church," is both arrogant and ignorant thinking. Frankly, from what I've observed, you won't even have the chance to try that most of the time. Our world has too many choices regarding church and general spirituality. Those young people will be out your door!

So what do we do? First, we remember from the very birth of the Church in the Book of Acts (Acts 2) that the Church is about a message (Acts 2:38), not about a particular structure. That message of God's love in Jesus Christ never changes, but how it is communicated may change. Second, just as the book of Acts also reveals (Acts 8:1), God has planned for His Church to be on the move and always "in process" as it continues to reach people with the news of Christ crucified and raised for us.

Some years ago I went to a seminar led by Dr. John Maxwell. As best I remember from my time there, he talked about the Lord's Church being three things: a **reaching** church, an **equipping** church, and then, the third thing that really made me sort of mad—a **sending** church. When I heard that last one, I thought to myself, "No! I've only got about 60 people in my church. We can't afford to lose anybody from our ministry." Do you see my error? It was in the pronouns "my" church and "our" ministry. Of course, it's the Lord's church.

How about if I replace the word "transiency" for "sending"? In other words, maybe our real mission is for people to pass through the Lord's church at Bethlehem—and then to be sent on to other people and ministries throughout the world with the encounter of Jesus and His mission that they've received through Bethlehem. I know where some of you are, right now. You're thinking, "But how will Bethlehem have the people to operate and the gifts and resources to support ministry in Bethlehem's community?" That's God's job!

HE has always been right on top of that job in our ministry. In 1989, I came to Bethlehem as their first full-time pastor in 18 years. Bethlehem had a little money in the bank that would take care of my salary for about 17 months, and then it would run out. (If we're doing the math on the basis of earthly spending habits and income levels back then.) But now, over 30 years later, I am still here. Amazing—in a way! Yet, NOT SURPRISING at all! The LORD has been in charge of making sure that this ministry would continue.

Here's what I've learned:

- **Transiency is hard. There's no denying it. I need the Holy Spirit to fill me with deep faith to bring me through it.**
- **Some transiency in ministry might be because of how we're doing ministry. That calls for constant reflection, repentance, and God's grace to do things differently and better.**
- **Transiency is an opportunity. God brings people to our ministry to grow closer to Him and become equipped. Then, sometimes, God sends them away from Bethlehem to the places where He wants these people to minister.**
- **Even through transiency, the Lord knows what He is doing with His Church.**

4

MANY POLES IN THE WATER

What's the best way to catch fish? Some people say it is all about using the right kind of bait. That's true, but I have a different answer. The best way to catch fish is to have multiple poles in the water. I find that strategy to be true not just for fishing but also for ministry in urban, low-income places. Perhaps in your community your ministry attracts people just by mainly serving people in your Sunday morning worship ministry. But in the community where I serve, the church is not just a religious community resident but also a place where people gather socially. It is a place where parents are looking for help raising their children, and it is an important voice and force toward change for the community. As we serve in this way, yet keep our main motive as reaching people with the Savior, we've found that the best way to Biblically "catch fish" (Matthew 4:19) is to have multiple poles in the water.

There's a personal aspect of this and a congregational aspect of this kind of fishing.

On the personal side, how many people do you call on each week to specifically try to help them get to know the Savior through issuing an invitation to Sunday worship? I have observed that there is a greater chance of getting someone to come to Sunday worship in proportion to the number of calls I make to people during the week. Don't see this as my own mechanical manipulation of the Holy Spirit. I'm not saying that at all. Moving people is God's work. Yet the Holy Spirit uses people like you and me in this mission field called Earth. Why else were the disciples SENT with the Good News of the Gospel, instead of the Father in heaven just skywriting the Good News of Jesus in cloud form or sending a Divine massive text or Instagram today in our technology age? There is no substitute for pastors and people reaching people each week with the Savior *and* an invitation to worship.

Why the invitation to Sunday worship? Why make that an important goal—to get people to Sunday morning worship? I am in no way saying, "ATTENDING SUNDAY WORSHIP = SAVING FAITH IN CHRIST." There are three vehicles through which the Holy Spirit works on people that happen in the context of Sunday morning worship. First, of course, the Good News that Jesus Christ gave His life for our sins at the cross and the Good News of His resurrection are both communicated constantly in Sunday morning worship—in songs, Scriptures, prayers, a sermon, the Sacraments, confession and forgiveness, etc. The outcome of that effort is God's work, according to Romans 10:17.

Second, in Sunday morning worship people encounter God's love horizontally as well as vertically through the fellowship of God's people in their words of encouragement, their embrace, and their presence. How true it is that the Lord often speaks powerfully through a brother or sister in Christ to someone who comes to worship carrying hurts and encounters people in God's house who listen to them and point them to Christ.

There's a third vehicle through which the Holy Spirit works on people. After we give our invitation to come to church for worship, the Holy Spirit works those words into a "movement of action" in people. That is, coming to church is a matter of intentionality. We can make invitation after invitation to people about Christ. We can declare to them what a difference He makes for life both now and in life forever. While the confession of faith that the Holy Spirit leads that person to make with their mouth is great news (Romans 10:9), I think there is something even deeper about the confession that people make with their feet when they come to God's house. It takes their words and lets them live in action. As faith becomes living in actions, it deepens. There is no substitute for us being "Christ's ambassadors to people" each week as we invite them to church.

The idea that having more poles in the water is a better opportunity for catching fish also has a congregational side to it.

While we can't be everything to everybody, I think churches need to wrestle with Paul's fishing approach in 1 Corinthians 9:19–23. I find it to be very on target. Just as one size doesn't fit all, one approach doesn't fit all. At Bethlehem, for example, we use basketball as a tool to reach young men for Christ. Our music ministry is also particularly tuned to reach those for whom music is God's vehicle to bring the Good News. In the summertime, when kids are hanging out on the streets, that's where we go with our Taking Jesus to the Streets ministry. The families in our neighborhood don't have a lot of good, wholesome, family-friendly activities. They don't have a lot of money. So in the summer we also host free carnivals where families can have fun and get free stuff—as we share the Gospel with them.

Parents also need childcare for their kids in the summer when school is out. We have another outreach approach where we raise funds to provide a free summer day camp so that we can make connections and share Christ. During the schoolyear, we offer a free, two-and-a-half hour afterschool Christian program for the children in the charter school that operates in our ministry building to provide parents with supervised childcare before they get off work. There is also a free children's Musical Theatre Camp that we operate every June for the sake of building relationships in Christ. You've got the idea. I know it might even sound exhausting, but this strategy has worked— having "many poles in the water" brings more opportunities for us to have conversations with people to talk about our Savior!

Somebody is thinking, "How do you afford all of that as a small church?" The answer is partnerships—partnerships with other churches and visionary Christians outside of our church! I'll write about partnerships and funding in other essays. But for now, hear this—I rarely have trouble finding partners, even financial supporters, to help us when we are passionate about a new way of sharing Christ with *new* people *outside* of our ministry.

Here are some lessons learned:

- **Of course, a ministry can try to do too many things and end up doing nothing well. But maybe it's time to think about "stretching" a little more beyond what we currently are doing.**
- **Of course, anybody who comes to faith is the result of the work of the Holy Spirit. Yet, God uses people to do His work. We've seen this strategy work with people, just like it works with fish. Having "more poles in the water" brings more opportunities for catching fish.**

5

~~WE CAN'T~~

Those two words, "We Can't," needlessly stop too many urban ministries and stop too many of us who work in them. WE CAN'T because we don't have the facilities to do ministry—like a gym, or a stage, or a useful sanctuary, or a good gathering space. WE CAN'T because we don't have the stuff that we need to do ministry—like a good sound system, instruments, gym equipment, etc. WE CAN'T because we don't have the people for ministry—singers with great voices, a musician, people who can do a dance ministry or drama ministry, volunteers to run an outreach program, coaches, young adults, etc. (We don't have 20 people for every job in the church; instead, we have 20 jobs for every person in our church!) Most of all, WE CAN'T because we don't have the money (enough said).

Just as Jesus taught the disciples when planning to feed 5,000 families, "Bring what you have (the two fish and five loaves) to Me." And we remember from John 6 that the Lord did the rest, so the lesson is a vital one:

You can't stay focused on the people or things you don't have. You need to pour yourself into the people you do have and, by their recruitment and reach, trust God to bring forth new leaders for the future.

People. Pour yourself into the people you do have. Are there one or two people in your church who will help you once a week? That's the way our first weekly outreach program at Bethlehem started. Today we call it "BBO" (Bethlehem Bible Outreach), but when we began, it was simply called, "Wednesday Program." Every Wednesday, two consistent members of Bethlehem named Mildred Holland and Marge Hoffman, along with a few others occasionally, would join me in our single church van to bring neighborhood kids to church. After a little gym time, we would teach the kids Bible stories. The evening would conclude with cookies and juice before we'd take the kids home. We started out with about 10 kids. Once word got around the neighborhood, the numbers grew to 25, then toward 40 kids. Over the years, we sometimes had over 100 kids!

In our first year when we hit the 40-kid mark with just three adults, we weren't thinking, "WE CAN'T do this—it's too many kids for just three of us." We weren't thinking, "WE CAN'T do this every week—a three-hour commitment every week?" And we weren't thinking, "WE CAN'T do this. Where is the money for the cookies and juice going to come from for all of these kids every week?" WE JUST DID IT because God told us, "YES, YOU CAN!"

Sometimes, training adults in ministry comes "in process" as we pour ourselves as leaders into new leaders—WHILE we're all doing the ministry together. If we had let all the "WE CAN'T" barriers stand in our way, or tried to plan the program to death, we never would have started it. Is today's BBO program stronger than it was back then? Probably. Could all three of us do today what we did when we were 30 years younger? Probably not. But we decided that a lack of people wouldn't let us say, "WE CAN'T." God blessed what we were at the time.

Over the years, our Wednesday night BBO program has grown more effective with better programming and even more trained leaders, and it has subdivided into other children's programs. Additional adult volunteers eventually jumped into the program with us—and God provided again! Also, out of the Wednesday BBO ministry came our Gospel Choir, our youth basketball ministries, and a growing van ministry. Thirty years later, some of our main church leaders (who were children in 1989) are adult leaders at Bethlehem! The Wednesday BBO ministry concept also later birthed current ministries such as our Taking Jesus to the Streets ministry, our Ephratha Activity Center ministry to the children of Ferguson/Jennings/Baden communities, and our Bethlehem After School (BAS) program. A program of three people who trusted God and wouldn't let "WE CAN'T" stop them has now evolved into programs with over 50+ leaders that minister to a multitude of children!

Facilities and Stuff. You say, "WE CAN'T have a Gospel Choir ministry. We don't have a musician and a band." Especially today—UNTRUE! Pour yourself into what you do have! You probably have someone in your church who has some musical gifts. You certainly have someone in your church, or among the people you know, with technology gifts (just ask your kids). Pre-recorded tracks of most Gospel songs are now available on the Internet. Somebody you know has a boom box, or you can find a "karaoke" sound system at some of the big box discount stores. Most of these units have Bluetooth capability that enables you to download the tracks from the Internet and make them available for your worship service. You have a microphone at your church. Use what you have to get started. In time, as people get excited about the music ministry, you will receive financial gifts to help your music ministry grow, which will even lead to a church musician. Why not try to get one of your new young people involved in taking piano or drum lessons? It's a long range view, but that young person could one day be your church musician.

Some years ago, a pastor said to me, "If we had facilities like yours, we could have an outreach to children as well. But until the Lord blesses us with a bigger building..." I disagree. Pastor, do you have a few retired members who could join you in spending two days a week at a local grade school? Could they help for 90 minutes after school to help local public schoolkids with their homework? That local grade school principal would be thrilled with such an effort! Think of the relationships you would make with those kids! The next step would be for the children to come to an activity at your church, and then, and then, and then...!

Money. You say, "But WE CAN'T because we don't have funding." That doesn't have to be a barrier either. The next time you're in St. Louis, please visit us at Bethlehem Lutheran Church. I would love to show you our ministry, where still only one out of every six ministry dollars comes from our Sunday offering plate. Our people give, but the income they give from is limited. So God has raised up an army of ministry partners to enable Bethlehem ministry to be all that it can be. Without these ministry partners, I wouldn't still be a full-time pastor at Bethlehem. God did it!

If you visit us, I'll show you our sanctuary that was a former bowling alley. It was built for $250,000, and today it is paid off. It never would have happened if we believed, "WE CAN'T." I'll show you the one church van that God multiplied into five church vans. That would not have happened if we let WE CAN'T stop us. Next, I'll show you the 96 new houses in our housing ministry. Along with our partners, we've brought $70 million of total development to our community in less than 15 years. Those homes never would have been built if we believed, "WE CAN'T." If you happen to be around in June, you can see our Musical Theatre Camp, an incredible children's ministry. You'll see our sanctuary transform into the bedroom of Peter Pan, or we'll go "under the sea" with the Little Mermaid. None of that would have been possible if our church said, "WE CAN'T."

The reason why we don't let WE CAN'T barriers stand in our way at Bethlehem isn't because we are people of such strength, but rather because we have a GOD who is "able to do exceedingly abundantly more than we could ever ask or think…" (Ephesians 3:20). Of course, we're talking about ONLY that which is IN ACCORDANCE with HIS WILL! There is no WE CAN'T in Him. And guess what? If you're a Christian, OUR Lord God is also YOUR Lord God! So enough with all of the WE CAN'T thinking!

6

THE KEY TO GREAT MINISTRY PARTNERSHIPS

In recent years, it's become very popular for church members in the United States to travel overseas for a week of ministry work in foreign countries. These trips do provide service and much-needed labor to places in need. But the real benefit isn't in what the groups do, but rather in what the groups get to see, hear, and experience on that mission field. The same is true about missions here in the United States.

Every church needs to be involved with ministry partnerships beyond themselves. Small, urban inner-city churches like us could never exist without partners who share with us their labor and especially their resources. That is an indisputable fact. For larger churches, the partnership with smaller churches often gives their members experiences and missional opportunities in a culture vastly different from their own. Sometimes when you "go away" to serve in a place different from where you live, you become more aware and open to serving opportunities that are right in your own community.

There are many factors necessary to forming and keeping strong ministry partnerships. Another chapter will take up that topic in more detail. But for this essay, I want to hold up something most vital among urban churches in helping ministry partners get involved in your ministry:

Help your partners see what you see and experience what you experience.

Providing data about the people you serve and how often you serve them is important in a partnership. Faithfulness and accountability are also essential in a partnership ministry. Stories that communicate to others what you see when you do ministry in your place are critical. But when you can enable partners to have experiences and partake in ministry with you and see what you see—that's the best!

Over the years, I've seen amazing things happen when people walk in the shoes of those of us who serve daily in urban low-income areas. In the area of social ministry, I remember years ago when some suburban Christian friends brought some groceries for a "family in need" whom we had just started working with. One of our members went with our friends to the place where the family was staying. After going into their home and seeing no furniture, they asked if the kids had beds (they had none). Within three days, the suburban couple made sure a load of used furniture and new beds was on the way to that family's home. It all happened because God used the opportunity for people to "see what we see." Then He opened those people's hearts and helped them see they had been blessed with resources to help.

When partner church members see how Bethlehem reaches out with the Gospel in the summertime in the St. Louis housing projects through our Taking Jesus to the Streets ministry, they respond with things like funding for the snacks and the little give-a-way gifts. But they also respond with their presence and sign up each year to help us during these evening events. One man commented to me some years back, "If you all can go out on the streets with the Gospel for 10 nights in the summertime in 90-degree heat, I sure can volunteer for at least one of those nights to maybe help make your work a little easier." During our Bethlehem Bible Outreach to children, some small groups from our sister churches also take charge of individual nights and bring the lesson. This enables the sister church to carry out their mission of spreading the Gospel, and it gives our weekly volunteer staff a night off from teaching. What a blessing!

Even when people have seen what we've seen, as far as opportunities for ministry, sometimes their help takes different shapes. Some people will partner with us on the "front lines" of outreach. Other friends will support us on the "back side" in ways that many would never think about, but are so vital! For example, a partner friend who is an accountant gives of himself to help our treasurer keep accurate financial books. When other partner friends heard that some of our old church pews were falling apart, they fixed them. A contractor friend who is a wonderful Christian man has also helped us whenever we've had some maintenance issues that were beyond what we could handle. He sends construction workers from his company to take care of things for us!

Another friend of our ministry many years ago summarized this kind of help when he said, "I don't feel comfortable getting out on the street with all of you on some of your mission projects. But I can help you on the 'back side' with my gifts and abilities behind the scenes." That thinking is right on target with the Scripture. First Peter 4:10–11 reminds us that we all have different gifts, and they are all needed toward the mission of helping people know the Lord.

This is God's Church at its best—when each of us works together, using the gifts that the Lord has given us, as we respond to the opportunities we see to spread the Gospel!

7

TIME MANAGEMENT

I know you have avoided reading this essay because you were thinking, "Here's where Schmidtke scolds me for being in my office too much and not being out on the street enough."

OR

"...for going to too many community and pastor fellowship meetings and having no time to just call on people."

OR

"...for working too much at the church and not spending enough time with my family."

OR

"...for not starting my sermon early enough in the week (if I'm a pastor) and for procrastinating (whether I'm a pastor or not)."

OR

"...for not managing the freedom of my schedule well and often hanging out at home too much and not getting ministry work done."

Let me first picture the challenge. In my mind I'm picturing a congregation, but some of the same observations work for an urban community ministry. Very possibly, the people you have in your church are limited in what they can give you, as compared to others. They're great people, but they have LIMITS.

Like you, we have great people. But they are *LIMITED in the financial contributions* they can make to the ministry. It could be because they're older and on a fixed income; it could be because they are very young and raising their families; and it could be because they are on a poverty level income and need more from the church than they can give to the church. But let's be real, they are LIMITED FINANCIALLY. Some churches can get everything done that needs to get done in their ministry because they can afford to pay for it. But probably for you, like here at Bethlehem, no matter how many chicken fundraising dinners or bake sales you have, there is a finite income level from your people and even your community.

Like you, we have great people who are probably very *LIMITED in talents, experiences, and abilities.* You might have some older people who have the talent and the experience to fix the toilet or change light fixtures, but they don't have the physical strength and ability to do that any longer. On the other hand, you may have some young adults in your church who are strong and able, but they have never led the team in charge of Vacation Bible School (VBS). They can do it, but it will require someone to lead them through all the planning steps involved in putting together a great VBS. Further, you might have someone in your church who is willing to be your treasurer or handle the insurance matters for your church, but honestly, they just don't have the experience and talent to navigate that kind of business piece.

Early in our ministry, we had some simple property matters in our old cathedral-sized church that needed to be taken care of. For example, lightning made a hole in our tall bell tower. Yet, 80 feet below, we didn't know exactly what had happened. All we knew was that there was water raining down inside of the bell tower. Consider this situation:

The members I had at this earlier time in our ministry could not physically crawl into that bell tower.

Our money was so tight that we couldn't afford to pay a contractor to see if there was real damage or maybe the "hatch" on the flat roof had just blown off.

I had some new young adults who could have crawled up the ladders and maneuvered around the bells, but THEY HAD NO INSURANCE. What if they got injured? Lawsuit!

This all happened before we had relationships with sister churches. So, at 27 years of age when I was in decent shape (that was back then!), armed with my insurance policy and my seminary training on "How to Climb a Bell Tower," I went up the tower and saw that there was, in fact, real damage. I didn't do anything amazing or different than you have probably done a hundred times already in your ministry. But do you see what I mean regarding the challenge? Do you see the LIMITS in our churches regarding talents, experiences, and abilities?

Here's another challenge that is so often forgotten. We have great people, but they are *LIMITED in TIME.* Think first about the quantity of time available. Some of the young adults in our congregation work two jobs in addition to their job of being a parent when they get home. They have less time than I do at 57 years of age and my kids are all grown! One of the challenges at Bethlehem is that there aren't hardly any of "me" (with time available) around. They would have more time if they didn't have two jobs, but that's their reality. Plus, in a lower-income community context, let's be real—the jobs that many of our young people work are often the second- and third-shift jobs. This interferes with the very times when most church ministry takes place. Further, if someone has volunteered to sing in the choir and be at rehearsal on Monday nights... and volunteered to teach on Wednesday nights for the Bethlehem Bible Outreach kids ministry... and also somewhere in there be in a small group Bible study, do we really want to try and get them to volunteer for the Friday night youth group event?

Bethlehem is a ministry that is about 90% African-American, both in the make-up of our congregation and in the make-up of our mission field/ community. If a new African-American, solid Christian man comes to our church, what do I want him to do? Where would I like him to donate his volunteer time? a) Fixing the toilet. b) Cutting the church lawn. c) Cleaning up the building. d) Working on our evangelism team. e) Mentoring some of our children and youth in one of our youth programs. f) Coaching a team. There is no (g) "all of the above" answer.

Most people would say, "Use that man in d, e, or f." I agree. Yet, "a, b, and c," are jobs that still need to get done. Let's say the man says, "Pastor, I can do whatever you want me to do. You decide." What's your choice? Also, how do you accomplish all the other vital stuff? This is the challenge of time management in a small urban ministry.

If you decide that YOU'RE going to do all of the "a,b,c" work, you not only will not get it all done, but also you'll run out of time for your pastoral calling, sermon prep, etc. And you'll not have the time to be a good husband and father yourself. If you say, "We'll just pay to someone to do the other options," with what? Most small urban ministries don't even have money to afford the ministry basics. If you say, "We just won't fix the toilet," then in time you'll have vermin, and the health department will be on your back. If you say, "We just won't cut the grass," the city forestry department will cite you and then charge you.

This isn't simple, especially when you realize that most inner-city churches have inherited property and buildings that are way beyond what they can easily take care of. Some churches say, "Let's get our youth to do this." Okay, but, IF YOU EVEN HAVE YOUTH, who will teach the youth what to do? Who will supervise the youth? What happens when the youth say, "I don't want to do this"? And they stop coming to church altogether because they want to be youth, not the church's "slave labor"? Add one more thing— most people who grew up in a church context were taught that individual congregation members are to take care of all of their property and business matters themselves, internally, with no outside help. Or to put it in another way, there is a badge of honor in saying, "We handle our business."

SO WHAT DO WE DO? I don't have specific answers for every place, but here are some thoughts to chew on:

- **Small urban congregational ministries in low-income areas don't work the same as congregational ministries located in** various areas and with different financial, educational, and age demographics. Realize this. Don't beat yourself up because the people in your church may not be able to handle all the business of the church by themselves.

- While as leaders we try to keep raising the level of our people to be strong, active servants of Christ, we realize that to be an active church reaching people for the Master, our LIMITS may mean that we need outside help to accomplish some matters. It also may mean that some things just don't get accomplished as quickly or as well, until God sends more help to our ministry.

- It is vital to raise up sister church partnerships and friends of the ministry outside of the congregation who will volunteer and help the ministry to be all that it can be.

- While property matters must be attended to and while running programs is important, as leaders, we must help keep the work of pointing people to Jesus as the priority of everything we do.

- We have found it to be true in our community that having the church, not as just a religious institution but also as a social institution for our families, is a real asset. In a time when there are so many unhealthy and dark places where families might turn, raising your family at the church is a strong strategy. Of course, separate family time must occur. But because the streets and our society are becoming such dangerous places, spending extra nights at the church in Godly programs might be a good way to share family time. This intentional family strategy can help with some of the ministry needs of the church.

- Having youth in a church family is great. Yet, having people in the 45–65 age group (people who are finished raising their kids and who often have more available time, income, and life experience) is significant for the workload of a church.

- Consider everything that has been shared above about the TIME MANAGEMENT of the church, especially as it does or doesn't fit your context. But then, trust the promise of Psalm 127:1.

8

GROWING SOMETHING "URBAN STYLE"

*U*rban community gardens have become something more common today. In the past year, some people created one not far from our church. They tore down a derelict building and then decided that the new open lot would become a community garden. Let me put forth a disclaimer right away: While I have had gardens before, I am not currently a gardener. At the same time, as someone who has spent 30 years in this community and who has run a lawn business for about 12 of those years, I think I can speak in general as an educated man about soil and how things grow in an urban community. Stay with me... we'll get to ministry talk in a moment.

Here's a lesson in Community Gardening 101. If you had unlimited money and could totally clear the lot plus about a mile around of the "urban weed fields"... and if you could pay to truck in massive loads of rich soil to replace the junky soil that was there... and if you could install an automatic sprinkler system for watering... and if you could afford to put great fencing around the lot to keep away the rabbits and the other animals... and if you could hire 10 gardeners who could daily take care of this garden for you, then... uh uh. *You're in an inner-city ministry—and very likely, YOU HAVE NO MONEY.* So let's think about this in a different way.

For something useful to grow in that new vacant lot, it won't be automatic and it won't happen quickly. (Weeds will grow in it automatically, but I am not considering them "useful.") Think about some of the steps that will need to be taken:

1. Most urban lots don't clean up all the old junk remaining from former house foundations very well when the house is being demolished. So there will be debris, bricks, glass, and rocks that will need to be removed from the lot for you to have a productive garden.

2. Very likely, the soil is contaminated. In days past, especially in the city, there was much carelessness about what was allowed to go into the soil. (That's why so often today you see more urban open lots sitting vacant for a while. Over the decades, the soil becomes very polluted, and the environmental cost of cleaning it up is more than the lots are worth.) You will probably need to build up the soil with some minerals to get something good out of it.

3. As you work the soil (tilling and raking), it will take some time to remove all the little weed seedlings. While this will be a continual fight, you can rake them out now or pull them out later as they grow into weeds.

4. Now for the planting of the garden. What crops will work best in the area? Some crops that work well in one part of the country don't do so well in others. You will need to study your region to know what will grow best.

5. As young seeds sprout, how will you protect them from animals? Rabbits love the first leaves of a bean plant. If the first leaves get eaten off, the plant might as well be pulled out; it won't produce beans.

6. A productive garden will take consistent and generous watering to encourage growth.

7. If your plants aren't getting enough contact with the sun, they won't grow well. You might have to cut back some trees on your lot. Contact with the sun is essential to growth.

8. Then, finally, comes the joy of harvesting!

Whoa! That sounds like a LOT of work. IT IS! That sounds like a harvest won't come overnight. IT likely WON'T! Can you skip steps or take short cuts? Of course, you can. But doing so will probably not give you the strong, sustaining, and productive long term garden you are hoping for. **Urban gardening is just like urban church ministry, especially if you** are coming to an existing urban church and God is planning on using you to resurrect it. Let me share a few comments that line up with the gardening steps above.

Step 1 – Yep, there will be CLEANING WORK to do in the old soil. **There may very well be some old-time church traditions and outdated ministry approaches that will need to be cleaned out for the Holy Spirit to grow something new in this place.**

You probably already know the kinds of things I'm talking about, but let me throw you a list to help you in your thinking. While the Gospel never changes and the Word of God never changes, new perspectives might be needed regarding your church's mission, how you worship, the music used in worship, the vitality of small groups, how your church is governed, having a missional thinking treasurer, etc. You often can't clean out everything immediately or at the same time, but there must be a cleaning process for productive growth to happen.

NOTE: Here is a point of discussion. Some people say, "Let the old church die and start a new mission." Others say, "Transform the old church to a new church." Yes, I know. Some people heavily reason that new churches grow faster; they're nimbler and can do what is necessary for ministry. I don't disagree with some of that thinking. Yet, I think about the positives associated with the "old" Bethlehem I came to 30 years ago with a goal of church transformation in mind.

- I began with a school building that had a GYM in it. We could have never afforded to build a gym or buy one if we were starting brand-new. Our gym has been the entry point for a ton of young people who, now 30 years later, are some of our main adult leaders.

- I began with no monthly financial note on a new building or even monthly rent. As a church that today takes in only about $1,100 weekly in the offering plate, there is some significance to that savings.

- I came to a congregation with a history and some pre-existing potential financial connections—including people who moved away from Bethlehem, but still care about it and want to help.

I wouldn't necessarily have all that in a new ministry. Starting a new ministry also has advantages. I just want to give you something to think about.

Steps 2 & 3 – As you clean out the old and "pull weeds," you better have something strong and sustaining to pour into the soil so that it doesn't boomerang back to contamination. Check out what Paul told Timothy in 2 Timothy 3:10–17. As he warned him about attacks and spiritual predators, he also told Timothy how to be strong—let God through His Word strengthen you and build you up!

The "spiritual minerals" that will keep YOU strong as a church leader, the spiritual minerals that will give continual hope to your current congregation, the spiritual minerals that will bring healing to the lives of the new people you meet as you reach out with your ministry are all the same—the solid, unchanging Word of God, the "power of God unto salvation for all who believe" (Romans 1:16)!

Don't take what I just told you for granted! All of that cleaning and strengthening enabled our "urban ministry garden" to continue to the next step—planting.

Step 4 – **Just as certain crops grow better in particular areas of the country, your ministry approach regarding how you sow the Gospel into new people will be unique to the community you are trying to reach.**

The Lord has you on the scene of your community to learn what this approach is. Books like this one and ministry seminars are available to encourage you in your work, to give you ideas, and to challenge you with common ministry issues to think through. But you are God's man or woman on-site in the community where the Lord has placed you. You need to put in the time and do the research. You must know whether your community is a poverty-level community that will need financial help for almost every program that you do. Or is it a gentrifying community that has money but just needs guidance in their priorities? You need to know if your community is made up of mainly single moms with kids, or singles, or elderly folks, etc. You need to understand the "buttons" that, if pushed, attract people.

For example, our Bethlehem community is mainly comprised of single-parent, low-income families with two to three kids. That fact tells me the ministries that help parents raise their kids are going to be attractive and meaningful to the new people we're trying to reach. Thus, a big portion of Bethlehem's outreach ministry is aimed at kids—they are our entry point into families.

Additionally, we have learned the buttons to push that capture kids' interest in our African-American community—activities that include food, going places, and performance and competition. Thus, as we design or tweak weekly ministry lessons, we do so with those attraction points in mind. Of course, we want to introduce people to the Savior and teach them God's Word. In our world, for example, that may mean involving people in drama and musical performance groups. (You can teach a lot of theology and make it stick through Biblically accurate songs that "have a beat.") It also could mean having a Bible tournament competition to learn Scripture.

Maybe these ideas are also the kind of seeds you will plant as you bring Christ to your community. Maybe your planting approach will be totally different. How you bring the changeless Christ does need be mindful of and unique to the place where you do ministry. See how Paul did this very thing in Acts 17:22–34.

Step 5 – **As new growth begins in the ministry where you're serving, remember it is brand-new growth. While it has appeared, it may need your help to be protected from attacks of the enemy until it gets stronger.**

I remember when my wife and I ran alongside our sons as they learned to ride a bike. Even when we took the training wheels off, our kids still needed us to run beside them, holding on to the bicycle seat until we could release them to ride on their own. Sometimes things got a little "wobbly," and they needed us there for support. It's like that in ministry. Be sensitive about "still being there" for new leaders who are developing. Be sensitive about being there for new Christians also who are developing.

Many adults in our church today first came to Bethlehem as children. AND when they came as children, they were the only people in their home who were in an active relationship with Jesus Christ. Their parents might not have helped them wake up for church on Sunday mornings or reminded them of church activities. Those kids needed US as a church family to be in their life and "parent" them in a spiritual way. Sometimes that meant searching for them when they started to wander away. Sometimes that meant even getting a little confrontational with them when they started to go in wrong directions. You can do that AFTER you have first built a loving relationship in Christ.

Some say, "But I'm not their mama or daddy. That's someone else's job!" No, remember the picture of Ephesians 2:19. It says all of us who believe in Christ are "members of God's household;" that is, we're family. Young plants will need older, stronger plants to help them along.

Step 6 – **Plants need watering.** Yes, yes, yes! I picture "watering" in one word—ENCOURAGEMENT! Isn't it refreshing when someone tells you that you matter? Isn't it refreshing to know that when you were gone, you were missed by the family of God? When you have a problem, isn't it refreshing for someone to want to help you for free, with no strings attached, and you won't owe them anything? (That's GRACE!) Isn't it refreshing to have people who cheer you on and tell you not to give up— whether through a phone call, a thoughtful note, or a hug? When you blow it, and you're beating yourself up over the sin, isn't it refreshing when people don't try to further slam you, but instead take you by the hand and lead you to the certain mercy of God for the sake of Jesus' life as payment for our sins? Isn't it refreshing to have people in your life who don't focus on your faults, but encourage you in all the possibilities regarding what the Lord may have for you? Enough said.

We all need the watering of encouragement. Today, maybe more

than at any other time, the Church of Jesus Christ needs to be abundant in watering people's lives with the Gospel of Life and Fresh Starts! This naturally leads to the final step.

Step 7 – Plants don't grow if they're not getting enough S-U-N. Plants need the S-U-N. Do I even need to say much about this?

Connecting people to a fellowship like Bethlehem is important. Helping people grow in their knowledge and practice of God's Word is vital. But it is the S-O-N who gives life!

This is what each of us needs in our lives. This is what every new person that we reach out to needs in their life. MORE JESUS! MORE JESUS! MORE JESUS!

9

"GIFTED" IS NOT ENOUGH

A few years ago, we were hosting one of our summer Taking Jesus to the Streets outreach nights at a local city park. These events are like a one-night mobile Vacation Bible School and include a lesson, music, small group activities, and refreshments. We start off with music. Using a booming sound system, singers from Bethlehem do about three or four contemporary Gospel songs to draw a crowd to our ministry area. When we sing outside, we use pre-recorded music tracks. It's so much easier than setting up a whole band.

On this particular night, as many people were gathering, we noticed a nearby group of adults in the park enjoying a Sunday night of talking, drinking, and barbequing. (Okay, in truth, there was more of the second activity of that triad going on than the other two. But they weren't hurting anyone, and they were very open and welcoming of us to do our ministry.) As we were transitioning into our final song before our main message, one of the men in that group motioned for me to come over and talk to him. I walked over and he said to me, "Rev, you should have Shirley sing. Could Shirley sing a song once you're done? It'll be Gospel. Shirley can really sing!"

Usually, I am very cautious about giving the microphone to anyone I don't know. (I've had some experiences with that that didn't turn out so well). But this time, something told me, "Let Shirley sing." I called "Shirley" to join us. Of course, she was shy and a little hesitant. But with lots of encouragement from the crowd, she came forward to sing. Shirley was incredible and had a great voice! She actually sang a Gospel song that we had sung in worship that morning. So much giftedness!

Afterward, all of us encouraged her to come to Bethlehem on a Sunday and sing. We wanted her to maybe even join our choir. She was so GIFTED by God! I got Shirley's phone number and followed up with her for about six weeks on a weekly basis. Well, Shirley never made it to Bethlehem for worship or to sing. I saw Shirley at the neighborhood gas station about three months later. We talked. Shirley still has never come to Bethlehem. You might have already guessed some of the other details of Shirley's life. She is so "gifted," but also has so many strongholds of the enemy on her life that she just can't break away from. You know what I mean.

Here's my point in telling you this true story: just being GIFTED is not enough to serve the Lord in ministry. That's equally true even if you don't battle some of life's demons that Shirley battles. To serve the Lord with the GIFTS that He has given us, a mixture of a few other attitudes and circumstances are needed.

Discipline and maturity are needed to use your gift well in the Lord's service. You could be GIFTED by God with the gift of teaching. Yet, if you lack the discipline to study your lesson each week to teach, and lack the simple maturity to say "no" to other commitments on the day that you chose to teach your small group, your service won't be fruitful—no matter how GIFTED you are.

Availability is also a vital consideration in order to use the gifts the Lord has given you. Tonya was a gifted youth leader. She could identify with junior high kids and really had a heart for them. She led the church's junior high ministry for three years. But then her mother got seriously sick. Someone needed to attend to her mother almost daily. Nobody else in the family would take on this labor of love. Tonya did. You've got the point—although her giftedness in working with youth still continued, her availability changed for this new season in her life.

Some people are gifted in incredible ways. They have the discipline to do what is needed to use their gifts. Yet, their unavailability to serve sometimes keeps them from serving effectively. Sometimes availability issues arise because we don't do a good job ordering our lives so that we can serve in the areas where we are gifted. At other times, God moves us for a season to a different kind of service and changes our availability to serve in a particular area.

Passion and desire are also needed to serve in powerful ways, using the gifts that the Lord has given. A person can be GIFTED by God in a certain area. They can have the discipline to serve effectively. The Lord has given them availability to serve. BUT—they just DON'T WANT TO DO IT! It's the opposite of those famous words of Psalm 100:2, "Serve the Lord with gladness." The problem is often exactly what Paul spoke about in Philippians 2:4, "...do not merely look out for your own interests, but also the interests of others." Only God can change this kind of heart. The way back for a heart like this is found in the words that follow in Philippians 2:5–11... LOOK TO our SAVIOR, JESUS!

Think about these things as you personally serve the Lord. Consider these other attitudes as you build your ministry team at your church that serves with you. **"GIFTED" is NOT ENOUGH.**

10

THE VALUE OF "100"

In recent years one of the phrases of the street has been, "Keep it 100!" That phrase means whatever a person says or does must stay 100% true and authentic." No stttrrrreeettttccchhhhiiinnng what the real truth of something is. "Keeping it 100" is right on target with our Lord and with ministry in His Church. First, with our Lord. Truth is what God values from us, even when we've failed Him as we've sinned. Through Christ, God has made a way for us to be 100% truthful with Him as we confess our sins, knowing that HE WILL FORGIVE US on account of Jesus' death for our sins. First John 1:9 makes this crystal clear.

Now, let's talk about "Keeping it 100" in ministry. Here is something so simple, I'm almost ashamed to even write it. Yet, it is so essential to practice, if you want to see any kind of progress in ministry.

REALNESS about where you ARE is the PRELUDE to getting to WHERE you want to GO.

Please pay careful attention to the first words of the next sentence. US PREACHERS (yes, I have put myself in this same category)—although we are totally real in the pulpit—are sometimes known for being LESS THAN REAL outside of the pulpit, particularly when we talk about ministry. I can't tell you how many times I've been at a conference and overheard a preacher telling some other brother preacher that he "has 200 people a Sunday" at his church—when in truth, he might have 75 a Sunday and perhaps 200 only at Easter. How do I know? In that particular case, I've been to his church several times, and I know for sure that he isn't being totally "100"!

I'm not getting down on preachers. Many of us in the church, both lay people and clergy, often aren't real and "100" about what things are. The areas where we often wander away from realness have to do with ministry numbers, ministry effectiveness, and ministry tracking.

Ministry Numbers. I know—numbers aren't the only measure of ministry, but they are important. If the numbers remain the same in a ministry, why is that? If the numbers are declining, why is that? If the numbers are increasing, why is that? These are fair questions. Maybe we won't always be able to discern the exact reasons for numerical change. Whenever we're dealing with people, especially people in transient places like urban areas, ministry response consistency is often a moving target because people's lives change so quickly.

Yet, taking time to be "real" about the numbers is useful toward honoring the Lord with our best ministry as we "go into all the world to proclaim the Gospel." (Mark 16:15) For example, we need to ask why the numbers are going down in an afterschool kids program that we start at 4:00 p.m. Let's say we find out that the local public school started a new program from 4:00–5:00 p.m. Thus, maybe we need to think about changing the timing of our program. Being real about ministry numbers helps us at least think about the possibility.

Ministry Effectiveness. Sometimes changes in our ministry numbers direct us to think about our ministry effectiveness. Here's an example. Why have the young adults started to disappear from our church? Why are they starting to worship at other local churches outside of our denomination? Sometimes we want to answer those questions with comments like, "Well, there are theological issues with the churches that our young people have gone to. We must preserve our doctrinal purity!" That answer misses the issue. It's not about changing the truth of God's Word. But in such a situation, we need to intensely listen and learn how to more effectively communicate God's Good News of Jesus to the 20s and 30s and 40s of our church. If we're in denial and not REAL about the fact that they're leaving, we will likely never think about how we can be more effective in reaching them. We'll never get to "the place that we want to go"—a church that speaks the Gospel to all people in the ways that they need to hear it!

Ministry Tracking. Jesus gives us the cue for this reminder when He says in John 10:14, "I am the Good Shepherd. I KNOW MY SHEEP and My sheep know Me..." We've got to be REAL about the "WHO" of our ministry. When there are 200 people in church, are they the same 200 people who were in church last Sunday? When there are 10 people at a small group Bible study, are they the same 10 people who were there last time? If not, WHO was missing? WHO was present? Has anyone checked on the people who were missing? Have we tracked WHO was present to notice if someone has been missing for the past three meetings? If we just track the total number, it could be that someone was gone and we didn't even know it. Maybe they were gone because they were hurting about something. Maybe they were gone because they were angry about something at the church. Maybe they were gone because they had a physical accident and no one in the church family has checked on them. If WHERE WE WANT TO GO is to be a GROWING FAMILY where NOT ONE PERSON IS LOST or missing, tracking people in ministry is essential! It's part of REALNESS and finding the truth about where people are and what's going on in their lives so that we can bring them the healing words of Jesus and keep them strong in the Savior!

A growing ministry, a strong ministry, a close family ministry, and a ministry that the Lord will be pleased with values REALNESS and isn't afraid of it. For REALNESS drives us back to the Head of the Church, our Lord, and seeks wisdom from Him as to how we can minister to others in a better way.

REALNESS about where you ARE is the PRELUDE to getting to WHERE you want to GO.

11

YOU NEED A CONSISTENT DIVERSION

For me, my diversion is officiating basketball and cutting grass. For you, it might be something totally different. But here's an important truth for longevity in an urban ministry:

Consistent Diversion Activities are Necessary Help to Keep Balance

The key word in this encouragement is CONSISTENT. There will always be way more work to do in an urban parish than you can ever complete. People will always be in need of you. What will be your "getaway"? Of course, going home to your family is a vital retreat. Yet, sometimes it is hard to keep unfinished work from creeping into your home. Also, because of the nature of shepherding people, it's also hard not to answer your phone. In a larger parish with multiple staff, members can take turns being "on call" for emergencies. But in the case of most urban inner-city churches, let's be honest—you are the staff. Even if you do develop lay leadership to handle ministry matters, nevertheless, it will not be easy for you to have a consistent getaway time. You need this time with your family. But you also need time for YOU, where you don't need to exchange the responsibilities of being a church leader for the responsibilities of being a spouse or parent. It needs to be regular and consistent, and not easy for you to postpone or cancel.

Some years ago, I got into officiating basketball and cutting grass in a lawn business. I get so much out of both activities. As a basketball official, I can't easily cancel at the last minute when I've committed to take a game. I am forced to actually carry it through and "leave the ministry" for a couple of hours, which is great for my mental health! Further, usually nobody knows me (certainly not as "Pastor") where I officiate. For two hours, I just get to be "me," with no direct pastoral responsibilities. It's a nice break.

Once I get behind my push lawnmower, it's so loud that I am unable to hear any cell phone ring. I do check my phone about every 45 minutes, but imagine being "unavailable for calls," even for just a short time! I don't cut grass with music playing in headphones, just the roar of the lawnmower (with ear plugs to protect my hearing). Peace. Quiet. A break. The grass keeps growing, I must say. So while I could postpone one day, I can't ignore cutting grass for a group of days.

These diversions make for a consistent pause from my intense ministry life. Both of these activities bring exercise to my body, the opportunity to work up a sweat, and a feeling of accomplishment when I'm finished.

What will be your CONSISTENT DIVERSION to your intense ministry work? You know what works for you. But make sure that you find one and do it. It will be a special "sabbath of refreshment" that the Lord has for you!

12

SIFTING IS NECESSARY

Remember the Bible picture of sifting wheat? Here's the basic concept—imagine a pile of VALUABLE wheat and UNVALUABLE chaff (in the same pile). If you throw it up in the air, the wind will blow away the lighter, UNVALAUBLE chaff, while the VALUABLE, heavier wheat drops to the ground.

Sifting is separating what is valuable from what is not valuable. Being able to sift through what is most VALUABLE for your ministry versus what is not as VALUABLE is so vital, because there is never enough time to be at every meeting or do everything.

For example, it is important for us to collaborate in ministry, especially when ministering in urban inner-city, low economic contexts. At the same time, SIFTING in collaborations IS NECESSARY. A ministry leader could spend every moment going to every community meeting and every pastors' alliance meeting—and meet with every social service organization—and never get anything done in ministry within their congregation, including doing hardly any outreach to their primary community ministry area! You must SIFT!

Some people who want your time have great programs and services, but they may not be a vital fit for the Gospel ministry you are doing. Or they might be a good fit for you one day, but they are not the best fit for the ministry you are doing today. You must SIFT through good programs and helpful people that are not necessarily in line with your main mission of bringing the Gospel of Jesus Christ to people. Many years ago, I toured a huge community organization that was started by a Lutheran church in a major metropolitan area. They were big! They had a multi-million-dollar budget and services for housing, daycare and employment, etc.

When we finished touring their "empire," I asked, "So what is your

Gospel ministry like that is connected to all these great things you do to make people's life better?"

They said, "This is our Gospel outreach ministry."

"No," I clarified, "I'm wondering about your Vacation Bible School, kids Bible programs, and small group Bible studies where you connect all of these people to the Lord." They didn't have an answer for that, except to say that all of this "HELPING THE LIVES OF PEOPLE" stuff was their outreach. They hadn't SIFTED what they were doing. Remember what Jesus said in Mark 8:36? "What does it profit a man to gain the whole world, yet forfeit his soul?"

I understand. Connections with other entities also sometimes lead to support; and dollars are almost always short in every urban ministry! But we must SIFT. We only have 24 hours and 365 days regarding our time. We have a finite amount of it to use in ministry. While all kinds of community programs can help us reach people, always remember that our primary work as Christ's Church is to bring Christ to people and encourage people to be connected to a local Christian congregation so that they can be supported and grow in their faith.

By the way, that's what we really measure and where we want to see growth. Elsewhere in this book, you'll read about all God did in starting our housing ministry, Better Living Communities. We're grateful to God for His work of 240 total new residences in our community and over $70 million of development in less than 15 years. But let's SIFT that and be clear. It is just "eye candy" to our real work of trying to share Christ with all the people of our new community. We must SIFT through priorities in ministry to keep our mission of sharing Christ FIRST!

One other encouragement about SIFTING: There is personal SIFTING needed in how each of us spends our time. One of the most practical lessons four years of seminary taught me was how to SIFT. Let me explain. When I first went to Concordia Seminary, I was really overwhelmed by the reading. There was no way that anybody could read everything the professors wanted us to totally and thoroughly read. After about a year, I understood

SIFTING. In the same way that no one at seminary could possibly read everything, nobody in a congregation has the time to read everything that needs to be read, make all the weekly visits that need to be made, do all the planning that needs to be done, and take care of all of the items on the "to-do list" that need to be taken care of.

So what do you do? If you have money, hire help. But since most of us in the urban scene don't have unlimited funds, learn to SIFT! In a given week, plan out the best use of your time for that week. SIFT! Some things may need to wait until next week. SIFT! You wish you could spend 10 hours visiting, but you only have seven hours this week. SIFT! You've got the idea. As you SIFT and give the Lord your best each week in ministry, don't live with anxiety about not getting everything done. I love the words of the Apostle Paul in 1 Corinthians 3:6 that remind us of who is in charge for progress in ministry. Paul said, "I planted, Apollos watered, but only God gave the growth." Amen!

13

INVITING PEOPLE TO WHAT?

The movie trailer was great! This was a movie that you were planning to see for sure when it came out in two months! Everybody was talking about the opening weekend of this new movie! But then you went and saw the movie. As you came outside, you couldn't figure out how the movie trailer that previewed the movie was so good, but the movie itself was so bad! Sometimes our ministries can be just like that.

We work so hard and spend so much money trying to be friendly to people in our community, inviting them to Sunday worship and other church activities. But then when new people attend, they never come back because "WHAT" we invited them to didn't connect with the people we invited.

I know where your mind is. Here comes the pushback, "But the Gospel of Jesus Christ is something that everyone needs" (YES!)..."The Gospel meets every person in their most critical need, the forgiveness of their sins" (YES, I agree!)... "The Gospel is the power of God unto salvation, according to Romans 1:16" (YES, totally true!) But how we present Christ and the ways we use to do it are sometimes confusing to new people. We mix up our historical "sitz im leben" (German for "setting in life") from the life context of those we are inviting to our church. We get hooked on the historical position we grew up with, and we don't understand the life context of the people we're inviting.

Think through some of these situations:

Situation #1 – It's our 100th anniversary as a church. Our heritage is German and Protestant. We now reside in a totally young, African-American community. We want to celebrate the church anniversary as an effort to reach out to the new people of our community. That is our goal. We decide to have an outdoor festival serving sauerkraut and bratwurst with a German "oom-pah-pah" band playing. While that might be on target for a "reunion event" of former German members, how well does it work as a community outreach event in a young, African-American community?

Situation #2 – We want to reach kids in our area. We decide to sponsor an open gym night for people in the community. Many people come. Yet, within the first 30 minutes, in our gym there have been 10 curse words, and the gym has taken on the "urban cologne" fragrance of weed (brought in by people who were smoking before they came). We immediately close the gym saying, "You can't do this stuff in our gym."

Situation #3 – Your church has just completed a canvass of the community. Ten families indicated they would come to Sunday worship next week. Three of the families showed up. You are an older, traditional Lutheran congregation. These families are young, African-American moms and kids. They don't understand the hymns. They like the sermon. But the worship is too difficult for both the moms and their kids to "connect" with. These three families never return for another visit to your Sunday morning worship.

You're probably already mad at me for writing down these thoughts. Please, hear me out. Have you ever considered the "WHAT" of WHAT you're inviting people to? Let's be clear—we NEVER, EVER change the GOSPEL OF JESUS CHRIST. The Word of God always stands. But HOW we communicate the Word of God in music, preaching, teaching, and in other parts of worship matters. It matters how we're thinking about cultural contexts and how we're making our ministries more family- and kid-friendly (if that is the new clientele we're trying to reach). Have we thought about the "WHAT" of what we're inviting people to? According to the Scripture, what CAN change? What should NEVER change? Sometimes we don't even have this conversation; we just decide that the "WHAT" of what we've been will be the "WHAT" of what we always will be. But where does that get us, if the new people around us who don't know Christ aren't interested in the "WHAT" of how we've always imparted the Gospel?

I love how Paul showed that the APPROACH in bringing the unchangeable message of Christ crucified and risen is open to change. Go to Acts 17:22–31 in your Bible. See how Paul was especially sensitive to the WHAT of the people on Mars Hill. He connected with them in verses 22–23, noting that they did care about "god" (even though they had been caring about something that wasn't the true God). I love how Paul thinks of his hearers in verse 29 by referring to them as the children of God, just like him. Paul does all this as he brings forth clearly who the true God is. I believe before Paul ever spoke on Mars Hill he thought about the WHAT and the HOW he would use to invite his hearers to know the true God.

I find Jesus to be sensitive to the WHAT of how He will share the Good News of new life over and over again in the people He meets face to face. In John 4, he speaks to a woman whose mind is on WATER and offers her "water" that will take away her thirst forever (John 4:10, 14). In John 6, Jesus begins with the "WHAT" of helping people satisfy their physical hunger as a prelude to telling them He is the Bread of Life, the only thing they need (John 6:35).

Now notice that nowhere in this essay have I told you to replace your organ with drums and a keyboard, or replace your hymns with only contemporary Gospel music. I haven't said you need to change your liturgy or that your pastor needs to stop wearing his robe and just wear a button-down shirt and slacks, or... or... or. My guess is that there are probably some changes that you could make to your "WHAT" that would help you better connect with people in your community who don't know the Savior. But I don't live in your community or pastor your church.

My plea to you is this. Start thinking about life from the perspective of the new people you are inviting to your church worship services and ministries. How can you best connect with them? Be willing to do whatever it takes to connect them to Jesus the Savior. Rarely does changing our "WHAT" happen overnight. You might not even have the people or financial resources to accomplish a lot of immediate changes to your "WHAT." But let the beginning of this movement toward a stronger and better ministry of the Gospel begin today as you think about the question, **"INVITING PEOPLE TO WHAT?"**

14

DEAR PASSIONATE PEOPLE LIKE ME...

Dear Passionate People Like Me,
  I know how you are. Whatever you decide to work at in life, you work at it with 200% of yourself. You will put in more than the time needed for the task because you want to see it succeed. You will sacrifice yourself for whatever the ministry is (and many times even your own health). You usually "don't take 'no' for an answer"; there's always a way to make this work. I totally "get ya!"

Yet, in the midst of the positive side to all that passion, adversity and conflict often show up (as in any ministry). Our passion makes for a very pressure-filled situation... especially when disagreements arise, people aren't coming through as expected, or the project isn't going as planned. Then things happen quickly. We let destructive words fly. We sometimes cast blame and fault. We can even challenge each other's commitment to the ministry. We stop being on the same team.

We passionate people would say, "Somebody had to say something about this." Or, "I just had to get my feelings out." Or, "I wasn't that loud... it's just who I am.' Or we add, "Okay, then I'm never going to say anything again." There are probably a hundred more excuses that I've put out there for yelling out my feelings in a passionate rage when things went south in a ministry. Here's what I am learning (present tense verb—I still am learning this):

Instead of Yelling It... Write It, Sit on It, and Sometimes, Throw It away.

Our childhood saying was wrong—"Sticks and stones may break my bones, but words will never hurt me." Words do hurt. Cutting words can make a volunteer quit and not come back. An out of control "blast" can burn bridges to people who could help the ministry. "Giving someone a piece of your mind" might make you feel better, but it also could close a door for a long time to minister to someone. Speaking without first thinking and even praying could cut off a relationship with a funder to the ministry. Do any of us, especially after we've cooled down, really want to hurt the other person we yelled at?

Instead of Yelling It... Write It, Sit on It, and Sometimes, Throw It away.

Here's how this progression works. Take a pen and paper, use your thumbs on your phone's keyboard, get on your computer—whatever your preferred writing method is—and get it all out by "talking" on paper! Tell it all. Just let it flow. BUT make sure there is no way this rant could be sent to the other person, even accidentally. (You probably don't want to do an email or a text!) Rather, type the message in a document. Then, if you finally decide to send it later, just cut and paste it.

After you've written it, SIT ON IT. It could be wise to SIT ON IT overnight, or for a couple of days, or a few hours. During that time, get away from it but also reread it. One of your goals is to be able to think about not just *what* you've said, but also *how* you've said it. Another goal is to *think about the person* you're writing. How will that person receive what you're writing? Did they really mean what they said in the same way that you heard it? What's the wisest next move for this relationship? Even if they were wrong, do you want the relationship to continue? If so, you might need to temper your words.

How can you make your point AND reconcile the relationship? Is there something you could have done different in the heat of the moment that might not have set things off? Also, as you SIT ON IT, pray three prayers:

1. *Lord, please guide this entire mess.*
2. *Lord, please work on changing this person that I had conflict with.*
3. *Lord, change me and humble me in the midst of this conflict.*

After having taken some time to reflect on what you've written, you might get some counsel from close friends. They might see things from a different perspective.

Finally, if your response isn't the way the Lord would want you to respond, DELETE it and DON'T SEND IT. You could craft a new response or just send a simple, "I'm sorry we had words. I'm praying through this. I value you as a friend."

Now for the "urban flavor" in many of these conflicts. This might not be true of the situation that you're in, but I've witnessed these circumstances in many urban conflicts—both WITHIN the urban community and WITH PEOPLE OUTSIDE of it. Think about these observations:

Many times, people equate loudness in an argument with control or the attempt to have control. The louder the response, the louder the first person will become.

Sometimes, people insist on getting the last jab in. So if I keep trying for the last word, the other person will always have one more. (Somebody has to let things end.)

Sometimes, my perception that I won an argument is my "self-esteem compensation" for my being self-consciousness about my lack of education or my lack of being respected by others. It's like this sometimes... maybe I didn't understand all the words that you said, but as long as I told you off or "cursed you out," of course I won the argument! That's sometimes how we feel.

Even when we know we're wrong, sometimes it's hard to admit that we're wrong, and our attacks are our way of covering up our own faults.

Even if I think someone is wrong about something they've said, if I need them on my team to get the Lord's work done, sometimes I ignore their offensive comment because their value to my team in doing the Lord's work outweighs my need for satisfaction of setting them straight. P.S. I'm sure people feel the same toward me when I make offensive comments!

As I write the above observations, I'm not trying to go "all psychologist" on you. That's not my area. My hope is that something above might be helpful as you read it. Maybe some of it leads you to say, "Hmmm. That could be another way of looking at this situation." Possibly, one of these observations might help show God's path for you in this conflict.

15

THE LAZY WAY, THE INEFFECTIVE WAY, NOT JESUS' WAY

Jesus was incognito as He sat in the Church Council (Board of Elders) meeting as the chairman, Mr. Maxwell, called the meeting to order. "Folks," Chairman Maxwell said, "we've got a few problems to address.

Here's the first item. Church attendance is down. People just haven't been coming to worship."

"Don't people realize that this is their responsibility as a Christian to be in worship every Sunday?" Mr. Jacobs responded.

Chairman Maxwell suggested, "Maybe we need to go out and make some calls on people and see what's going on?"

Mrs. Johnson quickly rejected this idea. "But you know that our church neighborhood is very dangerous after dark," she said cautiously. "We shouldn't be out on the streets."

Chairman Maxwell replied, "Maybe we could make some phone calls..."

Old Ms. Saunders jumped in. "Well," she said, "I just don't really feel comfortable about bothering people on the phone."

"But we need to reach these people some way..." Chairman Maxwell pleaded.

That's when Mr. Jacobs piped up. "Let's make a policy," he explained. "If you're not in church at least two Sundays over the coming three months, we drop you from membership because you're not really serious about the Lord."

WHAT KIND OF LOOK DO YOU THINK WAS ON JESUS' FACE?

Chairman Maxwell sensed they could not reach consensus, so he went on to the next item of business. "Well, there are some other issues for us to discuss. You all know that one of our teenagers is pregnant. She is already four months along and..."

"We need to do something strong about this right now, or else all kinds of teenagers in our church are going to be pregnant!" Mrs. Johnson interrupted.

"I agree," said Mr. Jacobs. "I move that we make a policy to immediately not allow her to take the Lord's Supper until she can come and meet before this church board!"

"I second that motion," Mr. Thompson added. "Also, by the way, can you ladies put out a message within the congregation that no members should be giving this young lady any baby gifts? That would make it look as if we approve of this sinful behavior!" There were several nods around the table.

WHAT KIND OF LOOK DO YOU THINK WAS ON JESUS' FACE?

"The third issue," said Chairman Maxwell, "is the matter of our property. Lawrence Tyler and Matthew Moore started a basketball ministry in our gym three months ago."

"Yes!" said Mr. Forester. "They've been getting quite a number of young men into our gym."

"But it's not all good news," interrupted Mr. Jacobs. "Just this past Saturday somebody broke two lights in the gym while playing basketball!"

"And where are we going to get the money to fix those lights?" Ms. Saunders wanted to know. "We don't even have enough money in the plate every Sunday to take care of our bills. And you know none of those young men show up to our church on Sundays."

That's when Mr. Jacobs said, "I move that we make a policy to discontinue the basketball program until the young men in the program can raise the money to pay us for our broken lights!"

WHAT KIND OF LOOK DO YOU THINK WAS ON JESUS' FACE?

Does all of this sound extreme to you? Maybe. But it's not that far away from how congregations sometimes handle issues. We love to make policies and often think more rules will bring people into line. How totally off the mark we are to the world we live in today. People pause and then proceed through red traffic lights; they don't care about rules. People own and use illegal assault rifles; they're not intimidated by the rules. Even political leaders and celebrities break rules that the average person on the street would get locked up for breaking. Yet, they're not afraid. You see, they know that if you have the right connections, rules don't matter. Respect for rules has disappeared in our world. In the church today, if we think rules are the way to bring people into line, we are GREATLY MISTAKEN! This is especially true with our young people. If they don't like the rules we make, they'll simply leave our church, go to the church down the street, or stop being part of a church fellowship completely.

I'm not advocating for not having structure or parameters in the church. Whatever the Word of God says ALWAYS rules. I'm saying RULES CANNOT REPLACE the time-consuming and often difficult and deep sacrifice involved in the prayerful work of shepherding people.

Believing that making rules and policies can shepherd people is the LAZY way, the INEFFECTIVE way, and NOT JESUS' WAY.

Let's go back to the scenario I described above. Imagine that Jesus (remember, He's incognito) raises His hand and is allowed to speak in the meeting.

"May I tell you a story?" he begins. "What man among you, if he has a hundred sheep and has lost one of them, does not leave the ninety-nine in the open pasture and go after the one which is lost until he finds it? When he has found it, he lays it on his shoulders, rejoicing. And when he comes home, he calls together his friends and his neighbors, saying to them, 'Rejoice with me, for I have found my sheep which was lost!'" (Luke 15:4–6)

Do you see the message of the story? Shepherding people means having a passion for EACH person. It is a passion that includes going to wherever lost place they are, not waiting on them to come to us. It is a work that will cost time and effort. Depending on where the sheep is, the shepherd may enter some dangerous and intense places. The shepherd's search continues until he finds the lost sheep. And the shepherd may end up carrying the wounded sheep until it can again walk by itself. But what rules over this entire intensive effort is the vision of the victorious celebration of finding and restoring the sheep to the shepherd's fold.

What does that mean for church leaders doing the work of shepherding God's people, whether we are clergy or lay shepherds? It means:

- **We won't recover sheep who have wandered by simply making**

more policies and new rules with the hope that the sheep will come back on their own and fall into line. This is the way of ministry leadership that is both LAZY and INEFFECTIVE.

- We must GO TO the lost sheep, rather than believing they will one day return to God's family.

- **RELATIONSHIPS always precede all CORRECTION.** What relationships? Of course, our relationship with the person who has been lost and wandered away from Christ and His Church. We need to build a relationship with a wandering sheep before we come with words of correction. (This is why, as shepherd leaders, we always want to have strong relationships with the people we shepherd, even before they wander).

  You've probably heard the old phrase, "Nobody cares what we think until they see how much we care." Yet, the key relationship we need to be focused on building with a straying sheep is to help them see how much the Good Shepherd loves them, even in their present lostness (see Romans 5:8). This work of relationship-building will take our time and investment. The wandering sheep might even push back and reject us initially with something like, "Where were you when I was just starting to slip away? How come you didn't care to check on me then?" (Yes, ouch!) This shepherding recovery work won't be simple, but it will be worth it, according to Jesus.

- As shepherds, we will need to constantly come before our Father's throne and ask that He give us wisdom regarding WHAT to say to the wandering sheep, HOW to say it, and the PACE we say it.

- This is Jesus' way of caring for the people of His pasture. It is about RELATIONSHIPS, not just making RULES.

16

THERE ARE GOING TO BE SOME LOW DAYS

I love the definition of a valley: a low area between hills. Hills are on both sides of every valley. If you had all mountains, or hills with no low valley areas, that geography would be called a plain. But if you're going to have mountains and hills, by definition, you have to have valleys between them. What is true of geography is also true of life and ministry. When you ask a person, "How are things going?" and they always answer, "Great!"—they're not really being honest. Everybody has low days and hard days.

Maybe you're having one right now! There are days when it feels as if the ministry we do is totally ineffective. There are days when people are impossible, and you would just as soon get in your car, start driving, and never return to where the Lord has placed you. Some days are about personal failure, when you look at bad decisions you've made. Days when you realize that you haven't been the spouse or parent that you should be. Days when you realize that although you've opened God's Word every day for your ministry, it's been a long time since you've opened God's Word so that it can speak to you. In these moments, know in advance that the enemy will seek to get you alone—away from other Christians who could encourage you and point you back to the Savior. When the enemy gets us alone, he often gains overwhelming power to lead us away from our Father and into selfishness, depression, and sin.

In those times of darkness, remember the words of Psalm 27:1–3. I like to start with verse 2, "When evildoers came upon me to devour my flesh," they weren't successful. David says, "My adversaries and my enemies, they stumbled and fell." In the same way, verse 3 says, "though a host encamps against me, my heart will not fear; though war arise against me..." Those words make me think beyond physical attacks. They make me think of Ephesians 6:12 where God says through Paul, "For our struggle is not against flesh and blood, but against the rulers, against the powers, against the world forces of this darkness, against the spiritual forces of wickedness in the heavenly places."

Doesn't that match up? The most difficult attacks and bouts with darkness in our personal lives and in our ministries are really not the people and the circumstances we see and touch. They're the temptations, disappointments, discouragements, and moments when we think that there is no hope—all of which attack our spirit. Hold on, my brother! Don't give up, my sister! David says in the last line of Psalm 27:3, that even in the face of all of that, "I shall be confident." How so?

NOW read Psalm 27:1! It has the reason for our strength. David says, "The Lord is my light and my salvation..." He clears the darkness with His shining love and grace for us! "Whom shall I fear?" No one! "The Lord is the defense of my life; whom shall I dread?" Same answer—no one! How can we know that? Because through His work at the cross and His resurrection, this saying is true, "Christ has destroyed death and has brought life and immortality to light through the Gospel." (2 Timothy 1:10)

What does that mean for you and me? No matter what we're going through, no matter how deep the pain, we have this truth in 1 John 4:4, "Greater is Jesus who is in us, than he (the devil and all his darkness) who is in the world." One of our deacons at Bethlehem, Deacon Terence Nash, says this line in almost every one of his prayers: "Thank you, Father, for KEEPING us." Through depressing times... thank you, Father, for KEEPING us. Through the pain of people's words... thank you, Father, for KEEPING us. Through hopelessness when it seems there is no solution to problems... thank you, Father, for KEEPING us. Our God is faithful in KEEPING US!

There are going to be some low days. But your low day is merely the prelude to the next mountaintop the Lord brings you to! Until we get there, "Thank you, Father, for KEEPING us."

17

STUDYING PEOPLE or SERVING PEOPLE or BOTH

*M*y colleague, Pastor Gerard Bolling, made this insightful observation about people in most urban ministries. He said, "Some people in the church are STUDYING PEOPLE. These are the people who are weekly in small group Bible study and study on their own. They are our most Biblically-educated members. Other people in the church are SERVING PEOPLE. When there are basketball tournaments to run, church workdays, tasks like ushering and van driving and coaching, etc., these people are faithful in this essential work. From the perspective of the actual ministry aspect of the church, the SERVING people are the backbone of the church. It would be hard to run the programs of the church without them. People are usually mainly STUDYING PEOPLE or mainly SERVING PEOPLE." Is that a similar picture of what you see in your ministry?

If STUDYING PEOPLE is door #1, and SERVING PEOPLE is door #2, what we really need in urban churches today is door #3—people who are BOTH STUDYING PEOPLE and SERVING PEOPLE!

As leaders, we must keep working at leading all our people to become BOTH STUDYING and SERVING PEOPLE! "Whoa! Whoa! Whoa!" you say. "In our ministry, I'm just glad to get people to come to Bible class. Why do I need to keep pushing STUDYING PEOPLE to SERVE when we're always 10 volunteers too short in most every ministry? I don't know if I should push SERVING PEOPLE to become better with STUDYING…"

Here's why this principle is so essential:

SERVING PEOPLE need to be STUDYING PEOPLE for the sake of "QUALITY CONTROL" regarding what's being taught or shared in ministry activities.

Let me explain. Every ministry program constantly presents moments to teach God's Word. For example, when a coach is leading basketball practice, there are teachable moments from the Word of God about how to resolve conflict (with confession and forgiveness), how to work as a team and think of others ahead of yourself (Philippians 2:3–4), how to be careful in how we speak (James 3:1–12), etc. This is in addition to the opportunity when you get to share the Gospel with a player, and then reach their unchurched parent through the ministry of the basketball team.

If coaches are just SERVING PEOPLE and not also STUDYING PEOPLE as well, we miss a great opportunity for ministry. Also, we miss teaching Biblical ways of handling life. Other serving ministries present the same opportunities. In van ministry, there are lessons in patience that can be taught. There are also direct Bible teaching opportunities in church afterschool programs, where leaders need to know the truth of God themselves. In many of the basic church activities that bring people together, conversation always takes place. How much better quality ministry takes place when SERVERS are also STUDYERS who know and apply the Word of God for themselves and lead others to apply it to situations? There is no way the pastor can be present at every ministry to Biblically clarify and interpret every moment from a Biblical perspective. SERVERS also need to be STUDYERS.

SERVING PEOPLE need to be STUDYING PEOPLE for the sake of WISDOM in HANDLING THE ENEMY'S ATTACKS.

Here's something we can count on. Especially as a ministry program begins to have success, the devil is going to attack it. He will especially sow seeds of conflict, division, and discouragement among the leaders. When the SERVING LEADERS are also STUDYING LEADERS, they have learned to see these attacks for what they are. They are humble and have learned how to bury conflict through confession and forgiveness among one another. It makes sense—Scripture continually comes back to sin and grace. How relevant and necessary for pragmatic ministry.

SERVING PEOPLE need to be STUDYING PEOPLE for the sake of having the STRENGTH NOT TO GET WEARY.

Everybody gets tired in ministry. That is especially true with ministry in urban areas, where there is never enough staffing for ministry programs.

When SERVERS are STUDYERS, God's Word teaches us to balance our lives. God's Word invites us to handle our weariness with prayer and faith in God's promises, not with complaining, accusing others, or quitting. Recall when Jesus met the Samaritan woman at the well in John 4. Most of that episode took place when the disciples were getting food for Jesus and their team of disciples. Recall what happened when the disciples returned in John 4:31–34 and pushed Jesus to eat something. Jesus said in verse 32, "I have food to eat that you do not know about." Then again in verse 4, "My food is to do the will of Him who sent Me and to accomplish His work." Was Jesus rejecting eating food? Of course not! We have to eat to keep up our strength. But Jesus was reminding the disciples of another kind of sustenance. It's the kind recorded at the end of Deuteronomy 8:3, "...man does not live by bread alone, but man lives by everything that proceeds out of the mouth of the Lord." The Psalm writer puts it even more succinctly in Psalm 119:93, "For I will never forget Your precepts, For by them, You have revived me." Here's the idea. When I get tired, I can either keep my eyes on my worn-out self, or I can keep my eyes on the Lord's promises. He says, "I will revive you. Trust me, I will strengthen you. I love you." Here's one of my favorite promises that encourages me to trust the Lord and put my strength on automatic pilot in Him. Philippians 2:13, "It is God who is at work in you, both to will and to work His good pleasure."

Now for the other side of the coin. We need to encourage STUDYING PEOPLE to also be SERVING PEOPLE.

First, let's remember that GOD'S WORD IS ALWAYS TO BE PRACTICED and lived out in life.

Jesus said, "Blessed are those who hear the Word of God and observe it." (Luke 11:28) Go back and read over that wonderful section from James 2:14–18, where James says, "Faith, if it has no works, is dead," (2:17), and "I will show you my faith by my works." (2:18). STUDYING PEOPLE need to put into action and see what it means to "trust in the Lord with all our heart and lean not on our own understanding... the Lord makes our paths straight." (Proverbs 3:5–6) It works! STUDYING PEOPLE who know of the comfort of the Lord need to experience bringing that comfort of the Lord to others. Second Corinthians 1:4 says God "comforts us in all our affliction so that we will be able to comfort those who are in any affliction with the comfort with which we ourselves are comforted by God." God's comfort isn't to remain in us, but instead to go out to others through us. I am spiritually out of balance when I STUDY, but don't also SERVE others. If leaders ignore that truth, it will encourage spiritually sick sheep.

Especially in the inner-city, we need "all hands on board." STUDYERS SERVING MAXIMIZES the SIZE OF OUR OUTREACH.

It is a numbers game! Remember those famous words of Ecclesiastes 4:9, "Two are better than one because they have a good return for their labor." When we do ministry work with more people, both the OUTCOME and the WORKLOAD are affected. We can do more and reach more people on a project with 10 volunteers than five volunteers. Also, the load becomes easier with 10 volunteers than five volunteers. It's like when we run our summer community carnivals. We can run the carnival with 15 volunteers doing everything if we have to. But it's BETTER with 25–30 volunteers serving in teams. One team does set-up and then leaves, another team comes to run the carnival and then leaves when it is over, and another team arrives to pack-up and clean-up the carnival.

As STUDYERS SERVE, there is BIBLICAL LEADERSHIP and ENCOURAGEMENT that they can impart.

Have you ever planned an event where the number of people who showed up was far less than you hoped? When you have SERVERS present who regularly STUDY the Word of God, they can bring insights that people who aren't in the Scriptures regularly might miss. For example, a STUDY person who served at the event might remind us, "Let's not get bummed by those who didn't show up. Let's celebrate the ministry we did with the smaller group of people. Remember how _____ really grew through this event?" That kind of thinking is not just "put on a happy face" kind of stuff. No, it's really Biblical. God, our Father, has His eye on each person and every detail of our lives. Jesus said in Matthew 10:29–31, "Are not two sparrows sold for a cent? And yet not one of them will fall to the ground apart from your Father. But the very hairs of your head are all numbered. So do not fear; you are more valuable than many sparrows." I need that simple Biblical encouragement because, while we'd all love to have big numbers at events, we can still do great individual ministry as we value what the Holy Spirit is doing in individuals, just like our Father does!

About 10 years ago, we were setting up for one of our Taking Jesus to the Streets (TJTTS) summer outreach nights in a very rough part of North St. Louis. Just one street over from us there was a drive-by shooting. We saw it happen right across the vacant field from us. It happened quickly. The car pulled away, and it was over. Within about 90 seconds, about 12 police squad cars flooded the area. Of course, when we heard the shots, we all ran for cover immediately. But when it was over, there was a decision to make. Kids were looking at us, wanting us to still do our TJTTS program. As we were standing there sort of wondering what to do, a wise young woman (who was a STUDYER) said, "Well, let's get started y'all. What else are we going to do? God will take care of us." That was great Biblical leadership. We got started. We did TJTTS, while the cops did their investigation on the other street. A bunch of kids came and learned about Jesus that night. Like the woman who was the STUDYER said, "What else were we going to do?"

Make it a priority to help people mature so that they grow BOTH in SERVING and in STUDYING God's Word!

18

REMEMBER WHAT'S REALLY AT WORK

What I'm about to place before you, you already know. That's true of most everything I've written in this book, but you and I do need to be reminded of it.

- When two very talented servants of Christ continue to pick at each other, intentionally look for ways to wound one another, and put the worst construction on every word and every action, what's really going on is the SINFUL, DESTRUCTIVE POWER OF SELF.

- When you and I make personal choices to act in foolish, ungodly ways that we would normally never approve of, in those moments we're caught up in the SINFUL, DESTRUCTIVE POWER OF SELF.

- The reason why people sometimes break promises they've made, especially when you were counting on them, isn't always that they're bad people. Rather, it's because in that moment they gave in to the SINFUL, DESTRUCTIVE POWER OF SELF.

- When someone who has power goes overboard in their use of it, what's really going on is the SINFUL, DESTRUCTIVE POWER OF SELF.

- When you and I try to control and even force things to our liking and our timing, instead of surrendering it to the Lord, in those moments we are captured by the SINFUL, DESTRUCTIVE POWER OF SELF.

- When we isolate away from people in times of depression and try to handle things on our own and self-medicate, instead of relying on the Lord and the people He has sent to care for us, we are shackled by the SINFUL, DESTRUCTIVE POWER OF SELF.

This list could go on and on. I bring this before you only to encourage you in what to do when you see issues like these in people.

Don't try and treat just the surface symptoms. See the core problem—the SINFUL, DESTRUCTIVE POWER OF SELF.

Ok, so how do we get freedom from the SINFUL, DESTRUCTIVE POWER OF SELF? How do we help others gain their liberty from the chains of the SINFUL, DESTRUCTIVE POWER OF SELF? I find Hebrews 4:12–16 to be an incredibly practical word. Notice in verses 12–13 the power of the Word of God—it is "living and active and sharper than any two-edged sword." If I've got puffed up excuses about why I think I'm justified in holding on to my sinful selfish attitudes and behavior, the Word of God "pierces" right through them! More important is the hope of verses 14–16. Jesus, the Son of God and our High Priest who understands our "weaknesses" and our "temptations," can give us help—mercy, grace, and forgiveness—because of the death and resurrection of Christ! When the SINFUL, DESTRUCTIVE POWER OF SELF rules over me, it is that simple. First, I hear God's Word that reminds me when I've gotten off track and into myself. Then I bring my failures to the Lord in repentance, and I receive the great news that God isn't giving up on me, but is again forgiving me for the sake of Christ! What a God!

Wait a minute! What about the people in my ministry who are "trippin'" with the SINFUL, DESTRUCTIVE POWER OF SELF?

The strategy is the same. Our encouragement to "try and play nice with one another…" Or to say, "You really hurt this person by not keeping your promises…" Or to insist, "You need to watch what you say around…"—none of that will loosen this SINFUL, DESTRUCTIVE POWER OF SELF long term. Only the Word of God will do it. Contact with the Word of God is the key, and that's where the power is. It's especially meaningful when you can study with a person in a small group Bible study. I'm not talking about designing a study for the very issue that they're going through. Rather, engage them in a small group Bible study, and let them get into God's Word. In the process, God's Word will get into them and bring about change and freedom!

People will fight this. They'll make all kinds of excuses as to why they don't have time. BUT, the truth is, consistent, regular contact with God's Word—especially in a small group Bible study—is the best spiritual care we can give the people of our flock! There is no substitute for it.

19

A STREAM OF NEW VISITORS

I visited the same urban church three times over five years. One time, I preached at the church. On both other occasions, I was at the church simply because I had a Sunday off and was in the area. The Holy Spirit used what I saw at this urban church in those three visits to send me a vital message. What I saw was this: aside from a few members who had died, and a handful of new people who had joined the church over the five-year span, it was the same congregation of people.

The Holy Spirit told me to pay attention to that "sameness" and challenged me to ask, "Why?" Where were the new people who have been reached? Even if they came for only a short time, but didn't stay, where is the STREAM OF NEW VISITORS?

The same could be said about a kids program—where are the new kids? Or is the same crowd the same crowd every week? The same could be said for a small group. A small group that stays the same without filling its "empty chair" can easily become a clique. I know, I know. Reaching new people on a weekly basis is hard with all of the other things that need to be done in the ministry.

Yet, here's the truism—keep making REACHING people a PRIORITY!

Of course, there are some weeks when our ministries get so overwhelming with so much to do that we just don't make REACHING NEW PEOPLE a priority. But if that becomes the trend and the status quo, we're not "GOING" into all the world like Jesus asked us to do. The way our urban ministry looks today will very likely be the same way it looks five years from now.

Moreover, if our goal is to reach new people and then help them become committed disciples of Christ, that disciple process often takes time. Wise is the urban ministry leadership who views the people within reach of their ministry "IN STAGES." For example:

- STAGE #1—new people we are reaching out to every week and inviting to a Bethlehem program
- STAGE #2—new people who HAVE COME to at least one Bethlehem ministry
- STAGE #3—new people who have started to CONSISTENTLY attend a Bethlehem ministry program (usually a non-Sunday ministry)
- STAGE #4—new people who have started to consistently attend SUNDAY MORNING WORSHIP
- STAGE #5—new people who are also part of a WEEKLY SMALL GROUP or SERVING MINISTRY

You've got the idea. You know the STAGES that work for your ministry. I will talk more about this concept of growth in another essay. But for this essay, rewind to STAGE #1.

How about systematically prioritizing new people for the next six weeks of your ministry life? Here's what I mean:

1. **Target 10 invitations to a ministry event to people each week, for the next six weeks.**
2. **Keep track and see who is coming to your ministry events. Is it the same people? How many new visitors are you having? Are the new visitors coming back?**

Put your ministry work under a microscope and see what the Holy Spirit will show you! Insist on this not just for yourself (you must lead by example), but also involve all your leaders in this six-week emphasis.

The idea of a steady stream of new visitors isn't something I thought up. Yep! You guessed it. It's in the Bible. Turn in your Bible to Mark 1 for a simple snapshot of Jesus' ministry. After His teaching and a miracle in

Capernaum in Mark 1:21–27, what happened according to verse 28? Then what happened according to verses 32–34? Jesus was constantly reaching new people, according to verses 38–39. After resting, what did He do? Even as crowds were coming to Him, what did Jesus do? Did Jesus "headquarter," open His doors, and then wait on the people to come to Him? One thing I love about Jesus is that what He commands us in Mark 16:15 about reaching new people, He first put into practice Himself!

I said this already, but it needs to be said again. I feel for those of you who serve on the urban scene where your schedule is so overwhelming and there are always a ton of "people emergencies." But become personally stubborn and decide that as you order your week and assign your time, you will make reaching A STREAM OF NEW VISITORS your priority.

20

PUTTING FAMILY BACK INTO URBAN AREAS

Alecia Beth Moore, you also know her as "Pink", co-wrote with Scott Storch a song called "Family Portrait" that was released in December of 2002. Pink writes about coming home to a place that's supposed to be her shelter, but it's more like World War III with all the fights about money and family. In the song, she says she never knew what love could be and doesn't want to repeat the same mistakes in her own family.

The words are spot on regarding the difficult situation many families are in today. And, it's everywhere—in suburbs and urban areas, among the rich and the poor, both Christians and non-Christians—all have brokenness in their families. Sometimes having money can mask the damage in families.

For us in lower-income, urban areas, the absence of solid family life stands continually right in front of us. Well, "Let's have parenting classes!" is often the first response. Educating parents is important. There is some truth to that. Yet, the problem is more fundamental. Most parents who need parenting help and guidance won't come to a class. Worse than that, most parents who know their home isn't what it should be don't want to change enough to do something about the brokenness in their home. So what do we do? Of course, first, we pray and ask the Lord to turn around this epidemic failure that keeps plaguing our families. However, what happens with the children whose parents won't do what's needed to change their family life? If they continue in a family like Pink wrote about, there's a great likelihood that their future family will simply repeat the cycle they've grown up in.

ENTER GOD'S PEOPLE, THE CHURCH! The Church is the best opportunity to BE FAMILY to those who are "family-less" and TEACH WHAT FAMILY IS to those who are family-less.

First, let's think about **WHAT IT MEANS TO BE FAMILY.** That could be an entire book. But for now, think about these following five insights. Aren't they at the heart of what true family is all about?

1 – REAL FAMILY is about CHRIST'S LOVE. That's what we believe as children of God. For example, Christ followers are the best people to take care of one another in a family—see what our Savior did in John 19:25–27. Who did Jesus Himself consider to be closest to Him? See Mark 3:31–35. Who is essential to every family if it's going to be strong? Psalm 127:1 has the answer. What ties us together as family is the love that Christ has for us, so much so that He gave His life for us at the cross. Christ gives us the inarguable reason to treat one another with love and care. "We love because He first loved us," says 1 John 4:19. When any of us get tired of loving or caring for others, all we need to do is think about how the Lord Jesus loved us. His relationship with us is the basis for our relationship with others in our families.

2 – REAL FAMILY is about CONSISTENCY. Being consistent means having love and care for each other that operates day in and day out instead of hit and miss. It's the word the Bible calls, "FAITHFULNESS." FAITHFUL love shows itself in keeping promises and being there to support each other, especially when doing so might be costly and inconvenient.

Isn't that the kind of relationship consistency that is missing from so many families today? I'll never forget a 9-year-old girl who had a huge smile on her face one night when I picked her up for our Children's Wednesday Bible program. I asked her, "Yolanda, what are you giggly about tonight?"

She said, "Pastor, my mama is coming to get me Friday night to take me to the movies!"

You see, Yolanda, was staying in a foster home. Her father had really never been around. Yolanda had been taken away from her mother because she abandoned her child for an intense substance addiction. But at that moment, years of disappointment from her mother had melted into the excitement of a Friday night date with her. When I saw Yolanda the following Sunday, her giddiness was gone. I learned the story from her foster mother, and you might already know how this story went.

The mother was to pick up Yolanda at 5:00 p.m., but by six that night, no mother. Seven o'clock came and went, no mother and no call. By 8:00 p.m., there was still no call, no message, no mama. By nine, her foster mother put her arms around Yolanda and helped her get dressed for bed. I could tell you countless stories just as unhappy as this one—stories of parents who left their kids at home alone until 11:00 at night, stories of kids needing to find their own food, and stories of parents who didn't even attend their own children's high school graduation. Strong families are places where love can be counted on and where the word of family members is true and can be trusted.

3 – REAL FAMILY is about SERVING OTHERS. Here is a riddle. When is it easiest for me to share money with others? When is it easiest for me to help others? When is it easiest for me to love and care for others? When? When? When? Give up? It's when I know there is someone providing money for me. It's when I know there is someone who will help me. It's when I know there is someone who will love and care for me.

What often suffocates people in families from serving others and lures them into living only for themselves is the fear that "I" won't be taken care of. Think about a spouse who says, "I need to take care of myself, because my spouse isn't." Or consider a child who says, "I need to watch out for me." If they knew that somebody else was watching out for them, then they wouldn't have to watch out for themselves. They would be free to be a blessing to others.

Especially in many urban families, life has become an "each one for themselves" type of existence. That's why so many people struggle with experiencing the joy of serving others. But there is an answer for this. There is a drastic change of mindset when you come to know the Lord. Listen to 2 Corinthians 6:18, "'I will be a father to you, and you shall be sons and daughters to Me,' says the Lord Almighty." Think about that. If God has all power and all authority and He is over all things, has adopted me, and said HE will be MY FATHER who will take care of me, then I have the FREEDOM to SERVE OTHERS! Knowing my Father is taking care of me enables me to take care of others. I no longer have to take care of myself, because someone else (my Father in heaven) has my life covered. If everybody in our families thought like that, what difference would it make?

4 – REAL FAMILY is about ACCOUNTABILITY. The word, "accountability," is a cousin to the word, "truth." Without truth and accountability, any relationship is difficult, maybe even impossible. Accountability says, "When you've made a mistake, don't try to hide it. Own up to it and tell the truth about it." This goes directly against the "street code" of most urban communities. In the street code, a person *never* admits wrongdoing. In the street code, you never tell the truth about the wrongdoing you know about or the wrongdoing you've seen. "Snitches get stiches."

But REAL FAMILY is about just the opposite. REAL FAMILY is about honesty. REAL FAMILY is about transparency regarding where you've been and what you've done. Even when we've blown it by something we said or something we did, through Christ we have the courage to be honest and truthful about our failures. That great news of 1 John 1:9 gives us the courage to be completely real—"If we confess our sins, God is faithful and just and (because of Christ's death at the cross for our sins) will forgive our sins and cleanse us from all unrighteousness." If we can't be honest, truthful, and accountable toward one another, how can we ever learn to trust one another? Forgiveness from God and forgiveness toward each other open the door for us to be completely "100" with each other.

5 – REAL FAMILY is about RECOVERY. Most families have some form of family photos. Recently, we took such a picture of our family at the wedding of one of my sons. It's great to see the whole family together smiling. However, in every family, the enemy has the same goal—he wants to eliminate that picture. He wants certain family members to disappear. To do this, he'll sow seeds of conflict among family members. He'll create confusion. He will even try to get family members in the picture to turn to themselves and their own wants, instead of valuing family oneness.

This happens in EVERY family. The key question is, "What are you committed to?" Is it okay to let family members withdraw into their own anger and selfishness? Is it okay to let the family picture shrink and allow family members to go missing? Also, let's not forget the difficult and destructive role that pride takes when it comes into play. Pride remembers hurtful words. Pride never forgets painful acts and betrayal. Pride often refuses to forgive. But in moments like these, the Word of our Lord must rule.

Ephesians, 4:31 says, "Let all bitterness and wrath and anger and clamor and slander be put away from you, along with all malice. Be kind to one another, tender-hearted, forgiving each other..." But you say, "I don't feel like doing that. You don't know what they did to us in the family. You don't know how they hurt us." Let Ephesians 4:32 finish. Here's why we must forgive, and **here's why we must always be people who seek RECOVERY with people.** The Scripture says, "Just as God in Christ also has forgiven you...." Galatians 6:1 says it this way: "Brothers, even if anyone is caught in any trespass, you who are spiritual, restore such a one in the spirit of gentleness..." How powerfully we, in the Church, will be used when we are committed to the RECOVERY of people into the family of God.

THE CHURCH has a GREAT OPPORTUNITY to BE FAMILY

to people!

We can love others with **the same kind of continual love that Christ loves us with.** Unlike ordinary love that gets tired, runs out, and breaks, we continue to be filled with love from our Father God as He loves us with patience and forgiveness because of Jesus.

We can be **the CONSISTENT FAMILY that so many people need.** One thing is especially true about the urban family scene—brokenness is ongoing. How powerful our FAMILY LOVE can be when people witness us making promises and KEEPING THEM! When biological family members don't show up for games, school programs, concerts, and accomplishments, it will not go unnoticed when God's people show up at those same events to cheer others on! What is vitally important is CONSISTENCY! We began our "More Greater Things" ministry work to families in the Ferguson, Missouri, area after the 2014 riots that were broadcast on national television. A team of our members went into one of the housing projects there to host one of our Taking Jesus to the Streets ministry events (sort of a Vacation Bible School on wheels). Over 100 people gathered in about 20 minutes for our presentation of Jesus' Good News. One of the most common questions the families asked us right at the beginning was, "So are you going to keep coming in and working with our kids? Or are you going to be like the other churches who come for a day, and then we don't see them again for six months?" Just as each of us knows the importance of CONSISTENCY in our own family relationships, CONSISTENCY is vital in our ministry work to BE FAMILY to others.

We can be **the SERVING FAMILY that is so often missing from people's lives,** even when the serving is UNCOMFORTABLE or INCONVENIENT. Several times there have been young people in our congregation with no place to go because they were put out of their parents' house. Whole families have been put out of their apartments in emergency cases. Time and time again, I have witnessed God's people in the church stepping in to open their homes on a short term or even longer term basis. Sometimes the serving is something simple—helping with a bill, bringing someone groceries, or watching somebody's kids while they worked.

BEING FAMILY to people through serving has limitless possibilities. It is so important. People will never forget our service. Two Bible passages give us a mandate to BE FAMILY like this. David said in Psalm 27:10, "For my father and my mother have forsaken me, But the Lord will take me up." The Word of God also converts that principle into our work as God's people in Acts 4:32, "And the congregation of those who believed were of one heart and soul and not one of them claimed that anything belonging to him was his own, but all things were common property to them."

You're probably thinking, "This is an intense kind of living!" Yes, it is. It is time-consuming and often exhausting. You won't last in this kind of ministry if you are full of yourself—there's just not enough "self-return and reward" in it. Yet, if you will BE FAMILY to others, you will see contemporary miracles of the Holy Spirit in the lives of people.

Part of **BEING FAMILY to others also includes ACCOUNTABILITY.** This is a tough one. It is sometimes hard to bring the accountability of the Word of God into people's lives who have lived for so long apart from what the Word of God says. The dynamic of LAW-GOSPEL is vital. Here's a quick reminder of that dynamic. The law of God sets forth what His expectations are for us. When we fail to meet what God wants, it is sin. The Gospel is the Good News that when we confess our sins to the Lord, our Father in heaven forgives our sins because of Jesus' death on the cross and resurrection that paid for our sins.

Let's dive into a very real family situation to illustrate this principle. Jimmy and Lisa have four kids. They are not married. They live together. On one extreme, a church sometimes says, "These people are living in sin. Until they stop living in sin and separate or get married, we have no time for them." On the other hand, some churches say, "Let's just ignore this. God's love is big enough for any situation. The Lord will understand." Neither of those are God's perspective on how to be family to people.

Here's a place to start with accountability:

1. Let's build a relationship with Jimmy and Lisa and their family. If we have no relationship with them, there will be no opportunity for conversation. If the topic of two people living together came up in conversation, of course we would say that this is not God's will for a man and woman. But at the beginning, let's introduce them to our Savior and His love for us.

2. As we build a relationship with Jimmy and Lisa, let's be prayerful and planned regarding how we talk about God's plan for healthy, strong, and blessed relationships. It's easy to show the blessing of God's plan of marriage between a man and a woman.

3. Let's acknowledge that God's power, not our pressure, will be the only way lifestyles and behaviors change. That powerful faith comes to us only as we keep on, and keep on, and keep on growing in our contact with God's Word (Romans 10:17).

4. While we certainly acknowledge that to live life in intentional sin is dangerous, God's work of faith and a heart that yields to Him is on a timetable beyond our control. Our job is to love people and set before them WHO Christ is and WHAT He has done for them. What motivated the change in Zacchaeus in Luke 19:1–10? What brought about the turnaround in the woman described in John 8:3–11? Only one thing—when each of them came in contact with the love of Jesus the Savior. Jesus' love came, and *then* their changed behavior came, not vice versa.

We will come to places in relationships where our love includes speaking in very true ways about the seriousness of sin. But we will never have the opportunity to have that serious talk, without first having a relationship in Jesus with the person that we're talking to.

There are many translations for this approach of Christ's love today. It's needed with people who are confused about who God wants them to be sexually. It's needed with people who are battling addictive strongholds.

It's needed by those who have made their own selves their main god. It's needed by those who define the Christian walk as only attending church every Sunday. You're getting it. Accountability to God's Word is before *each one of us* as members of God's family. Our only hope is bowing before the Lord as we let His love overwhelm, fix, and control us.

Be prepared. This kind of BEING FAMILY to others will be filled with times of DISAPPOINTMENT. Which of the following have you experienced?

- Jason promised that he would come to Sunday worship, but now for the fifth time, he didn't show up.

- After Tatiana got pregnant and had her baby out of wedlock, she said it would never happen again... but it did.

- David had so much talent musically. He could really sing. Our choir needed an incredible lead singer like him. But he just couldn't stay away from drugs.

- When Lance says something today, you can count on it. But for six long years, Lance lied and then lied more to cover other lies.

- We invited Michele into our home to stay with us because she had no place to go. We took her shopping for the basic things she needed. Why did she still steal from us?

Whenever you and I choose to BE FAMILY in Christ to someone, it's guaranteed that we're going to face disappointments from the very people we're trying to help. That's the evil one's mission against our ministry. He wants to frustrate us and push us to give up on people. He wants us to stop trying to BE FAMILY and stop leading them to a relationship with the Savior. His aim is to get us to say three words, "I'VE HAD ENOUGH!" But even though the disappointments hurt us and try to capture our attention, Jesus wants us to keep our focus on RECOVERY.

You've never heard this story. It wasn't in the newspapers or on ESPN. It's actually so old that, back in 1976 when it happened, there was no ESPN! But I remember what happened at Trinity Lutheran School in Oshkosh, Wisconsin, during my eighth-grade year. The Concordia Lutheran School basketball team that I played for hadn't won a tournament in years. In fact, in the previous season we only won three games! But we made it to the semi-final game of the Trinity Oshkosh tournament that year. We were down by eight points with just a minute left to play, and the teams were in a timeout. All hope should have been lost. It would be understandable to think, "We gave it our all. We did our best. But it just wasn't enough." However, our coaches were the late Daryl Haake, and my dad, Bob Schmidtke. Their message during the timeout was a little different. "Keep playing," they told us. "You can come back."

You've seen this movie a thousand times already, but we did come back—and this was even before the three-point shot came into mainstream basketball! We won the semi-final game, went to the championship game, and then won the tournament! This is what I love the most about the message of Christ. I am a massive screw-up in sin when it comes to the things that I say and what goes on in my mind and heart. Asking for forgiveness for sin is part of my daily "to-do list" with the Lord. Without the grace of God, there would be no hope for me. But like Paul, the former Christian tormenter, said of his early life in 1 Corinthians 15:9–10 and like David, the adulterer, said about God's work in his life in Psalm 32:1–7, I am grateful that our Lord never stops being the GOD of RECOVERY!

Don't miss what I'm saying. Sin should bring shame to our lives. The purpose of guilt is to drive us to our knees in repentance. But Luke 19:10 says the LORD OF RECOVERY came expressly for this purpose—to BRING RECOVERY to what is lost in sin!

A simple, two-word question has become so important to me in my own life and in my ministry of BEING FAMILY to others. It's the question, "NOW WHAT?" Let's say you had an affair with someone with whom you were not married, and you acknowledge your sin. "NOW WHAT?" Yes, you did spread gossip and rumors and were successful in cutting another person to pieces with your sharp words. "NOW WHAT?" For the past seven years, you haven't been the parent to your children that you should have been. "NOW WHAT?" You were on your computer looking at some stuff that you shouldn't have been looking at. "NOW WHAT?" Again, you blew your rent money at the casino. "NOW WHAT?" You've had Matthew 7:3–5 disease again and again and again. "NOW WHAT?"

God's Good News of Isaiah 1:18 is that He doesn't leave us alone to deal with these messes. He doesn't give up on us! Through the sacrifice of Christ's life for our sins at Calvary, God is always in our life huddle saying, "I forgive you. Keep playing. Keep living. You can come back!" Psalm 118, especially in its first four verses, sets forth the Gospel truth of the entire Bible—God's forgiveness, His mercy, and His desire for our continual recovery out of the mess of sin NEVER ENDS! There is no more powerful and more needed message than that for us to share as we seek to BE FAMILY to those who have no real family.

As we are FAMILY to those who are family-less, how exciting it will be for God the Holy Spirit to use us for duplication purposes and TEACH WHAT FAMILY IS SUPPOSED TO BE to the next generation!

21

A MUST FOR YOUR MINISTRY DESKTOP

I recently toured "Hitsville, U.S.A.," the birthplace of Motown Records. Although, I've been to the Motown Museum in Detroit a few times already, this time I went with our Bethlehem high school basketball team and learned something I never remembered hearing about before. Of course, when you think of Motown, you think of its founder and leader, Berry Gordy. But our tour guide mentioned a woman named Maxine

Powell. Maxine was part of a team of people that Berry put together to train artists like Marvin Gaye, the Jackson 5, the Supremes, and Stevie Wonder. Wait a minute! Train stars like those giants? Yes. Berry's staff worked with his talented artists to develop them musically, help them with their dance moves on stage, and select clothing for their performances. Maxine worked in the department of Artist Personal Development, and her job was to work with artists on manners, social graces, and stage presence.

The underlying principle here is so important—just because a person has talent doesn't mean that they and their talent don't need developing. Or to say it in another way, Berry Gordy recognized that he was in the people development business, as well as the entertainment business!

This same principle should stay on the desktop of every leader in an urban church or ministry. Rare are the times when someone comes to our ministries whose life and ministry gifts from the Lord are developed. What is usual and more commonplace is that God uses us to develop the ministry gifts that He has put in people. I can't tell you how many times I have looked at other ministries and thought, "Why can't I have people in our ministry who can sing like that? Or lead like that? Or work with kids like that? Or can organize like that? Why can't I have as many musicians who can all play like that church over there does?" In turn, I know there are also other ministries who have said the same things about our church family. But let me repeat what I said a few lines above.

Rare are the times when someone comes to our ministries whose life and ministry gifts from the Lord are developed. What is usual and more commonplace is that God uses us to develop the ministry gifts that He has put in people.

If I have accurately described the landscape of urban ministry (and I think I have), then there is only one of two direction choices we can take:

We can spend our ministry life complaining and whining about the people we don't have and make that our excuse for not being able to progress in ministry.

OR

We can decide that among our priorities of working in the Lord's Kingdom each week, we will help people develop their gifts from God to use in joyful ways.

What does this mean? Specifically, you'll need to decide the particular ways in which to develop the people in your ministry. I don't know your ministry like you do, but only for the sake of example, consider these questions:

- Who needs vocal lessons in order to be the singer they can be?

- Who could be your next drummer or keyboard player or guitarist, if you helped them with music lessons?

- Who could be the next coach of one of your basketball teams, if maybe this year they came aboard as your assistant coach?

- Who could be the next chairperson of your church homecoming event, or basketball tournament, or "family and friends day"—if you gave them some mentoring?

- Who could become your next elder/deacons, or small group leader, or properties manager if you helped coach them?

You've got the idea! Now, permit me to be a "mind excuse reader." You're thinking something like:

- "But I don't have time to do all of the things that currently need to be done in our ministry each week. Where will I ever get time to add developing/coaching people each week?"

  RESPONSE—I understand. At least invest SOME of your time each week in developing people. If you don't, your leadership and circle of developed workers will never get larger.

- "I'm not even gifted to develop some of the areas where I need people to be developed. I don't play piano myself—how can I teach someone how to play? I don't know much about sports—how can I develop a new coach?"

RESPONSE—Who says it has to be YOU that does all of the actual coaching? Your work could be finding other coaches to develop your people. You just bear the responsibility of making sure it gets done.

- "I'll do it next year. Right now, I just have too much going on."

RESPONSE—I understand you might have to close out some things in your life as you make DEVELOPING OTHERS a new priority in your weekly routine. Yet, be careful of putting off this vital work. How true are the words of an unknown author, "One of these days is often none of these days."

What did you do with your time during the COVID-19 pandemic when all of us had to shelter in place? Was it just "down" time? Here's what we did at Bethlehem. I helped two of our musically inclined members to work on some simple praise songs for our Sunday morning worship. While both of these young ladies had the talent to play, they had never taken the time to sit down and do it. Now they had time on their hands, so I challenged them to practice these three songs. They worked hard on them. After about three weeks, they were ready. We used the ladies to play keyboard on the songs they worked on for two of our Sunday online broadcasts. Usually, our Minister of Music plays almost all our worship music. Now, guess what has happened? These two young ladies are learning new worship songs to play. This is how Bethlehem is developing more church musicians for our music ministry! Developing more leaders means more ministry can be accomplished! We could have put off trying to address this ministry need of developing more leaders. But we are glad we didn't.

A quote I found from a professor named Karen Lamb who teaches Oral Communication captures exactly the lesson I learned from this experience, "A year from now you may wish you had started today." True! True! True!

Here is our challenge—"WHO will you make time for this week to help develop the gifts God has placed in them? What time will you dedicate toward this? How will you do it? What steps will you take

toward doing it?" Don't leave these questions unanswered for one more day!

22

I NEED MY WEEKLY FAMILY MEETING

Acts 16:13 says, "And on the Sabbath day we went outside the gate to a riverside, where we were supposing there would be a place of prayer; and we sat down and began speaking to the women who had assembled." Would you join me in a little imaginary interview I'd like to have with the Apostle Paul?

"Okay, Paul, if I have this correct, you and your group—probably Silas, Luke, Timothy, maybe others—got together on the Sabbath day when you were in the city of Philippi. I understand you went out to a place by the riverside, expecting to find some Christ followers with whom you could gather for worship. NOW I'VE GOT SOME QUESTIONS: Weren't you tired from all the travelling? Weren't you maybe even tired of people by this time? I mean, we all need a break from people when we work in ministry. And since there's no synagogue in Philippi, wouldn't this have been the perfect Sabbath day just to chill and sleep in? Or if you wanted to pray and worship, why not have a little worship time among yourselves? I'm guessing that very likely you didn't even know this group of women who gathered down by the riverside to worship. Paul, WHY DID YOU AND YOUR GROUP GO OUT TO FIND OTHER CHRIST FOLLOWERS TO WORSHIP WITH? Inquiring minds want to know!"

I think I know the answer to my own questions. I'd say 99% of the time I feel just like Paul felt. (There is a 1% human side of me that would like to stay in bed and sleep on a Sunday morning!) Here's the bottom line. No matter if it's been a great week or a stressful week, a week when I personally won over temptation, or a week when I lost, a week when people have tested me to the limit, or a week when I felt as if I couldn't take it any longer, I have learned this:

I NEED MY WEEKLY FAMILY MEETING.

I need my Lord working on me not just VERTICALLY, but also I need Him to minister to me HORIZONTALLY! Just to be clear, my VERTICAL relationship with my Father in heaven is how He directly cares for me through the promises of His Word. He does this through the identity He has given to me as His child in my Baptism and through the assurance He gives that He is on my side, because Christ's death keeps covering my sins. That VERTICAL strength is unquestionable!

But there is another source of strength that our Father pours into our lives. He imparts this strength to us in HORIZONTAL ways through the ministry and touch of others in the name of Jesus.

The Bible is full of examples of people God uses to strengthen us in a HORIZONTAL WAY. See what Barnabas meant to Paul in Acts 9:26–27. See what Jonathan meant to David in 1 Samuel 20:12–34. The HORIZONTAL LOVE OF GOD the Lord brings us through other people is well-described in Hebrews 10:23–25, "Let us hold fast the confession of our hope without wavering, for He who promised is faithful..." There's the goal of life—that we may not give up on our faith in Christ, especially when adversity comes. But how do we hang on? How do we stay strong, trusting the Lord when we feel like giving up and letting go? Read on to verse 24, "And let us consider how to stimulate one another to love and good deeds..." The idea of the word stimulate is to "spur" and "cheer" one another on when we get lethargic or want to quit. We all get tired sometimes. I need you to encourage me to keep going as I trust and serve the Lord. In verse 25, the writer reminds us how this HORIZONTAL LOVE OF GOD occurs. He says, "...not forsaking our own assembling together, as is the habit of some, but encouraging one another; and all the more as you see the day drawing near."

WHEN WE GATHER—whether in worship, or small study groups, or serving groups, or even when you invite me to go get a soda to converse about how God keeps taking care of us—these are times when we can talk and encourage each other. I need your hug that reminds me everything is going to be alright because the Lord is in control. I need your ear to listen to my pains, and then I need your encouraging words that point me back to Christ. I need you to check on me so that I know I am not forgotten and so that I remember somebody cares for me in Jesus. I need you to come by my side when situations arise that are beyond me and I need help. I need you to correct me and call me back to what is important when I wander away from the Lord. It takes Christ's family to do this for me.

The place where I most consistently receive this kind of care, and can observe it in the largest way, is my WEEKLY MEETING in God's House. This is why it is such a downer for me when you aren't at worship or our small group meeting. I really miss you, because I needed to see you in order to receive, FROM you and THROUGH you, the HORIZONTAL LOVE of Christ our Lord.

By the way, if our small groups and Sunday morning worship can become places where people receive the HORIZONTAL love, peace, forgiveness, and acceptance of the Lord through us—it won't just be a blessing of strength for us alone. Our meetings will be coveted by all who discover them. God used the Apostle James to tell us a very important message about the VERTICAL and HORIZONTAL LOVE when James said in James 2:18, "I will show you my faith by my works." For most people, the means by which they see the VERTICAL LOVE of our Father in Jesus Christ is through first experiencing God's HORIZONTAL LOVE from us.

Some popular song lyrics illustrate the power of what gathering in Jesus' name can be for both Christians and new Christians. "Where Everybody Knows Your Name" came from the pen of Gary Portnay and talks about going to a place where the people welcome you and even know you by name. This is why I need my weekly family meeting. I need to come to a place to regroup in the mercy of God. I need to come to a place where sinners gather to again be changed back into forgiven saints. I need to come to a place where I know God's love will flow to me, and I will leave stronger than the way I came. This is what the Church of Jesus Christ is supposed to be when it gathers—a place where, in Christ, everybody knows my name.

23

WHEN BAR-JESUS SHOWS UP

You can count on the fact that he will show up. You can count on him to try to stifle the growth the Holy Spirit is bringing about in those whom you and your ministry are reaching with the Good News of Jesus. You can count on him to be disruptive and try to darken every time the Light of Christ shines in people. His name is BAR-JESUS.

"What?" you ask. Yes, I said, "BAR-JESUS."

He is both a real person from Acts 13 and a recurring metaphor of the counter-attack the evil one always launches against those who bring Christ's message of life. First, open your Bible or Bible app and check out Acts 13:1–12. Verses 1–3 begin with a "send-off service" for Paul/Saul and Barnabas for some mission work that the Holy Spirit is leading them to do. In verses 6–7, Paul and Barnabas meet a magician named BAR-JESUS and the proconsul, Sergius Paulus. Let's think about the latter first. Sergius Paulus was the governor of the province and a man of great influence.

Let me translate that to today's ministry scene. Sometimes the Holy Spirit will provide us with an opportunity to bring the Gospel to a leader. It could be the leader of a community. It could be the leader of a team. It could be the leader of a gang. It could simply be the leader of a family. These are big moments! If by the grace of God and the faith-giving power of the Holy Spirit, the leader embraces Jesus as their Savior, what often also happens to those who follow or are influenced by the leader? Correct. They often come to know the Savior as well.

Every person, no matter who they are, is a precious soul for whom Christ died. But pay attention when the Lord sends you "leaders" who

can impact others. It's a moment for great Kingdom magnification.

Back to Acts 13:7. Not only did God give Paul and Barnabas an audience with Sergius Paulus, the record says that he was interested in the Word of God! Wow! How exciting! Don't you sense the "open door" and great opportunity for the Kingdom? In ministry, we need moments like this—moments when we see growth and feel as if the Lord's promise of Isaiah 55:10–11 is true and real!

When was the last time the Lord gave you an open door to a Sergius Paulus type of person?

Don't miss it when the Holy Spirit gives an open door to a child in the neighborhood who has great influence with many other children in the neighborhood. It can be a huge opportunity for God's Kingdom!

Notice that Acts 13:8 begins with "BUT..." You knew there would be one, right? And that's the next part of the lesson:

Where God the Holy Spirit is doing great things and opening doors, there will always be a BAR-JESUS/Elymas, sent by the enemy to try and throw water on all the Holy Spirit fire.

Expect it. Pay attention. In one form or another, BAR-JESUS is always coming when the Lord's work takes two steps forward. What do I mean? What does BAR-JESUS look like? Let's say a child is starting to grow in their faith and embraces your ministry as the place where they are finding people who love and care for them. BAR-JESUS is the parent who uses "church" to punish their child for bad behavior. They say to the child, "You've been clowning around in school. I know you love to go to youth group. Nope! You're grounded from going to Bethlehem for three weeks."

Ouch! That's a BAR-JESUS move. I get the discipline that the parent is trying to bring, but that child needs MORE JESUS, not LESS JESUS in this moment. BAR-JESUS shows up in other ways. Sometimes when someone is new in Christ (or has been away from the Lord and is reconnecting with Christ and His Church), BAR-JESUS can be someone who tries to get that person to work or take care of appointments on the same day as small group Bible study or on Sunday mornings.

BAR-JESUS can even sometimes be a church member who sows seeds of gossip and negativity into the ear of a brand-new member of the worshipping community. BAR-JESUS can also encompass an assortment of life factors. You might have to move, or take a different job, or deal with a family issue or some other matters that personally DISRUPT your LIFE WITH GOD in a strong worshipping community. I love the way the work of BAR-JESUS is described in one version of Acts 13:8. It says that BAR-JESUS was "seeking to turn the proconsul (Sergius Paulus) away from the faith (in the Lord)." Do you see it now? There are many BAR-JESUS forces constantly pulling people away from the Lord! Sometimes they are so overwhelming, and they discourage us in our ministry work. However, there are still four verses to go in this story about BAR-JESUS. In verses 9–11, you can see what happened to BAR-JESUS. However, more important to me is what it says happened to Sergius Paulus in verse 12.

Peter made a confession of faith that "Jesus is the Christ, the Son of the Living God," and Jesus gave Peter a promise about ministry in Matthew 16:18 on the basis of that confession. Christ said, "I will build My _____; and the gates of Hades (or to use Acts 13 language, BAR-JESUS) will not _____ it." You fill in those blanks.

This message is to encourage you in your ministry. Don't give up when BAR-JESUS seems so big and bad or when BAR-JESUS tries to checkmate every ministry move you make! Don't step back from aggressive ministry, especially to all of the influential Sergius Paulus types the Lord puts in your path.

While the battle may be long, while there may be setbacks in the work that you do with the Sergius Paulus types, remember what Jesus said to Peter in Matthew 16. Christ is stronger than any BAR-JESUS.

Christ is more powerful than the real enemy behind every BAR-JESUS. He proved that when He rose from the dead Easter morning! Stay focused on the work of reaching people with the Gospel that the Holy Spirit has given you. And know that the promise of 1 Corinthians 15:58 is absolutely TRUE!

24

A SPIRITUAL PACEMAKER

They've become so commonplace today, but they are miracles of modern medicine. It's amazing to think I can have something inserted inside of me that senses when my heart needs stimulation and then gives it exactly what's needed to keep my heart beating properly and my life functioning. That is the basic job of a PACEMAKER. Now imagine this. Wouldn't it be just as incredible if there could be something inserted in our hearts and minds that would keep reminding us of the wonderful promises of God's love for us in Jesus Christ? Something that would call to our mind the right paths that the Lord wants us to walk? I'd call that a kind of "spiritual pacemaker."

Now get ready. There IS such a kind of SPIRITUAL PACEMAKER that God has given us—it's MUSIC. This is especially the case in the urban African-American community where we often sing without written music and worship on Sunday mornings because the lyrics have been committed to our hearts and minds. What a spiritual advantage it is when the lyrics to the songs we sing have taken up residence in our hearts. Let me explain.

I grew up going to a Lutheran grade school in the 1960s and 1970s. Part of our graded daily memory work included verses of Christian hymns. Almost 50 years later, I can still remember what I learned from those days at Immanuel Lutheran Church in Sheboygan, Wisconsin. But there was a bit of a problem back then, and it's the same problem with that pedagogy today in 2020. I knew every word of the hymns by memory (in the King James version) backwards and forwards. However, most of the time I missed much of the meaning, because I didn't know the big, antiquated words. Before you label me as a "hymn hater," hear me out. Today, I love hymns (we do sing one hymn every Sunday at Bethlehem). Armed with a master's degree level of education, and having attended seminary, I now understand the richness of the word choice of the hymn writers. For most of my youth, however, I didn't understand what I memorized.

Moreover, apart from my education, I probably still wouldn't understand everything in the hymns. They used words that I never used in conversations. I probably also have to admit that if there had been video games and all the other distractions kids have today, I might have cared even less—even though my parents insisted on earning an "A" in memory work. Oh yes, I know where you're going in your mind. That's the problem, right? The problem is that "parents aren't what they used to be" when it comes to raising their kids? Possibly true. But nobody has been able to change that issue en masse. At the end of the day, it's difficult for "little John" to retain a Gospel message in words that are hard for him to understand and aren't meaningful to him. The words that get implanted in a child's mind get forgotten easily.

How many Lutheran schools today are able to motivate kids to memorize hymn verses? Let's set aside Lutheran schools, because Lutheran schools have disappeared almost to the point of extinction, especially in urban areas. Are urban ministries and congregations able to implant the Gospel in kids by memorizing Christian hymns? At Bethlehem, we haven't been able to do it. I don't know of any urban place where this strategy is working strongly across the board. And what about children and youth who have never grown up in the church? They are even more disconnected from the way many mainline churches are communicating our faith through music.

It's not that our urban kids today can't memorize music lyrics. Ask a child aged third-grade and up who listens to rap music to give you the lyrics to a particular song. They'll give you an A+ recitation, not only with accurate lyrics but also with precise "bounce" and "voice inflection." Music is definitely a tool that could be like a spiritual pacemaker, even for kids. We can implant God's truth in songs so that the truth is called to one's mind and heart as people live out their faith in daily life. Think about the opportunity to implant the Christian faith into young people through music! Here's an example. Consider the following lyrics to three songs I wrote that we sing at Bethlehem:

> We can implant… the promises of God from a song they'll think
> about when someone starts shooting on their block: **"The Lord is
> my light and my salvation, Whom shall I fear? Whom shall I be
> afraid?"**
>
> We can implant… the promise of identity in Christ from a song
> I can sing even at my lowest moments of life when I think nobody
> cares for me: **"In dark times, You shine Your grace, That gives
> me strength for all that I face. When I am broken, You shine
> Your healing, To mend and repair whatever I'm feeling. Even
> when I've disobeyed, Jesus, You'll wipe my sin away, Peace You
> shine on me, Hope You shine in me, You'll never leave me!"**
>
> We can implant… the promise in a song that as I go through stuff
> in life, including when family and friends have abandoned me:
> **"Not far away, is my Father from above He's working everything
> for my good, Right by my side, is my Savior Jesus Christ walking
> with me like He said He would! Holy Spirit, filling me up with
> God's promises, peace, and power, Is my confidence to face my
> life every day, every minute, and every hour."**

What if solid Gospel truth could be implanted in people via music?
How powerful the Holy Spirit would use that tool to keep someone strong
in their faith in Jesus!

So what is needed for that to happen? The music itself needs to be
attractive to those we're trying to reach. In your urban context, you'll need
to research and understand what "attractive" means. If it's not attractive,
it won't be listened to, nor memorized. Just as important, the songs need
to be Biblically accurate to our faith in Christ. We don't want to implant
messages that are Biblically inaccurate. This discussion continues in the
following essay, "How to Eat Prime Rib."

25

HOW TO EAT PRIME RIB

My apologies in advance to those who are not carnivore meat lovers like I am. As I write this today, on our meatless Tuesday fast of our Bethlehem Consecration Week, I am struggling! To me, there's nothing like a perfectly cooked piece of PRIME RIB. It's the BEST meat! How does a person eat prime rib? It all depends on who you are. For someone like me, I am cutting generous mouthful-sized pieces. I have good teeth. I can handle them. My wife, whose mouth is smaller than mine, would cut some of my pieces of prime rib in half. For someone who has braces, they may have to eat even smaller, thinly-sliced pieces. What bite size would you feed to a 3-year-old? You've got the idea. Everybody can still eat the PRIME RIB. They might even be able to eat the same quantity of prime rib. But THE PACE and SIZE is unique. My size piece of prime rib would be too much for my toddler grandsons. It would make them choke. Everyone can eat prime rib, but the PACE and SIZE OF THE BITE matters.

Think with me about the Word of God and its central message of God's grace in Jesus as the PRIME RIB. Everyone needs this PRIME RIB. Musically, we don't ever want to change the PRIME RIB into anything but the PRIME RIB that it is. Yet, how it's eaten is a vital consideration. For most of my lifetime, we've often served the Gospel of Jesus Christ through music in Christian hymnody in only one bite size, and that's BIG BITES. The problem is that, more and more, those to whom we're serving the Word of God through music in our churches and ministries aren't spiritually grown men and women. Many haven't grown up in Christian families or even in Christian churches. Many are coming to our ministries with no faith background and without knowing much at all about the Lord except for a few religious slogans and clichés.

Further, let's be honest. Our young people who have grown up in the church have different life contexts than most Baby Boomers my age. Most young people today haven't had the rigorous catechesis that older followers of Christ had. Plus, let's be "totally 100"—it is a very different world to grow up in today. Young people and young adults have many more distractions. With social media and advanced electronic entertainment, they have a variety of options vying for their time. We live in a much more immediate culture that says, "Deliver me your message quickly. Let me get involved immediately. If not, I am headed someplace else, maybe even to the church down the street, and maybe not to a church at all!"

Today's world has had their attention span trained by television programming that lasts only about seven to eight minutes before a commercial break. And the music that attracts us—it better be on point and exciting. We've become used to high-quality video and musical flawlessness (that's why there is so much lip-syncing over recorded tracks). I'm not saying this world is right. I'm just saying this is the world that is. So whatever we put before people spiritually, especially in the preaching and music that are the hallmarks of the African-American church, it better be presented in edible bites that are easy for people to eat, or they will disappear from the table.

However, churches have reacted in different ways to this reality in which we live. Some churches say, "We are who we are. We've been singing our songs this way since 1930, and we will continue to do so, whether you sing with us or not." Other churches have watered down the faith and sing songs that no longer are the PRIME RIB of God's Word. They are choruses so full of generality that they could mean anything. I advocate for the third response. That is, let's always keep the PRIME RIB as the PRIME RIB. BUT, let's realize that it may be necessary for us to sing of God's PRIME RIB in simpler, smaller, bite-size portions of the Gospel. AND, let's be open to sing NEW SONGS as we EAT of the FATHER'S PRIME RIB with new beats and new song formats. At the end of the day—what's the goal?

The Bible doesn't mandate a particular kind of music or a particular song format. The goal is to PLACE CHRIST BEFORE PEOPLE in a

way that is understandable without lessening the message of who Christ is. Then the Holy Spirit does His work of bringing about faith.

You and I as ministry leaders must ask the Holy Spirit for wisdom to know what size and portion of God's PRIME RIB message is best to serve the people to whom we minister. Will you use Christian rap? Contemporary Gospel? Urban contemporary? Hymns? Music that is reflective? Music that "jams" and celebrates the life we have in Christ?

It will take much research regarding the people you are trying to reach. It will take much conversation and getting to know the people you are trying to share Christ with in order to understand how to reach them musically. It will take much wisdom regarding the musical resources you already have and what you can gain in order to effectively reach people with the Gospel. This will be both a short term and a long term project that you will be working on. Your approach will also always be changing, because people are always changing, although God's PRIME RIB served is always the same. This will take much prayer from you and your leadership to understand the best way to serve the Lord's PRIME RIB to your people.

26

CAN WE "SING A NEW SONG"?

In several places in the "songbook" of the Bible, the book of Psalms, the writers encourage God's people to "sing a new song." I spent a little time taking a closer look at Psalm 33:3, 40:3, 96:1, 98:1, and 144:9. What is meant by a NEW song? Walking back to the original Hebrew word for "new" in these verses, CHADASH, two thoughts seem to show themselves.

First, a "new" song has to do with a change of circumstance. You can see that in Psalm 40:1–3. The writer's song that was a cry of concern becomes a new song of praise completely due to the Lord's delivering strength and power in his life! That's a "new" song that we all know in so many ways, but especially because of the forgiveness of sins that we have in Christ Jesus. Our "new" song changes from hopelessness to confident forgiveness because of the Savior! What a great "new" song that the Lord enables us to sing EVERY DAY!

Second, some of these other passages in Psalms speak of a NEW song that we sing unto the Lord to celebrate our continual discovery of the depths of our Father's love for us and His sovereign, loving control over our lives.

So how do these truths transmit into the songs we sing today? While the songs we sing must always place God and His grace through Christ in the spotlight, do we have permission to sing of our Merciful Lord in fresh and new ways, as well as in the old ways the Christian Church has always sung about God's grace? Why not?

As we think about how God's PRIME RIB message of Christ can come to people in each context, there must be the freedom to ask, "Who is singing?" In our urban African-American context, many in our Bethlehem family are new Christians. They did not grow up in the faith, are younger in age, and are not versed in Christian church lingo (the many code words of our faith that longtime Christians know). They want to participate in meaningful worship immediately (not once they complete an adult instruction class or learn a certain liturgy). They also come out of the current eight-minutes-at-a time TV generation. Accordingly, I find that the best musical approach for us in worship and music is to present the Gospel of Christ Jesus in a manner that is SIMPLE and STRAIGHTFORWARD.

While it is useful to expose worshippers to some of the great hymns of the Church so that they can connect when they are in other places within the Kingdom of Christ, there is great value in ensuring that the music in worship is straightforward and simple.

Here are some personal thoughts about straightforward and simple musical worship. Very likely, you may passionately disagree with some or all of them. But these considerations have been helpful to us at Bethlehem regarding worship music for our young and urban African-American context. My hope is that even if you disagree, the Holy Spirit will lead you to think more deeply about music in worship.

Songs that are more straightforward and simple have this in common:

- **They never compromise or confuse God's Biblical message of His love for us in Christ.** The PRIME RIB always must stay GOD'S PRIME RIB.

- **They often use choruses and refrains.** I'm not talking about using choruses or refrains as a kind of mantra to call for the Holy Spirit. Rather, a refrain/chorus in a song that accurately states God's Biblical message is an incredible mnemonic tool for using music as a "spiritual pacemaker" for one's soul!

- **They are more accessible for new people to the faith.** At Bethlehem, I want to see new worshippers at church every Sunday, especially people who know little or nothing at all of Christ. Songs that are simpler and more straightforward with easier melodies enable new people to more easily participate in worship.

- **They give seasoned worshippers more time and moments to meditate, worship, and pray.** I believe I often have spiritual ADHD syndrome in worship. Sometimes six verses of a hymn are too much for me to take in at once. It is often hard for me to think through the grand message of all those verses, because the wording of some hymns and the quantity and depth of some hymn lyrics are just too much. When there is a song about God's amazing patience, I need time for it to not only clearly remind me of what God's amazing patient love is, but also to help me reflect on how that amazing patience refuses to give up on me!

- **They are often easier for musicians to pick up.** Finding church musicians today is a challenge that is becoming harder. Simpler and

A PLACE NOT FORGOTTEN

more straightforward music is easier for musicians to play. Many of today's contemporary Gospel songs have available "tracks" that can help ministries who don't have capable musicians to play them.

- **They are often easier to remember and carry with you beyond the worship service.** Interestingly, great Biblical preaching has a central theme and points that support what the central theme is all about. Shouldn't music be the same? Why does music have to be so complex and presented in so many images and metaphors that are beyond the life experience of many people today?

My prayer for you in these essays about music is that you put your ministry approach to music in worship under a microscope and consider the perspective of those you want to reach and encourage in their faith. Find out if what you're currently doing is the best way to reach new people *and* feed your current people. Don't do what is most convenient, if you know it's not the best musical approach to reach the people you're trying to reach. Don't do what other ministries are doing simply because they're doing it; your world is the world God has placed you in. You know your world. Those who aren't in your world, don't know about your world.

Never reduce God's PRIME RIB message in music from anything that it is, although how you portion it and the style you use to serve it may be unique to your context. From the Lord, we all have permission to "sing a NEW song," as long as our song is always about Him and His incredible work of changing our lives!

27

STOP & SMELL THE ROSES, ESPECIALLY NOTICE JUST THE BUDS

Someone new shows up for worship. Someone who has been gone for a long time returns to worship. Someone jumps in to serve that you never expected. Someone who was holding a big grudge drops it and forgives.

A grant that you were hoping for is funded. A member sends you a text and tells you how much you and your ministry mean to them. An incredible discussion happens in Bible class, and you aren't even able to get a word in yourself (it's so good). You have planned a big outdoor outreach ministry event where nobody shows up in the first 15 minutes, and you're about ready to pack up and quit, but then a huge wave of people shows up.

One of your deacons makes a hospital visit, and you never told him to go. You find out that some members solved an intense conflict with other members three weeks ago without your even being involved. One of your members drops off dinner for you and your family at your house, and you didn't know it was coming. Your church or ministry remembers your ministry anniversary, and you didn't have to remind them.

As you open the mail, there is a card from someone outside of your church encouraging you to keep going in ministry, along with a big check. Somebody you have worked hard with and invested a lot of time in advances in their Christian life.

I could go on and on.

What does this entire list have in common? These are "roses"—the ministry victories the Holy Spirit sends for us to smell to encourage us in our work for the Lord. No doubt, you have your own list. We need these for the hard days of ministry when frustration and exasperation with people and circumstances get a tight hold on us and discourage us! I'm writing this the day after I was in the midst of one of those low days. We need to remember the roses! Not only the roses, but the buds before the roses bloom.

Last night, a "bud" encouraged me. Two young ladies who have been worshipping with us showed up for our first small group confirmation Bible study session. Even when people have said, "I'll be there," the pessimist/realist in me sometimes wonders if they will show up. We all know the enemy wants them not to attend a meeting where God's Word will be front and center. The whole point of this essay is quite simple—make sure you take time to observe all of the roses the Holy Spirit is sending you. I know. Sometimes it's hard and sometimes we can easily fall in holes of depression. Ministry in the city is filled with the highest highs, but also the lowest lows.

There are three ways to help you smell the roses, even the buds.

First, one of my mentors, Rev. Arthur Schudde, showed me a drawer in his office desk when I was a young pastor. Inside were a bunch of cards and letters he had saved. He told me, "Make sure you keep the encouraging cards when people tell you how much they love you and how important you are to them. On the tough days in ministry, you need to just pull some out and read them." What great advice! These cards and letters were, in fact, sent by the Holy Spirit to you (through other people) for these very moments to encourage you to not give up, but to keep going as the Lord's faithful minister.

Second, for the past 30 years at Bethlehem, I look for one blessing on Sunday mornings that the Lord sends to encourage me. Bethlehem often starts Sunday morning worship, and then people gradually flow in. Sometimes at the beginning of worship there has hardly been anyone in the sanctuary! Just when I was about to get really frustrated in my spirit, God would move my eyes to see someone He had brought to His house who had been gone for two months or longer. Sometimes, the blessing has been seeing a child I never thought was a singer being used by the Lord to really sing and encourage all of us.

I think you have the idea. In 30 years of Sunday mornings, I can honestly say that I've never been to a Bethlehem worship service without at least one "rose" sent by the Holy Spirit to encourage me. The problem sometimes is that I get too focused on myself, and I miss those roses. The problem is sometimes my impatience to remember that every beautiful rose starts as a bud.

Third, every person doing ministry in urban areas especially needs close friends around them who HELP THEM SEE the roses. For me, that includes people like my wife, my son (here in St. Louis) and daughter, and other close friends. They are the ones the Lord has placed around me who, when I share my ministry frustrations, remind me of God's roses and encourage me to keep going. All this makes sense when you remember Hebrews 10:23–25. Look it up. Our meetings might be in the sanctuary, in small groups, out on the street, or in a gymnasium, but God uses all of those places to show us the roses that tell us, "Keep going. Keep serving the Lord in this place where He has placed you. Don't run from it! Don't give up! The Lord is with you!"

28

A MINISTRY OF TODAY

On Sunday, March 17, 2019, 11-year-old Trent Davis was worshipping at our church alone, as he usually did. Many children like him come to Bethlehem, even though their parents are at home on Sunday mornings. This Sunday was not unlike any other Sunday in the two years we knew Trent. On Monday, March 18, 2019, Trent was dead after being hit by a car as he was waiting for his school bus that morning. We were all so crushed and overwhelmed with grief when we heard the news from all the television reports that the young boy who was killed was our "Trent." That's the tragic way that life goes sometimes. This isn't the first inexplicable death that we've experienced in the life of a child. It won't be the last.

As we began our ministry to children a few decades ago, honestly, we did so with the strategic thinking that the way you reach families on the urban scene is through the children. Yet, this horrible tragedy does again place before us a present reminder:

Our ministry to children isn't just raising them up in the way of the Lord for "one day" when they are grown-ups. Helping children to know that Christ gave His life for their sins that they may have life is something that they need right now in the raw present of life. None of us can count on tomorrow.

So here's a simple group of encouragements to urban churches and ministries about a ministry to children.

If your community has children, be aggressive in your Gospel outreach to children. Hit the streets looking for children you can share the Gospel with.

Do programs like our Taking Jesus to the Streets street ministry that I've mentioned several times in this book. (Contact us if you want to learn about it). A program like this will often give you instant connections with masses of children in neighborhoods. Ask the children you already have in your ministry to tell you where their friends are, and connect with those new children. Another great resource is a van ministry that enables you not to have to wait on kids to come to your church, but instead you can bring the kids to your church for programs. As discussed elsewhere, be ready to "be a Christian family" to new children. You may very well be the only Christian family (sometimes the only real family) they will have.

See children as their own person in your ministry.

We have story after story in our ministry where a young person in our church was the only one in their household who was consistently part of a church or ministry. In some cases, we were never able to get the family into a regular relationship with Christ at that time. However, over a couple of decades, when the youth grew up and started a family, they decided to raise their family in the Christian faith. Some people overlook a ministry to children because children don't bring much immediate "return" to the congregation in tithes and offering, and they don't add to the volunteer workforce. In the first place, who knows if those children will make it to 18 years of age? If they don't reach adulthood, don't we want them to die in faith in Christ Jesus? In the second place, think of how a family heritage could change as this child grows up in the faith and then raises their children to know the Savior.

Sunday morning worship is key to our ministry with children.

While other programs like midweek Bible programs, sports programs, and youth groups can attract and nurture children toward Christ and a home congregation, I've observed that the litmus test of commitment and long term Christian growth happens via a connection to consistent Sunday morning worship. I think that's because the "horizontal" aspect of the Holy Spirit's work also powerfully affects the person. (See the "I Need My Weekly Family Meeting" essay.)

The tragedy with Trent also reminds us of the following truths:

Whatever we do in children's ministry, let's MAKE IT OUR BEST WORK!

Sharing the Gospel with a child takes a lot of creative thought. It takes work to fuse finding a meaningful metaphor or approach with bringing Biblical truth that is accurate and not "watered-down" to nothing. Further, when you teach kids the Scripture, doing it well takes a lot energy. You've got to be "into it." They'll know if you aren't. But here's the reminder again: let's make our ministry to kids our best work TODAY, because maybe tomorrow won't be there for them. Even more important, isn't this the will of our Savior? (Matthew 19:13–15)

Ministry to children needs good accountability systems.

Of course, we need good accountability systems in place to guarantee the safety of children we minister to. We want those who minister to children to be adults who will care for children and not harm them in any way. In addition, we need good information systems to keep our contact information accurate. Families in urban areas change their contact information often. Phones get turned off, and numbers change. Sometimes we've gone to pick up a child for a weekly ministry only to find out from neighbors that the family moved, but never left a forwarding address. At times, this has even resulted in our losing contact with this child.

Ministry to children is hard.

Kids will challenge you. Our programs usually happen after kids have been in school all day. They are restless and antsy by the time they come to us. In the same way, volunteer teachers often come to church youth ministries after having worked a full day. Remember that our ministry to kids may be the only Jesus message they get in a week. Our ministry to kids may be the only love that some kids receive on a given day. When we minster to kids, it's easy to lose sight of their long range growth as they mature into wonderful Christian adults. This is holy work that the Lord calls His best servants to do.

Ministry to children needs consistency.

My wife reminds me again and again that kids need schedules, habits, and routine. Great ministry to children means doing it week in and week out. It means showing up, not canceling (especially when leaders don't feel like doing it). When we get tired or are tempted to cancel out, all we need to do is remember how our Lord treats us. Lamentations 3:22–23 says that the merciful way in which the Lord treats us is "new every morning!"

Thank God for reminding us that even through the sad end of life for Trent, our ministry to children (as well as our ministry to every person) is a MINISTRY OF TODAY!

29

PARTNERSHIPS ARE GOLD!

Sometimes people have tried to make the Bethlehem ministry story to be the John Schmidtke ministry story. Nope! I reject that. In the first place, if God can make a jackass speak (Numbers 22:28) to bring His message, then the Lord can use anybody, even someone like me. In the second place, anybody who knows ANYTHING about ANY KIND OF MINISTRY knows that it takes a great TEAM to make ministry work. In our congregation we have so many team members, and I've mentioned the names of several throughout this book. There are exponentially more valuable team members than I've even mentioned who have made the Bethlehem ministry strong. Just as valuable as all the team members within the Bethlehem family are also the partnerships outside the family.

Partnerships really are gold! Urban churches and ministries won't make it without them. Even urban churches and ministries with endowment funds, if they are continually stretching to reach new people in the name of Jesus, will need partnerships. The costs of active urban church ministries will always be greater than what comes in the offering plate. So just resolve that partnerships with other churches, agencies, and individuals outside of your church family are needed! Not only are they needed from a financial perspective, but partnerships make us better. They're part of God's plan in Proverbs 27:17 for "iron to sharpen iron" in our ministries.

Partnerships are important for both sides of the partnership. If you pay attention, God will give you new ideas for your ministry from your partners. Your partners will help you get stronger. I've used some of our suburban ministry partner congregations to give me a vision for some better ministry procedures to work toward. Our suburban partner churches have also helped us learn the importance of planning and having longer range vision. On a personal level, partners can make you a better ministry leader. I owe a huge debt personally for all the business acumen three men have taught me: my friends Jack Gerber, Jack Klobnak, and Rick Bagy. They took me to a higher level in understanding how business works, a business understanding that my father, Bob Schmidtke, first began in me long ago. By the way, make no mistake about it. While the church's goal is to make disciples of Jesus, understanding the business side of the church as a not-for-profit corporation is essential. Blessed is every urban ministry leader who isn't a "know it all," but listens and learns from smart Godly men and women the Lord sends their way.

There are various kinds of partnerships—with individuals, with sister congregations, and with entities like foundations.

While hopefully all partners pray for each other, some partnerships to urban churches and ministries mainly give financial support. Other partners provide both financial support and volunteers to help us do ministry work. All kinds of partnership are valuable. Within volunteer work support there are varieties of help. The partnership of volunteers is usually powered by the giftedness and comfort level of the volunteers, in coordination with the specific work needed. For example, some of our volunteers help us with kids' ministries by attending the events. This experience is very useful and meaningful to some volunteers.

On the other hand, some volunteers say, "Being out on the street for a Taking Jesus to the Streets night or helping at a kids Bible program session isn't my thing. But I can help you with some of the property matters of your church." Having friends who simply come in on a Saturday and fix "this and that" is just as important! Like most inner-city ministries, Bethlehem is short both on the people resources and the skill sets to take care of all our property. How valuable it is to have friends who voluntarily give of their time and help us! It's just as important as money. There are projects that we would have to pay a service person to do, if not for our ministry partners.

Sometimes partnerships get creative. Not long ago, one of our sister church partners helped us by having a drive at their church to collect individually-wrapped snacks for our afterschool programs. This saved us a bunch of money!

The best partnerships are two-way, not one-way streets, especially among congregations.

Rev. John Brunette of Faith Lutheran Church in Oakville was our first Bethlehem congregational partner. John and I were classmates at seminary, and he initiated the partnership with me at Bethlehem. We've been so blessed by our partnership with Faith. They help us with both financial support and volunteer help. But it's a two-way partnership. What John knew (even way before other pastors and ministries discovered this) was that as people get more involved in mission in our Bethlehem world, the Holy Spirit helps those same volunteers to be "on fire" for missions in their own congregational worlds! That's the way it works.

So many other churches have followed the example of Faith in partnering with Bethlehem's ministries. Our other suburban partners bring so much to us. They tell me that Bethlehem brings them mission encouragement and fresh ideas about missions. One more important thing: financial gifts from our suburban mission partners are unrestricted. That is, they trust us at Bethlehem to know the best way to use their gifts. That is huge! I am so grateful to God for partnerships that are two-way streets.

Here's another reality that I have to mention. When the senior pastor or head of the organization is on board with the partnership, the relationship is so much stronger.

Take time and invest yourself in building that relationship and keeping it strong. Enough said.

Urban church leader, make the responsibility of both initiating partnerships and maintaining partnerships YOURS.

Don't wait on potential ministry partners to call you. Of course, in order for it to be a good partnership, both sides of the partnership need to buy into it. But you, urban church leader, be the initiator. Be the one who keeps reaching your partners with regular ministry updates and to tell them about the needs of your ministry. In many cases among both individual and congregational partners, your urban ministry is just ONE of MANY partnerships that bigger suburban churches have. We all know how schedules go in the fast pace of life and ministry. Urban ministry leader—you send the pictures, share the updates, and set up lunches with the partnering individuals and churches.

PRESENCE is so important in partnerships.

There's nothing like COMING TO the ministry place itself. When partners can visit the ministry site and participate in the actual ministry to people, this firsthand view is huge in helping the ministry partnership grow and stay strong. Having partners on the urban site can also often help you see how the ministry can become even more effective. Likewise, presence is also very important for the urban ministry to visit the home turf of the suburban congregational partners! Pictures and written reports are effective in telling the ministry story. However, having a live presence in a congregation on a "mission Sunday" where the urban ministry leader or a choir connects with the entire sister church can really get the suburban sister church more excited about the urban mission.

If you have the opportunity to be the mission speaker or to bring your choir for a congregational mission Sunday, here are a few things that will help put your best foot forward:

- Be yourself, but make sure you acclimate to the suburban congregation's mission world in how you communicate.

- Come prepared with your best presentation. Don't wing it; be strategic.

- Give the congregational partners concrete ways that they can become involved in the mission. Ask if they would sign up to help you on certain nights or save certain art supplies to use in projects, etc.

- Have a strong follow-up mechanism. It's critical to have some way to follow up on people who indicate they want to help, especially on the day of your visit. At the same time, most urban ministry staffs are not equipped to station someone at the urban ministry's phone to answer calls. I've found the best way for me to be able to capitalize on interested people who want to get involved is to either have them call the suburban church's office, or, even better, to speak their names and contact information into my cell phone so that I can follow-up with them personally. Then I pass on their contact information to someone on our ministry team. Whatever way you determine to do this, it is essential that you not lose these contacts.

Communicate! Communicate! Communicate!

Regularly communicate about the urban ministry that you work in. If it's not consistent enough, people will forget about you. Report on both what has happened in your ministry, as well as upcoming opportunities for friends to volunteer. Know the audience that you're trying to reach through your communication. What do they care about? What are the kinds of things they get excited about and want to support? Be transparent about both what has worked in your ministry and what has not worked. Not everything goes the way you planned. People don't believe everything is "great and okay"! At the same time, don't whine or make excuses for ministry that hasn't worked. Nobody wants to support a losing team.

Thank You Letters

Never, ever, ever, ever, ever forget to THANK people! Thank you letters for gifts should be sent promptly. People don't like to wait to receive feedback regarding a gift that they've sent or an event that they've volunteered for. YOU NEED A SYSTEM to keep from forgetting to say "thanks." Think about it. In most not-for-profits, there is often a full-time development person doing this job. That is just one more hat for you to wear in your ministry. When you write thank you notes, insert a paragraph about something great that happened recently in your ministry. People appreciate recent updates, and it reinforces why they gave a gift to your ministry, rather than to a different ministry.

Wow! That is just scratching the surface of partnerships. They are so essential. They make all of us better. They take a lot of work! They really are gold!

30

"I'M LOOKING FOR SOME ASSISTANCE"

The church office phone rang one morning. "Hello. My name is Doresha Tyler. Could you help me? My electricity got cut off. I have five kids. We're cold and we don't have any food."

Another day, I was just returning to my truck after paying for my gas at the filling station when a man came up to me. "Excuse me, sir," he said. "I don't mean any harm, but my wife and I are from Nashville. We came up here to go to Barnes hospital for some of her cancer treatments. Our car broke down last night. We walked all the way from Barnes (about 4–5 miles). We don't have any money. Could you help us with just a little money to get back home to Nashville?"

Someone in our neighborhood recently stopped me as I was leaving the church campus and said, "My cousin's step-sister's mama died of an overdose two nights ago. We're trying to raise some money to bury her. Could you give us some money for the funeral?"

Every urban ministry or church will face these kinds of requests. What do you do with them? Are they all real and true? Are they scams and hustles? How do you sort them out? Even if you suspect a "tale" is being told to you, and you decline to help, how do you deal with others' reactions? "I thought you all were church people." "God wants us to help each other." "What kind of church is this where you don't help anybody?" "How would you feel if it was your son that you were burying?"

Guilt can be a pretty powerful convincing mechanism to try and get us to give something, even if we think the story is probably not true. Whenever a ministry in a neighborhood helps Mrs. Jones with $250 on her electric bill, even if you tell her not to tell anybody, guess what is going to happen tomorrow or by the end of the week? Yep, about 10 more people will be on your doorstep looking for help! The more you learn about your community, the wiser you will become about how to handle social ministry requests. Realize that sometimes you will "guess wrong" and give someone assistance who didn't tell you the truth. Don't beat yourself up for it. Just learn from it and be wiser next time. At the same time, resist the temptation to become so worried about making a mistake in helping people that you choose not to help anyone.

For most of us, our resources for social ministry are not unlimited.

Therefore, we need to use good judgment about who we help and how much help we provide. You will be smart if you develop some social ministry giving guidelines in your mind and then be flexible about adjusting them as you keep on learning from individual situations and people. Rarely have I found two situations to be the same.

Although some people don't agree with this truth, I find a strong Biblical case to tie material resources to the spiritual food people really need.

What Jesus said in John 6:26–27 really makes me think. "Truly, truly I say to you, you seek Me, not because you saw the signs, but because you ate of the loaves and were filled. Do not work for the food which perishes, but for the food which endures to eternal life, which the Son of Man will give to you, for on Him the Father, God, has set his seal." What "business" are we in as God's people, the Church? Mark 16:15 makes it clear to me that our first priority is a person's spiritual life and knowing Jesus as their Savior. Helping them with the basics of life basics is a bridge to that spiritual life. But the basics must always be a *bridge* to the spiritual, not an *end* in themselves.

While we have a food pantry at Bethlehem, our mission is not to feed the world with physical food. While we have a gym at Bethlehem, our mission is not to primarily use our gym as a community center for our neighborhood. Rather, it is a bridge for people to come to know Christ the Lord. We help everyone in a first-time opportunity. However, ongoing help comes to those who want to walk with Christ. We define that as being part of worship and/or Bible programs at Bethlehem. Some people would say, "That's a very closed and parochial view of helping people." Maybe so to some. But I find the Word of God to place a special preference on those who want to be part of God's family of faith. A very important Bible passage to me is Galatians 6:10, "So then, while we have opportunity, let us do good to all people." Now get ready for the last phrase, "and ESPECIALLY to those who are of the household of faith." If we had semi-trailers full of food, perhaps our distribution philosophy would be different, but our resources are very limited. Galatians 6:10 sounds to me like there is a priority on those who want to know the Savior and walk with Him.

Accountability in social ministry is vital.

Keep records of when you're helping people with food, clothing, or finances. In the busyness of ministry, you will forget when you last helped. At Bethlehem, we don't want to create a co-dependency where people are relying on the church to provide for them on a monthly basis. If we had resources for this kind of ministry, perhaps we would look at it differently. Even still, assistance and ministry must go together. If people just want food or assistance, the agency they need is a public food bank or government energy assistance office, not the Church. Someone is thinking, "But this moment could be an opportunity for beginning ministry with someone." Yes, it could. If you want to help someone and then follow up by bringing the message of Christ, DO IT. But MAKE SURE YOU FOLLOW UP!

Recognize the seasons when people give.

Most social ministry donations of food, clothing, toiletries, and money happen from about Thanksgiving until Mother's Day. That's the season of giving. Summertime is usually quite dry, as far as receiving gifts for social ministry. Whatever you understand the "season of giving" to be for your ministry, be aware of it and use it to plan for needs throughout the year. You need a "Joseph philosophy"... stock up in seven plenteous years to sustain you in the seven lean years.

Be careful of becoming co-dependent with someone who chooses not to spend their money in wise ways.

This is a tough one, especially when it involves members of your ministry. And it will! Here's an illustration. How does your ministry handle the parent who spends $300 on a big birthday party for their 4-year-old but then is at your door two weeks later asking for funds for his electric bill? Know this as well—this example won't stay between you and the dad who came asking for help. Almost everybody at the birthday party will know the situation and wonder how that person got their electricity back on. Then they will find out your ministry turned the power back on. Further, the message they will receive is that the church can be "hustled" with a sad story.

I'm not saying that people don't make mistakes with money. We all do. I'm also not saying to refuse help to someone who has made an unwise move with money. What I am saying is that how you handle these moments will have far-reaching implications! Also, here is a reality—if a funder who gave you several thousand dollars finds out you allowed someone to "hustle" the church with the money they contributed for ministry, they may not be as excited about future contributions. It's something to pray and think much about.

Providing people ways to help themselves is a great way to do social ministry when you have the chance.

Some years ago, I knew a young man needed some help with a bill. This was a very unusual and unique situation for this man. I thought it was a good investment to help him, so we did. As I was giving him the money, he said, "Pastor, I am going to pay this back." To his face, I said, "Okay," but in my heart I thought, "We'll see." I have heard that response too many times, so I was ready to give the man the help he needed without expecting anything back.

Over the next four months, the young man did some work at the church to work off the help that he had received. This is something that he really wanted to do, and he paid off the debt. I also observed that the Lord honored what he did with some special blessings after working off his loan. God poured even more money into this man's life. Well done! Where we have opportunity to empower people to help themselves, it is most useful to them and a great story to share anonymously with funders!

Social ministry isn't simple. It takes much thought and prayer. I am a whole lot better at it now after over 30 years of ministry. I think the Lord wants us to keep social ministry as MINISTRY, not a new kind of handout.

What areas of your social ministry strategy might the Holy Spirit be causing you to rethink?

31

A WORD ABOUT COMPENSATION

Among the people who have affected my ministry is the late Warren Wiersbe, even though he never knew me. The closest I ever was to him was when I shook his hand at a ministry conference to thank him for his teaching. Among many truths I learned from him, I love one simple, but accurate truth he taught me from a distance about studying the Bible. Dr. Wiersbe taught that things repeated in the Bible are usually especially important. For example, the words of 1 Timothy 5:18, "The laborer is worthy of his wages," are an important truth because they are also found in Matthew 10:10, Luke 10:7, and 1 Corinthians 9:14.

In this essay, we're talking about compensation for those who work in the church. Okay, I need to get a few things off my chest. You may "love 'em or hate 'em." If the church was to pay every person for every work they did for the kingdom, we would go bankrupt immediately. Christ calls us to serve. Pay should not be part of everything we do. Here comes a tricky part—what should be "paid" service and what should not? The texts above seem to talk about full-time church work—when a person has made church work their full-time vocation. Let's begin by discussing different kinds of ministry in this essay.

Full-time vs. Part-time vs. Volunteer Work

The distinction, in itself, is not so simple. For example, what if someone's regular vocation doesn't pay them a livable wage? Can a part-time church job supplement that, especially a part-time job that needs accountability and consistency? That is, if a person needs to find a part-time job to supplement their income and they are gifted in youth work, instead of them going to work in retail for eight hours per week, could the church hire that person as a youth director for a program where they need consistent accountable leadership?

What about when the church finances are incredibly small versus the pay that a ministry staff person wants? How can we pay an amount that we don't consistently have? We all know horror stories of "fat cat" pastors who drive up to church in luxurious, expensive cars while their ministry struggles to pay the electric bill. At the same time, the Christian church of today, at large, is famous for wanting to do ministry in missional areas like inner-city communities, but then expecting those who work in those communities to live on next to nothing. Would God agree with the missional math equation that "working in a poor urban mission = living a life of poverty (for you and your family)"?

Yes, I know... the reward will be in heaven one day! So are any of us surprised when many excellent urban full-time ministry workers come to the city and begin good work, only to leave once they start a family? They leave for better paying suburban ministry positions because they've grown tired of looking into the eyes of their kids and saying, "No, baby, we just can't afford that." Sorry for the ranting. My point is that this is not a simple conversation.

Thus far, I've been zeroing in mainly on more full-time church workers, but some of these same thoughts are applicable to compensating anybody working in an urban ministry. I hope the following views can stimulate your thinking in a positive way.

We especially need our best ministry workers in urban inner-city areas.

For over 30 years, my ministry has been in the inner-city of St. Louis. Especially if you are not Lutheran, you need to know that our

national church body, the Lutheran Church-Missouri Synod (LCMS), is headquartered in St. Louis, and one of our main LCMS seminaries is also in St. Louis. A sad truth about inner-city Lutheran church work in St. Louis is that urban Lutheran St. Louis parishes have been used as the "side income gig" for ministry workers hoping to get called to positions at the national church headquarters or seminary.

They've also been used as the "side income gig" for some ministry workers who have come to our St. Louis seminary working on graduate work, as well as some Lutheran ministry workers in the St. Louis area looking for supplemental income. My point is not the airing of dirty church laundry, but rather this—if we as a church are really serious about ministry in inner-city urban areas, our leaders in these places should be among our brightest and best, not our "leftovers." AND when we call people to urban inner-city places, we should also have plans to support them—not give them two years' worth of salary and then tell them they need to "raise their own support" (especially when none of them have had hardly any training in fundraising).

When you think about it, it makes sense for God's people to place strong full-time church workers in urban areas. Inner-city areas have the most concentrated amounts of people. Because much inner-city work requires ministering across cultures, it is specialized, complex work that takes special training. It takes workers with an entrepreneurial and business spirit (I'll speak more about this in another essay). It is not the model of "Pastor, you take care of the spiritual piece. And the church council will make sure the bills get paid and that you receive your bi-monthly paycheck."

Ministry in urban areas is so varied because of the complexity of "people issues" (remember the situation with Tiana in the essay, "Ministry in Tangled Life Webs"). There's no way to teach young ministry workers at seminary or Bible college all the situations they will face. They are too varied in life experience, age, and also culture. I believe the only way to equip young full-time ministry workers in the city is to give them a good grounding in thinking Biblically, to help them gain an entrepreneurial business sense, and then to provide them with mentors who have lived in these kind of ministry contexts so they have someone to talk to.

In addition, while we need workers in these contexts who are both strong and charismatic in their leadership, workers also need to understand the importance of duplicating their efforts by pouring themselves into others. The mantra of John Maxwell from the first seminar of his that I attended continues to be one of the most important reminders to my ministry (even 25 years after I first heard it), "Never do ministry alone. Never do ministry alone. Never do ministry alone."

In part-time ministry, why would we pay for a job to get done in ministry?

Some people in the church would say that there should be no paid part-time jobs in a church. Well, let's think about that. Here are some factors regarding why we might pay a person to do a part-time job in our ministry:

1. *We need a certain expertise that a person has.* We need someone who can keep books with accuracy and excellence. OR, we need somebody who can play keyboards or drums or organ for our worship time. OR, we need someone who can write good curriculum for a program we have begun, and we can't find workable curriculum from a Christian publishing company.

2. *The job requires consistency and accountability.* We need a van driver who will be present to drive three nights a week. Our program is dependent on it. We can't find volunteers who can make that size of a volunteer commitment. We can't handle having to find a replacement driver when the volunteer calls off at the last minute. OR, we need a leader who will plan regular youth events for our young people. These are just a few examples.

3. *Sometimes the "church market" makes pay necessary to get a quality person.* This is especially true in music ministry. It is labor-intensive when it comes to preparation and rehearsal time. If all the other churches are paying someone $250 a week to play for rehearsals and

worship services, to believe that you will find someone who will play every week with no compensation is probably not realistic.

4. *Sometimes volunteers won't fill the job we need for a particular ministry to take place because of the size of the commitment.* A good example of this is the van ministry at our church. Some dedicated adults who deeply love the Lord donate their time once a month on a Sunday morning to pick up and take home worshippers with our church vans. Without these individuals, our Sunday morning worship would be significantly wounded. Some of our children's programs need van pick-up service three nights per week, but this is a commitment that volunteers have not been able to give. Thus, we need to pay for this transportation job to get some of our kids to our programs.

Finally, what are the factors involved in how much the church pays someone for work?

1. Budget – Let's begin with the easiest issue. We can't pay an amount that we don't have or can't consistently raise. No need to say more about this.

2. Education – In some jobs, getting a degree or advanced degree boosts your salary or hourly wage. Not really so in most urban church ministries. It's not that the worker isn't worthy. The issue is really the first point above.

3. Experience – This can be useful if it helps with greater ministry output. A person who has had 20 years of experience raising money for ministry might possibly be a good reason to pay that person well as your development director.

4. Performance – This is probably the biggest factor determining how much we pay people. Here's how it works. While I may think you are a valuable ministry worker, if your performance on the job isn't strong and doesn't give me a story to tell to raise money to fund your

position, your compensation will be limited. On the other hand, if the children's ministry program you are leading keeps growing, you "enable me to pay you better." I will be able to take your story and bring it to potential funders with the message, "We need _____. Look at the incredible ministry work that she's doing. We can't afford to lose her in our ministry. Can you help with a gift for us to keep her at Bethlehem?" I'm not saying that's the right way it should be. I'm just saying that's the way things work.

5. Attitude – Even when someone has some skills useful to our ministry, if they are constantly complaining, focused on themselves, and filled with negativity, not only am I less likely to pay them well, their employment on my staff will not be long term. On the other hand, I constantly look for opportunities to bless people who have grateful attitudes. Maybe I can't give them a high hourly wage, but when I receive a blessing, I pass it on to them as well, all because of their Godly attitude.

6. Replacement Cost – Sometimes we find that we've possibly made a bad hire. Sometimes there's someone on our team who has a bad attitude or isn't as strong in their work as they could be. BEFORE you release them, think about their "replacement cost." That is, what will it cost you to replace them? Are they replaceable for a cheaper cost? Would it cost more to replace them? Think about this factor as you consider what you pay people.

7. Understanding Job Flexibility – The church can never pay people what they're worth. The funding just isn't there. Yet, a powerful "perk" of working for a ministry is the flexibility. As my kids were growing up, I got to see almost every one of their daytime school programs because I had the flexibility in my schedule to be there. Friends and family couldn't do that. That was important to me. The flexibility of working for the church should also be understood in thinking about compensation. It really is important.

8. Paid Service vs. Volunteer Service for Christ – For 30 years I have spent almost 90 minutes every Wednesday night picking up kids for our Bethlehem Bible Outreach kids program. This isn't in my job description. I don't get paid for it. I just do it because it is part of my volunteer service to my Savior as John, not Pastor Schmidtke. This is something that church workers need to constantly be aware of. Most of those who work for a ministry arrive after having worked an eight-hour workday. They give their volunteer service to the Lord out of gratitude for His kindness. As people who get paid for working in ministry, we must make that distinction and have that same heart of service. Honestly, to the person who works at our church only when they're paid and doesn't do volunteer service, I'm already looking for your replacement. You're not serving in the way the Master wants you to serve.

It's easy to see why thinking about what we pay people for certain ministry work takes much meditation and prayer for wisdom from our Father in heaven.

32

REACH THE CHILDREN, REACH THE FAMILY

If you have children, think about how many adult friends you have made through your kids. What happened when your kids were part of a sports team, or a play, or took swim lessons, or when you were on a committee at your child's school? I would reason that while you were on the sidelines at these events, you very likely met some other parents you never would have known except through your kids. That's the way life works—kids are often an entry connection point for adults and families. Actually, this strategy has been used by the Lutheran church to reach families for decades. In many cases, before a Lutheran church was planted in a location, first a Lutheran school or Lutheran pre-school was planted in that very place! Kids brought families together. Then, from those relationships, the forming of a church emerged. Even if you can't afford to plant or have a Lutheran school, the strategy of REACHING FAMILIES through REACHING CHILDREN still works. In fact, in urban areas like our North St. Louis community, I think beginning with a ministry to children is exactly the right strategy.

In our neighborhood, the most plentiful people resource is children. The people resource with the fewest opportunities for things to do is children. The people resource that doesn't have their guard up or suspicions about the church, and is the easiest to reach, is children. You will need to find out if that's demographically true for your community, but based on what I've seen in urban, inner-city, low-economic areas, there always seems to be children.

So if we're going to reach a community with the Gospel through an outreach to children, let's be crystal clear about what kids need. While open gym play time, youth groups, free sports teams, music theater camps, afterschool programs, and field trips to here and there will certainly attract kids, what young people need most is JESUS! It is our message of Jesus the Savior that distinguishes us and makes us unique. Think about it. Big organizations like boys/girls clubs and YMCAs do some of the same kinds of activities with youth that we do. Many of them even have funding and facilities that are far superior to what we have as church ministries. But never forget what we have that they don't have:

We have the Good News message of Jesus; we have the love of Christian caring adults running our programs; we have the powerful Holy Spirit working behind the scenes to create faith through every moment that we spend with children. Honestly, from a power standpoint, nothing compares to what we have from the Lord!

However, as we work with kids, we must *use* the powerful spiritual advantage the Lord has given us! I'm not talking about hitting kids over the head with the Bible or dry, uncreative, and boring Bible lessons. I'm talking about the powerful fusion of new life that happens when God's Word and

God's Spirit are fused through our ministry to children.

Let me show it to you from God's own Word. Take a quick read of Ezekiel 37:1–14. Pay special attention to God's promise in verse 14, where the Lord says, "I will put My Spirit within you and you will come to life!" That's as much of that great promise as it takes for me to get excited about sharing Christ with kids who are broken, kids who have been given up on by many people, kids who have been discarded even in their own families, and kids who are craving for love. Life-giving healing is breathed into their lives as we bring the love of our Lord to them through God's Word. Here's how God works.

When He works on a person, did you know that our God works through both a FRONTAL campaign and BEHIND THE SCENES campaign?

Check out what happened with a centurion soldier in Matthew 27:54 at the crucifixion of Jesus. ON THE FRONT, this soldier saw the innocent Jesus give His life on the cross for the sins of the entire world. He heard what people said against Him. He also heard the love Christ spoke about them, "Father forgive them for they don't know what they are doing." This centurion even heard one of the criminals hanging next to Jesus say, "This man doesn't deserve to be here," and "Jesus, remember me in Your kingdom."

ON THE BACK SIDE, as the hours at Calvary took place, God the Holy Spirit was suggesting faith within this man's heart. Maybe this centurion supervised putting Jesus on the cross, and maybe at that time this centurion didn't pay "this Jesus guy" much attention. But within just a few hours, after the FRONTAL view of the Savior's love and the BEHIND THE SCENES prompting of faith by God the Holy Spirit, this military commander says, "Truly, this was the Son of God!" All praise to our God for the victory of faith!

When we teach a Bible lesson with children, did you know that same FRONTAL and BEHIND THE SCENES power of God is at work?

Why are we surprised when children believe in Christ their Savior? Why are we surprised when God pours hope into their hopeless lives through the Gospel? Maybe they are the only person in their family to know the Lord, but look forward 20–25 years as they stay with Christ's church and start their own families. They're speaking Joshua language by then. "As for me and my house, we will serve the Lord!" (Joshua 24:15)

Never let this key principle fall into the background in your ministry to children—it's not enough to just keep children busy and out of trouble with church activities. It's not enough to have them feel like the church is their second home. We must always sow the seed of God's love in every meeting we have with kids. We will trust the BEHIND THE SCENES power of the Holy Spirit to grow faith out of that Gospel seed.

Now let's get down to practical matters. Some people will criticize having a ministry toward children as our main outreach strategy. (By the way, as the church grows and the children grow into youth and adulthood, the church's nurturing and outreach programs need to increase to meet people at different life stages.) Let me place before you some advantages and challenges regarding a dynamic outreach ministry to children.

Challenges

- Kids don't bring immediate "return" to the ministry in increased tithes and offerings, more adult workers, or adult leadership.

- Ministry to kids is not an easy road. Most kids who are on the streets and accessible to our ministries haven't had much love, attention, or home training from their parents. They often have significant behavior issues. If you're someone who says, "I raised my kids already. I ain't raising anybody else's kids for them," then this ministry is not for you.

- Kids ministry is very labor-intensive. It will take your best creative Bible teaching in order to be effective. Many times, it involves not just having an event at the church; it also involves picking up the kids for the event and taking the kids home afterward.

- If you're going to do an event that costs money, be prepared when none of the kids will bring any money. You will have to figure out how to pay for events that cost.

Advantages Kids Bring

- Kids bring fresh energy to a ministry. Kids often ask us, "Why not?" to dreams that we've sometimes already deemed "too big" for us.

- Young people are some of the best evangelists there are. When I pick up children for our Bethlehem Bible Outreach kids ministry, not a week goes by when some kid hasn't said, "Pastor, can we go pick up my friend, _____?"

- Children are "formable." They are open to learning and growing. Children are a great beginning place for starting a strong music ministry.

- Young people give ministries hope for the future. While the kids we pour Christ into are definitely part of the church right now, it's exciting to envision future adults who grew up learning God's Word. It's exciting to see the church as a missional people on the move to reach more people for Christ!

- Programs for children are among the most "fundable" ministries when we approach foundations and individuals for support for our ministry work. People want to invest in children who represent both present and future ministry.

- A ministry to children will refine your entire ministry approach in bringing the Gospel to people. If our teaching, preaching, and music is attractive to kids and clear enough for kids to understand it, it will work with any age group.

- Kids are forgiving and give more immediate forgiveness when we mess up in ministry. They don't hold long term grudges like most adults do.

- As has already been said, kids are the best access into adults and families in the community.

- If you are well-known by the kids of the community through your ministry to them, your safety, even in high crime areas, has just increased exponentially. When you are on a rough street and "little Tommy" sees you, I've found that all of the other tough customers on that street will respect you and not harm you. They may not be interested in Christ, but they respect you for "doing something positive" with the kids.

- Here's a big one for a ministry to children. If you stay at an urban ministry for a long time, you will foster an incredible reputation in the community and among the people of the neighborhood. People don't forget those who are trying to help them toward a better life.

- Don't forget the greatest advantage—when we share Christ with children, those children have the ultimate confidence of Romans 14:8—"whether they live or die, they belong to the Lord."

Maybe you're convinced that you need to launch a new outreach or create a stronger outreach to the children of your community. My guess is one of your first concerns is something like, "What do we teach these kids? How do we find useful lessons that will be meaningful to them?" Such curriculum that is sensitive to an inner-city African-American culture, while being firmly grounded in God's Word and focused on Jesus, is not always easy to find. We would be glad to talk with you about this and show you some of the studies and lessons that we have developed at Bethlehem. Contact us.

33

A PLACE WHERE RECOVERY IS NOT A CLICHÉ

*B*eginning in the early 1990s, the word "RECOVERY" started to be identified more and more with Christian churches in the United States. I believe its emergence with church ministries can be strongly tied to a program called "Celebrate Recovery" started by Rick Warren and John Baker at Saddleback Church in Southern California in 1991. Celebrate Recovery became the heart and soul of Saddleback's ministry as it reached thousands and helped people come out of a variety of addictions and come close to the Savior. Some churches embraced this program and began "branch" Celebrate Recovery programs at their churches to help people become free from addictions. For others, the concept of "RECOVERY" from a multitude of life maladies has become a new way of talking about the liberating Gospel of Christ and the work of His church.

With all of that said, I fear that for many ministries, putting the words "church" and "recovery" in the same sentence has become more of a preaching and ministry cliché than a reality of how the church carries out ministry.

Biblically, the Church of Jesus Christ has always been a place about RECOVERY for people and their lives, beginning with the addiction of sin. Remember the woman caught in adultery in John 8? Jesus received her, forgave her, and then sent her on her way with the encouragement, "Go. From now on, sin no more." There also certainly seems to have been a recovery that Jesus worked in the life of Mary Magdalene. Luke 8:2 notes her as someone "from whom seven demons had gone out." By John 20:11–18 after Jesus' resurrection, it is Mary Magdalene with whom the Savior has a special moment of spiritual intimacy near the tomb of His resurrection. The Apostle Paul has his story to tell of recovery through Jesus in Acts 9. The impetuous Peter is in a long term program of spiritual growth and recovery when you chronicle his journey from a raw and salty fisherman in Matthew 4:18–22 to an unfocused follower of Jesus in Matthew 16:21–23, to a fickle, fearing disciple in Matthew 26:69–75, to a recovered, useful shepherd in John 21:15–17, to the fearless, bold apostle of Christ in Acts 4:7–13, 18–20.

As urban ministries residing in places of significant spiritual darkness, we have a tremendous opportunity to be places of recovery for people! However, there are some particular ministry adjustments to make in becoming a place where people can leave strongholds of sin and be strengthened in the Savior.

Here are some attitudes necessary for a church to become a place of real recovery.

Judgment Is the Means, Not the End.

Of course, as God's people, we judge sin. We judge that stealing is sin. We judge that all sex outside of marriage (of body, mind, and heart) is sin. We judge that bearing false witness is sin. Forsaking the assembling of the people of God to worship is sin (i.e., it is not the will of God). But here's something vital to get right—judgment (God's Law) is NOT AN END; it is a MEANS. If we treat it like an END, then we become like a holiness club. That is, the church would be a group who always gets everything right in their lives. The problem is that nobody would be able to be a member of that club because "all of us have sinned and fallen short of the glory of God." (Romans 3:23) When we treat judgment as an END, we often "grade" sins. We say this one sin is worse than this other sin. No, according to God's Word, all sin needs to be confessed before God to receive the forgiveness that Jesus won, even though different sins may have different consequences in this life.

When we treat judgment like an END, we may encounter someone who is caught in a particular sin and decide that because they've done this certain horrible, unthinkable act, there's no hope for them. At best, they will only be able to become a second- or third-class Christian and member of our church.

That might be our sad judgment, but it's not God's kind of judgment. Second Peter 3:9 tells a different story from God's perspective. It says that the Lord is "patient toward you, not wishing for any to perish but for all to come to repentance."

If that is to be our attitude toward confronting sin, then our attitude is always one of hoping for and working toward recovery (meaning repentance and the cleansing forgiveness of Jesus). That approach permeates how we confront someone who is caught in sin.

In Galatians 6:1, I find one word so vital in capturing God's approach to talking to someone else about their sin. The verse says, "Brothers, even if anyone is caught in any trespass, you who are spiritual, restore such a one in a spirit of..." here comes the word... "GENTLENESS."

Gentleness means I'm not just concerned about WHAT I'm going to say, but also HOW this person will hear what I'm going to say.

I am careful about the words I choose, the way in which I say them, and the timing when I share them. What's going on in their life now? While unconfessed sin is a dangerous state for any of us to be in, a sensitivity to timing when we talk to people is key. Also, think about this... what is this person's maturity and experience in the Christian faith at this time? What size "bite" can they handle as I bring God's Word of Law to them about their sin? Some might say, "Give them God's truth, and let the chips fall where they may." I would counter, "Well, if the goal is RECOVERY through confession and forgiveness, wouldn't an approach that was more thoughtful and sensitive be a better way?"

I'm not talking about softening what the Lord says. I'm talking about always speaking with the goal of recovery. The goal is recovery! The goal of judgment isn't embarrassing the person before the church. Judgment is only a MEANS for the person to see their sin and then look to their Savior! The END is that they are FORGIVEN and RESTORED by Jesus! That segues well into the next attitude we need to believe in our urban ministries.

The Gospel Completely Frees Us. Do you believe that "the blood of Jesus God's Son cleanses us from all sin," 1 John 1:7? Do you believe what God says in Isaiah 1:18, Isaiah 43:25, and Hebrews 8:12? Is it true that when God forgives us for Jesus' sake that our sin is removed and no longer attached to us? Then, why in the Body of Christ (the Church) do we so often refuse to treat people (who have confessed their sin and believed the forgiveness of Christ) like total recovery from sin has truly come? Wasn't Christ's blood enough? It either was, or it wasn't. God's answer is, "IT WAS!" For us to be a place of recovery, we need to learn that confession of sin and the forgiveness of Jesus TOTALLY FREES US to move forward in a new life with a clean slate, led by the Holy Spirit!

A place of recovery is a place where people don't look down on people with a forgiven past.

It's a place where we accept one another, just as God, through Christ, never tires of accepting us, even when we've sinned. If David showed up at our church on a Sunday morning, would we embrace him or keep our distance from him because he was an adulterer? If Abraham showed up at our church, would we receive him, even though he made a baby with his wife's servant? What about Judah, head of the family from whom the Savior came... could he be a member of our church, even though he slept with his daughter-in-law? Don't forget the woman God used in a key way to help His people take the city of Jericho... could Rahab be a member of our church, even knowing how she had made her income? You've got the point. A place of recovery is where we love one another deeply and without hesitation, no matter their past! We rejoice that they joined us in laying our sins at the cross and finding mercy from our Savior. That is an attitude of recovery. Only God the Holy Spirit can cultivate such a place of recovery.

Everybody is in Recovery from Sin. None of us can ever forget that. Remember that Paul said in 1 Corinthians 15:10 only "by the grace of God, I am what I am." Wasn't this Jesus' point in John 8:7? How useful this attitude is for us as we minister to others! **When I look at you, or when**

you look at me, we see one another on the same level, eye to eye, as sinners saved by the same Savior.

We're constantly dependent on His grace to us. I understand your recovery, even if it is from something sinfully different than what I am recovering from, because I am in recovery myself through Jesus, just like you!

Accountability. In a place of recovery, where the spirit of recovery lives, accountability is welcome. We help each other to walk in God's ways. There is freedom for you to check on me and see how I'm doing in my walk with the Lord, and there is the same freedom for me with you. We pray about the true "100" challenges and demons we're fighting through the resurrection power of the Holy Spirit. What kind of church family can we be if this spirit flows among us?

Recovery is a Process. Being declared right and forgiven of our sins by God for Christ's sake is a decisive moment of release through the Gospel. But because we continue in sinful bodies and in a sinful world, constantly needing God's grace every day, our lives of recovery are always in process. This is vital for us to understand as we live together in a community of believers. A drug addict is always a drug addict. They live in dependence on their "higher power" every day to make it through THAT day. I find this picture to be powerfully accurate as to what recovery is for me in my life and in the life of every Christian. Every day with Jesus. Every day I must come to Him with my sins. Every day He forgives me. Every day His Spirit fills me and guides me to make this day a new and better day. But without Him I can do nothing. (John 15:5) On the one hand, yes, that kind of living does diminish WHO I AM. On the other hand, it actually surges and expands WHO I AM because of HIS DWELLING IN ME! HIS DWELLING in me makes WHO I CAN BE limitless!

Here is the underlying rule in a place of recovery:

A place of recovery is a place where WHAT GOD SAYS ABOUT

US through Jesus is what rules, not what we say about each other or what we say about ourselves.

I think such a fellowship of recovery, as described above, can be an incredible place for people to find healing in Jesus and then thrive!

P.S. There Will Be Relapses. In a perfect world, people recover from their maladies, addictions, and sins, and never go back. Memo: this world is not perfect. Remember what Paul said in Romans 7:18–19. Those relapses will be times of disappointment for you as an urban ministry leader. When those relapses occur, remember two essential things. First, relapses don't just happen to others; each one of us relapses in keeping our promises to God every day. The grace that you and I need is the grace we need to show to people in our ministry. Second, be clear about your courses of action when someone you love relapses. You really have only one of two directions to go. You can either give up on that person, or you can start over with them in the mercy and compassion of our Father in heaven. Our Father would have us do the latter!

34

10,080

Sounds like a lot doesn't it? But so many times it feels insufficient. The figure 10,080 is how many minutes each of us has every week. Nobody has more. Nobody has less. In this time, we need to eat, sleep, love, spend time with the Lord, worship with our families, go to work, serve others, etc. Sometimes it feels as if they last forever. Sometimes it seems that we had only 1,000 minutes to get done what we needed to get done. But the 10,080 minutes are the same every week.

Now here's the topic for this essay: HOW WILL YOU USE YOUR TIME? Let's narrow it down even further. You say, "Of course, we must sleep, eat, spend time with our family, spend time with friends, exercise, etc." How will we find balance between our ministry time and our non-ministry time? Because most urban ministry work (outside of Sunday worship) is very flexible in scheduling, two diseases are easy to catch. One is LAZYITIS. You know the thinking on this one. "I don't need to go into the office. I can just work from home (even though I'm not as productive and people can't easily find me)." Or "They can't really pay me what they should pay me, so I'll just take some extra time off." Or "Most of my programming is from 4:00–8:00 p.m., so the rest of the day is mine." Think about that. Really? You only work a 20-hour week, plus your Sunday morning responsibility?

It's easy to catch LAZYITIS working in an urban ministry place, because in many urban ministry places the "staff" is just you, or maybe you and one other person. It's easy to get into an unproductive work life routine.

A lack of productivity and lack of ministry results could reveal your LAZYITIS. But when you're in an inner-city setting, and there is a great lack of productivity in your ministry because you honestly have not been putting in the time, there is a convenient excuse escape. It goes something like this—"This community is so hard to reach with the Gospel... people just don't follow through... they just don't show up... I don't have any support in this place." Yep, I've heard all the excuses. Don't misunderstand me. I totally agree with what 1 Corinthians 3:6 says about who is responsible for results. Yet, every one of us in ministry can be responsible for faithful ministry—making our calls on people, leading our Bible studies, caring for people through their life challenges, equipping people to think and act like Jesus, and leading people to the foot of the cross. Maybe a good way to provoke thought about LAZYITIS is to have you chew on the question I try to ask myself each week before the Lord:

"This week, did I give my very best to bringing the Good News of Jesus to people?" God knows and we know the answer. What are you doing with your 10,080?

At the other end of the spectrum is another disease—

WORKAHOLISM. I could write pages and pages about this. It is one of my addictions. It's easy to catch because there is infinitely more work to do in urban ministry than there is time to do all the work. There is always another person to call on. There is more study needed for a lesson or sermon. There are always meetings to go to, both in your ministry and in your community. There are new ministry connections and partnerships to make. I have had an affair with my ministry to the detriment of spending time with my wife and my kids. I'm now trying to do better with my grandkids and in the latter years of my marriage. Thankfully, I have a forgiving family.

With this disease, I need to come before the Lord and confess, "Lord, I was out of balance this week. Help me work more balanced and work smarter by equipping others."

Let's focus on the 10,080 minutes that is dedicated to ministry. How will you and I use our MINISTRY TIME?

Will we use our ministry time on PEOPLE or TASKS? Both are needed.

What I mean by TASKS are things like preparing the church bulletin, writing thank you letters, preparing Bible studies, preparing sermons, writing grant proposals for ministry funding, etc. Those are all TASKS. But in an urban ministry, as a ministry leader, you may very well be the point person meeting with repair people, dealing with city inspectors, doing some minor repairs yourself, and taking care of other property issues. Do you feel the time demands getting deeper? I remember early on in my ministry when we didn't have a church properties board and couldn't pay for grass cutting or outside maintenance. I spent some of my Saturday time making sure that the grass was cut and trimmed for Sunday morning worship. Some would say that is important and that a clean and attractive entrance really matters for Sunday worship. After a while, I decided that in stewarding my time, that TASK wasn't as important as preparing for Sunday worship. There are TASKS that need to be accomplished every week. I do not believe in compromising on the TASK of sermon preparation.

Yet, choose PEOPLE over TASKS.

Be a ministry leader who makes calls on people. Check on PEOPLE who have missed Sunday worship or one of your weekly ministry events. Get to the hospital to see PEOPLE when they are sick. When a visitor has come to worship or a ministry event, make a follow up phone call or visit that PERSON. Your office is an important place for ministry, but make sure to get out of it and go see PEOPLE to encourage them in Christ.

There's no one in the Bethlehem family, or about to come into the Bethlehem family, that doesn't know Lynette Penny. Some know her as "Ms. Penny." Others just know her as "Penny." Ms. Penny is *obsessed* with contacting people (I am saying this positively!). She'll contact you at the beginning of the week about church, and then for sure on Saturday you're going to get a call from her. She wants to see if you need a ride for church on Sunday from the van ministry, or if you're going to get to worship by your own transportation. Also, you might as well answer your phone right away, because if you don't, she's probably going to blow up your phone with calls until she reaches you! Penny is a blessing for our outreach at Bethlehem and a great reminder to keep on choosing people over tasks, especially when the list of life tasks is overwhelming. She is an asset for any ministry team to keep upholding a passion for reaching people with the Savior in front of the entire church as a necessary, regular part of what each of us does with our 10,080!

35

DIFFICULT PEOPLE

Every ministry has them. Who is the person who lied about you? Who is the person you can prove was talking behind your back? Who is the person who seems to always take the side against you in any discussion? Who is the person who may have even tried, or is trying, to get rid of you?

I'm talking about difficult people. It is so easy in those moments to say to yourself, "That person messed with the wrong _____," and then begin to plot a reverse offensive plan to not only prove them wrong, but also embarrass them in front of everybody, take them down, and maybe even rid them from the ministry! Have you been there? I have. Just being real! In truth, I think all of us go there sometimes.

Some people think ministry leaders are "Teflon-coated" and everything just bounces off us with no damage. You know, "Sticks and stones..." No. the truth is that difficult people can hurt us, no matter how much we might deny that they have gotten to us.

Join me in thinking through how to deal with difficult people in a way that honors God.

We Must Love Difficult People in Jesus.

Yes, I know this is really hard, because attacking words and actions hurt. But think about Jesus who, to save you and me, "endured the cross, despising the shame..." (Hebrews 12:2) Think about Jesus, "who has endured such hostility by sinners (us included) against Himself, so that you will not grow weary and lose heart." I love what Luke 19:41 says about Jesus: "When He approached Jerusalem, He saw the city and He wept over it." When was this? It was actually in a joyful circumstance—Palm Sunday. He was riding on a donkey descending from the Mount of Olives and getting ready to enter Jerusalem to begin the week when He would die. The crowds were cheering for Jesus, saying, "Blessed are You, Jesus! Blessed are You who comes in the name of the Lord!" After having been so mistreated by difficult people, and now with a big crowd behind Him, it would have been so easy for Jesus from a human perspective to say something like, "Yeah! Let's go into Jerusalem and 'kick butt' on all of those Pharisees and Jewish leaders. They're all jealous of Me. All a bunch of haters!" But Luke 19:41 says, "When Jesus approached Jerusalem, He saw the city and He wept over it."

What was He weeping for? Jesus was weeping about all the people of Jerusalem who would not receive Him as the Savior. His tears were tears of loving disappointment. In Luke 19:42 Jesus' tears become words about the people of Jerusalem, "If you had known in this day, even you, the things which make for peace!" At the very end of Matthew 23:37, Jesus mourns over the problem with the people of Jerusalem. Do you see it now—the underlying feeling of Jesus' heart for people who had been so DIFFICULT for Him and made His life so painful? Jesus never stopped loving them.

On our prayer list, under the category of "things" we need God's help with, isn't this in the top five? "Help me, Lord, not hate and not want to get revenge, but to LOVE difficult people, just like Jesus did." Prayer is the way we must go regarding this matter. We will need LOVE POURED INTO US.

It won't just emerge from us naturally. That's why in moments like this, the two words the writer to the Hebrews uses at the beginning of Hebrews 12:3 are the only place for us to begin: "Consider Him..."

We May Have to Restrategize.

When a football team has played the entire first half and their game plan of running the football hasn't worked... AND THEY WANT TO WIN THE GAME... then, often at halftime they RESTRATEGIZE and try to pass the football in the second half. If we want to win the game, sometimes changing strategy is absolutely necessary. The stubborn person who says, "Nope, this is what I do, and this is the way I do things," might very well keep doing what they're doing. It's a free country for us to do what we want to do! But, very likely, that stubborn person is going to lose the game.

Ministry is always about WINNING THE GAME, or more precisely, sharing the Gospel so that people come to faith in Jesus and stay in faith in Jesus.

Other goals like getting revenge on people who have hurt us, teaching them a lesson of who's boss, or quitting on them because "I can't take them anymore," might very well may make us feel better, but they won't WIN the game that our Lord wants WON! What does our Lord want us to do? See what Jesus told Peter to do three times in John 21:15–17.

To care for difficult people may take some new strategizing. For example, in my ministry, I found that when I talked to one difficult person, what I said always got twisted. So I changed my communication method with this person and always emailed. That way, if they contested or tried to twist what I said, I always had a written record of it. Even when I spoke to them face to face, I tried to follow it up with an email to confirm what was said. I know you're thinking, "What a hassle!" It was, but it did work better.

Here's another strategy. The person with whom you're having challenges may be in a ministry-serving position that is not suited for them. I knew one person who was a great crisis, emergency, short term helping person. He was the best at staying with you through an intense and unexpected time. But when it came to a long term assignment, he didn't do well with that. The problem was that he really just wanted to have the "title" of chairman of this board.

Restrategizing how we minister to someone may mean using an approach similar to the one we have with our children. When a son is born, we might throw a basketball in his crib, envisioning the next LeBron James. But then as he begins to grow, we may need to restrategize and see the unique gifts God has given him and then help him develop those gifts. Blessed is the parent who restrategizes, rather than forcing his kid to live life a certain way so that he can live through his child. Blessed is the ministry leader who is committed to winning by caring for people, even when it means restrategizing. This is not easy work.

Pass Them to Others to Care for.

I'll never forget "Ricky." This is a true story, but his name wasn't Ricky. Ricky was a talented young man in high school, but he had a smart mouth, was full of himself, always had to have the last word, and loved to put others down to lift himself up. I had no use for Ricky. I truly tried with Ricky many times. Most of the time, I wanted to beat the mess out of him (yes, I know that doesn't sound very pastoral). On the other hand, another man in our ministry named "Dwight" was a friend of Ricky's and had a very effective way with him. Dwight could get Ricky to do what was right.

Sometimes, we need to pass our "Rickys" to a "Dwight."

Isn't that the great thing about Christ's church? The Lord has created us as a body with many different gifts (1 Corinthians 12:12–31). The only thing that gets in the way of someone like me passing Ricky to a Dwight is me. I need to lay down my pride to think that I am the sole connecting point for all ministry and let the "Dwights" use their gifts.

Pray the Right Prayers.

Some years ago I was having trouble with a difficult person who wasn't even part of our congregation, but was a part of our larger ministry. When I was on a morning walk one day, the Holy Spirit indicted me in my mind as I was praying. I had been praying and praying, "Lord, please change this person" when the Holy Spirit put into my spirit, "John, there's another prayer that you need to pray in this situation." That prayer was, "Lord, please change ME as I work through this difficult situation."

Maybe this is so obvious to you, but that moment was meaningful for me. I'm not holding myself up as someone who always does and says everything right. No way. One of my favorite people in the Bible is Peter. He's always saying the wrong thing or stepping in mud. That's me, only worse. My life is one big apology! But when I'm dealing with a difficult person who I KNOW has hurt me, who I KNOW has done me wrong, many times my prayer has been about THEM. No, the right prayer also includes, "Lord, change me. Change me in how I am saying things. Change me from always looking for the negative. Lord, change me from remembering E-VER-Y-THING they've ever done to me. Change me and make me the instrument of your healing for me and for them." Amen.

36

THE VITALITY OF BIBLICAL AUTHORITY

In 1989 when I came to Bethlehem Lutheran Church, this once big congregation of 2,500 people had dwindled down to about 30 worshippers (90% of whom were commuters, not in the neighborhood; 90% were elderly; and 90% were Caucasian, though we are located in a predominately African-American neighborhood). Unfortunately, that's not an unusual picture of what happens to many older mainline Christian churches located in inner-city areas. For all practical purposes, Bethlehem was in a 17-year pastoral vacancy prior to our coming. Part-time and retired pastors who were faithful and worked hard served the church, but their time and energy were very limited.

When Sharon and I came to Bethlehem, we had no idea if we were coming to bury the church or to see something new come forth. As I considered the call to Bethlehem, I found the church had several useful things going for it. Although our 1,100-seat church building had a lot of issues, Bethlehem also had a four-story school building with a gym. Bethlehem was also in an agreement with the Head Start program that enabled it to gain some income through renting out some of its classrooms. Bethlehem also had a great heritage of former members and people who attended Bethlehem school and cared about Bethlehem. In addition, the church had a small endowment fund with cash available to support a full-time pastor for about two years before the money would run out. Most of all, Bethlehem had a group of about 30 strong, tough, faithful worshipping members who had not left for the suburbs as the community changed. They said they were committed to trying one more time to make aggressive ministry in the community work.

However, there was one thing Bethlehem had lost in the years of its decline and pastoral vacancy. Our church had lost the authority of the

Word of God. Don't misunderstand. Bethlehem believed the Bible is the Word of God. We still do. But what we had lost is the truth that the Bible is the authority for our faith and life as individual Christ followers and as a church.

The principle that God's Word decides everything is a must for any church or ministry to hold strongly to, no matter where it is located.

Think through what this truth means. In the first year of my ministry at Bethlehem, one of my aims was to begin an additional Bible class during the week. I reported on this goal at one of our monthly Board of Directors meetings. Amazingly, I received push back from a few board members. They were concerned that leading this additional new Bible class would keep me from visiting our shut-in members as much as they wanted them visited. As discussion in that particular board meeting began, the chairman of the board called for a vote on whether I would be allowed to form and lead a new Bible study at Bethlehem. I stopped the chairman and reminded him that this wasn't a "voteable" matter. God's Word had already spoken the command to spread the Word of the Lord. I had to remind our membership that if God's Word spoke to an issue, it wasn't up for a vote. That discussion came about because, in our Biblical ignorance, we had lost the authority of the Word of God.

More important, the Word of God, not only MUST decide everything among God's people, but also the Word of God is the one authority that can speak to so many life matters in this world that even the Church often gets confused about. Let's look at a few.

RACISM. God's Word cuts through all of the tension and baggage that sometimes make even churches become uncomfortable in crossing this world's racial and cultural lines. What can anyone say and what discriminatory separation can anyone make among people when God's Word speaks in Galatians 3:26–29 with such clarity?

CLASSISM. It is very human for people who have more money or more societal power to consider themselves above those who do not. What I've found among good Christian friends who are millionaires as well as good

Christian friends who live at a poverty income level is that they respect, care for one another, and get along, because they have embraced the words of David recorded in 1 Chronicles 29:14. The Word of God makes everything so clear!

SELFISHNESS. This is probably the greatest poison of life. How tempting it sometimes is for all of us to make our life aim our own desires, pleasures, and whatever we want. Yet, 2 Corinthians 5:14–15 makes God's plan for us so clear. We are to live for Him!

THE PRIORITIES OF A CHURCH. "But Reverend, we need to vote on this and decide if this is what we want to do as a church… after all it's our money, our property, our church! We need to decide if this is what we want to give our time to." No, check Ephesians 2:19–22. Whose household, whose family is the Church? HIS priorities need to be our priorities, even if they sometimes make us uncomfortable.

Some years ago, I was trying to help another church grow stronger in their outreach to their community. We had planned a series of Sunday afternoon canvasses to reach their community. I was there for the events. Some of our Bethlehem family members were there. But the members of that church wouldn't go to the community with us. I understand that walking the streets may not work for everybody's comfort level. Instead, invite people every week to worship; make some phone calls to people you know who aren't living close to the Lord; invite someone at your job or in your neighborhood to a church event. You decide the manner in which you obey Jesus' words in Mark 16:15 when He said, "Go into all the world and deliver the Gospel to all creation." But don't just DO NOTHING with that Word from our Lord! How hard it sometimes is for churches to look beyond ourselves and our own comfort and see those who don't know Christ! Oops! There's the Word of God again, when we think only of ourselves—check out 1 Corinthians 10:24.

CHANGES IN OUR CHURCH. Let's be honest. All of us have our own preferences for what we like and how we like things to go. That's true in life. That's also true about our church home. There are many factors involved in the status quo of how our church operates in worship, in outreach, in responsibilities, and with regard to the commitment of being a member, etc. One factor is "taste"—I like this kind of music or worship, rather than this kind of music or worship. Another factor is "fear"—something new or doing things a new way may scare me because I may not like it as well. Laziness can make me not want to give change a chance. In order to do greater things in our ministry, it may cost me more of my time to volunteer; maybe I don't want to do that. Ignorant judgment also sometimes keeps people from trying changes. They say, "Well, that's not the way we do things as Lutherans," even if the proposed change is in step with the Word of God.

Two important observations. First, note that all these factors regarding change have to do with ourselves and what we want or don't want. Self is never to be at the heart of our lives as Christians. See Matthew 6:33. Second, when God's Word is the authority and God's Word has spoken about the proposed change, that settles it. We all bow before God and His Word... EXCEPT if your church does not practice Biblical authority. The authority of God's Word in our churches is vital!

Although we are people of different ages, different races, different levels of Christian maturity, different life experiences, different preferences and tastes, different bank account levels, different languages, etc., God's Word reveals to us the one Savior, Jesus Christ, who enables us all to become one with another. We all bow before what the Lord says!

One more thing. I am a Lutheran Christian. I think Martin Luther was a great man, and God used him powerfully to remind the Church of the importance of the grace of God and encourage the Church to be people who read, study, digest, and seek to live God's Word. I embrace the motto, "Only grace, only faith, only Scripture, only Christ!" Lutherans have some great traditions. BUT I also say that God's Word, the Bible, always trumps Lutheranism.

37

A VARIATION ON 1 PETER 4:8

First Peter 4:8 says, "Love covers a multitude of sins." How true! Now, if I may borrow that phrase from the Scripture:

"Excellent, prepared, Biblical, Christ-centered preaching covers a multitude of young pastor sins."

I bring this to your attention because I personally know that it's true. I don't say this believing that I am such a great preacher. The best I can say is that I try every week to be the best communicator of the Word of God I can be. And, even after 35 years in the pulpit, I still study every week from the original languages, and I still try to sit at the feet of other preachers via books, recordings, and seminars so that I can keep growing.

The point I want to make to you in this essay is to encourage you to give prime attention to your preaching and teaching of the Word of God. Receive this encouragement as a brother who has spent 30 years in the inner-city.

I know you have so many important matters that compete for your time in ministry. I know you need to give attention to your family. I know you need personal time with the Lord. I know you need your "me time." When you're in the homestretch of preparing a solid message for Sunday, I know it's hard on Friday and Saturday when your family and friends are playing and you're zeroed in on birthing a vital message to the people of God for Sunday morning. Because we who serve inner-city parishes are often by ourselves, it would be so easy not to prepare well for your Sunday sermon. Don't do it. Giving attention to your preaching and teaching is not only right in the eyes of God, but it's also something God uses in powerful ways in your relationships with the people of your church.

Early in my ministry, a woman (who has since gone to be with the Lord) didn't really care for me. I don't think she disliked me personally. I think it troubled her because the Lord wanted to use me to lead Bethlehem through some changes. She was also a smart woman. She knew that the Bethlehem with 30 longtime worshipping members in 1989 wouldn't last more than about one more decade or so (many people were in their eighties). However, I believe she wanted Bethlehem's congregation to live on, even beyond her lifetime. If she could have put it in words, I think she would have said:

"Pastor, can't you just leave things the way they are at Bethlehem until after I die?" (By this she meant "who" comes to our church, the traditional way we worship, the ministries we have, etc.)

New worship styles and new people who didn't look like her or act like her were hard for her to get used to. Giving attention to reaching new people, rather than just giving attention to those who were already in the Bethlehem family, was hard for her. Seeing Bethlehem crossing cultures in ministry was hard for her.

By the way, I know from the grapevine that she wasn't alone in some of the above opinions and preferences. Add to this the fact that I was a young pastor with a young family. I didn't always say things in wise, politically correct ways. Sometimes, I got out of balance in how I used my ministry time. Sometimes, I spent more time out on the street trying to reach new people in the community with the Gospel than I spent with our shut-in members and didn't visit them as frequently as some in the church would have liked me to do (and probably as frequently as I should have). True! True! True!

This woman could easily have left Bethlehem and transferred to another suburban Lutheran church and felt more comfortable. What kept this woman at Bethlehem? What gave a lot of those wonderful older saints great patience with the John Schmidtke of his mid-20s? One day, some courageous older saints from this group told me the answer. They said they stayed because they received a solid Sunday morning sermon from the Bethlehem pulpit. That's why they didn't want to leave. All praise to God the Holy Spirit!

I could write a separate book about all I've learned through the years about preaching God's Word in an urban inner-city parish. But for this moment, I just want to encourage you in your preaching or your teaching. Give time to it. Make it your best every week. Have the discipline to "go away" from everything else to be alone with the Lord. Study and learn for yourself and then for the sermon you will bring. Go deep. Let the Holy Spirit lead you. Preach the text of God's Word, not your opinions or what you think "will preach" and get great response. Work on your delivery, and don't read a spiritual lecture. Use great illustrations, but don't let your illustrations and stories overshadow the truths of the Word of God you bring. You can't preach like God's Word has incarnated you personally if you haven't been away with the Lord that week for God's Word to incarnate you personally. The "why" is Biblical. You have been called to "correctly handle the Word of Truth." (2 Timothy 2:15)

Now for the by-product of strong preaching. It will be used by the Holy Spirit to make people more patient with you as a pastor, more accepting of your leadership, and more willing to put God's direction ahead of their personal preferences. Most of all, it will be used by the Holy Spirit to give people hope and confidence that, because of Christ's continual forgiveness and mercy, they can continue to go forward with life.

38

THE GROWTH PROGRESSION

A few years back, I had to think about a new way of looking at people in our ministry. Why? I was getting MAD and EXASPERATED WITH PEOPLE.

- I would see "Jimmy" who took three steps forward in his spiritual life and in our ministry. I was looking forward to his next three steps of growth. BUT INSTEAD, he took two steps backward.

- I watched "Martina" who had so much talent, so many gifts from the Lord! She had finally started to step up and be the leader in our ministry I thought she could be. BUT THEN, she disappeared again. With no communication, she started showing up late for ministry events and soon not even showing up at all. It was like an addict trying to recover who relapses backwards into a binge.

- I can even remember the first Sunday that "Cedrick" came to our church. He was so excited about our ministry and wanted to jump right in and get involved. I was thrilled to have a possible new worker in our ministry with such fresh energy! He even made it to a ministry event that first week, and then to his second Sunday in a row at worship. BUT his life at Bethlehem never went any further. He got distracted with a new job opportunity and a relationship that finally sprouted.

Have you ever found yourself feeling frustrated like this with people in your ministry? What depressed you wasn't just their decline in personal spiritual growth with the Lord, but also the fact that YOU NEEDED THEM! You needed another dependable person in the ministry. You thought this person could be one of your next leaders to help you! When my heart gets "teased" with the hope that more help and hands for the work of the Lord might be on the way, but then gets disappointed, sometimes I honestly get gun shy about being hopeful with people. It's easy to let the enemy flood our hearts with pessimism and negativity when the next new "someone" comes to our ministry, or the next longtime "someone" tries to come back again into our ministry. On the outside we might be smiling and encouraging, but on the inside, we honestly have the kind of attitude that asks, "Okay, how long will you be around this time?"

That kind of attitude may be truth-based and might even be a personal mechanism to protect our hearts from getting hurt again, but it doesn't contribute much toward leading that person into a growing and consistent life of service to the Lord in our ministry.

I needed to begin seeing people in a different way. I have found it so helpful to intentionally see people in something I call, "THE GROWTH PROGRESSION."

Actually, this GROWTH PROGRESSION flows right out of what Jesus teaches in Mark 4:3–9, 13–20 regarding how the seed of the Word of God is received by people. Jesus said in Mark 4:15 that some people basically do not respond to the Word of God. There are also some people more like rocky soil, according to 4:16–17. They will flash a strong response to serve, but when the going gets rough, they step back and fold. Still further, there are people, see verses 18–19, who start growing and serving, but then they are attracted to what they think is a better offer—the cares of this world. Eventually the cares of this world ultimately choke the Word of God, and they stop serving. The last description in this picture from Jesus is in verse 20. God's Word finds a place to grow and thrive in the good soil. These people become some of the real "gifts from God" He sends into our lives to serve with us, encourage us, and relieve some of the ministry load. True! True! True! My colleague Pastor Gerard Bolling gave me a term to describe this last group—he calls them the "soldiers." That's what we need in our ministries, more soldiers! We can all agree on that.

Here is the big question. Was Jesus describing "stages" of soil or the kinds of soils people will always be? Can people/soil who begin as "hard soil," "rocky soil," or "soil where weeds are allowed to grow," ever change and become "good soil" where the Lord and His Word grows and thrives with consistency?

Think about how the Bible would answer that question. The Word of God tells us the answer. Our God constantly shows that He can take a Genesis 12:10–20 deceptive Abram and make out of him the Romans 4:16 Abraham who is the "father of all of us who believe." Our God can take the Genesis 18:12 laughing Sarah and make out of her the Hebrews 11:11 Sarah who believed God's promise, even the 1 Peter 3:5–6 Sarah, who is a model for Godly women. Our God can take the greedy, evil, selfish Zacchaeus and make out of him the new Luke 19:8 Zacchaeus who makes restitution and has a generous heart. On the basis of those examples and so many more, I say, "Yes, though we might be 'rocky soil' today, through the mercy of God in Jesus, the Holy Spirit is able to change all of us to fruitful and productive 'good soil.'"

Often this fabulous change the Holy Spirit brings about takes time. As I wait on Him, I make sure I don't get in His way, lashing out at people when they back away from serving. I've decided that seeing people from the perspective of the following GROWTH PROGRESSION levels is helpful for me to continue to stay positive and not give up on them. There are three different steps in God's GROWTH PROGRESSION of leading people into commitment to Him: SPECTATORS, SOMETIMERS, or SOLDIERS. Here are some definitions:

SPECTATORS are people who come to our ministry and may very well be very excited about our ministry and might even volunteer for one or two ministry events. BUT they mainly just watch the work get done. They are mostly consumers of the ministry experience. They jump in and help only in those rare times when their schedule and an opportunity to serve coincide. It's not that they are bad people. They might even be pretty regular at worship. Yet, when it comes to serving and helping in the work of ministry, they have very low commitment.

SOMETIMERS are people who have more commitment than SPECTATORS. They cheer on the work of ministry and are very proud of the ministry work their church does! For a time, they will even plan their life around opportunities to serve. SOMETIMERS will even step forward to start a new ministry. They will have great excitement! BUT while they might be involved strongly for five or six weeks, then they step back and disappear for two or three weeks. When you follow up with them, they often have an excuse. They say, "Well, things happened in my life." Or, "I'm just going through a lot of stuff right now." MEMO TO EVERY ONE OF US—according to the very words of Jesus in John 16:33, we will always have "turbulent stuff" going on in this earthly life. It's the nature of this life! Real serving means not waiting until things quiet down. It's serving through the "turbulent stuff" as we rest on the strength of Jesus (John 16:33). SOMETIMERS "tease" leaders with their great talent and potential. But they disappoint us because their commitment is hot and cold. Some SOMETIMERS could become SOLDIERS simply by being better at organizing their life—seeing life in bigger chunks and then keeping the schedule of commitments they make.

SOLDIERS. It's not that SOLDIERS are perfect. It's not that they never take "pauses" in their serving life. But SOLDIERS are "all in" when it comes to the work of Christ. SOLDIERS think of His desire for them ahead of their own desires of what they want to do with their lives. SOLDIERS are the people who find their own replacement when they can't serve, or they still show up at the event, so as not to let down the ministry effort. SOLDIERS know the importance of their presence to the rest of the team. You just can't replace being in worship with the family and being at events where the family serves. SOLDIERS are people the leaders can invest in and depend on. SOLDIERS are the backbone of any ministry. They are the most valuable people in your ministry. Here's one way I often easily recognize a SOLDIER—they check on me as a leader and then step in to make my load lighter. More important than a great financial giver is a SOLDIER. Yet, guess what? Most SOLDIERS are also the best financial givers to our ministry.

Let me help you envision this threefold description of people in an even sharper way by unfolding how SPECTATORS, SOMETIMERS, and SOLDIERS operate.

When it comes to CONSISTENCY in serving:

- SPECTATORS watch ministry more than they participate in ministry; yet they are very interested and positive about ministry taking place.

- SOMETIMERS cheer on the ministry and sometimes act like SOLDIERS in ministry; they contribute to the ministry, but they do it in spurts.

- SOLDIERS are dependable to "be in the game" and carry the cause of ministry day in and day out in whatever way they are needed to serve. SOLDIERS have the attitude of Isaiah in Isaiah 6:8, and they mean it!

When ADVERSITY comes, either to the ministry or to people's personal lives:

- SPECTATORS often move on to something else and something easier when the going gets tough. They often jump from one thing to another, sometimes even from one ministry/church to another.

- SOMETIMERS will either stop serving altogether (as they recede into their life burrow until the storm passes), only serve at a distance, or serve only in very selective circumstances.

- SOLDIERS stay strong. They keep serving through the adversity; they know that on the other side of every valley is a new mountaintop! They keep their eyes focused on the Lord, not the present hard circumstance.

When the CARES OF THE WORLD try to get the attention of God's people away from the Lord and His ministry:

- SPECTATORS quickly let their eyes move away from ministry to whatever is newest and most attractive. When you ask a SPECTATOR to commit to helping in ministry, they sometimes say something like, "Well, maybe I can help, but I don't want to commit. I don't want to disappoint you in case something else comes up in my life." (What they mean is, "...in case I get a better offer to do something else with my time.")

- SOMETIMERS often are like SPECTATORS in this situation. They have one eye on the world and one eye on Christ and His ministry. They want to help. They do serve in ministry. But they often have "miss out disease." They think, "Ministry will always be there to do, but these other opportunities? If I don't take advantage of them, I might never get this ticket to the game again... I might never get this overtime offered to me again, etc. (Hmm... God has no control over helping SOMETIMERS in extraordinary ways at other times? Maybe meditating on Ephesians 3:20–21 and Matthew 6:33 might be useful. What would God say about this through these Scriptures?)

- SOLDIERS. It isn't that they aren't tempted by the cares of the world. It is rather that they have learned to keep both of their eyes on Christ. They have surrendered their will to say, "If God wants this opportunity for me, He will provide it for me at a time when it fits into my life and doesn't disturb my serving Him." SOLDIERS have also surrounded themselves with Christian brothers and sisters who have permission to confront them when they start to follow the "cares of the world" and then direct them to turn back to Christ.

When it comes to BUILDING A MINISTRY ON:

- SPECTATORS, it is virtually impossible. You can do some isolated events with SPECTATORS, but not ongoing consistent ministry. The only way SPECTATORS and ongoing ministry works is if you can pay a large enough staff who can basically run the ministry on their own, and then SPECTATORS sort of show up when they want to show up and get in where they fit in.

- SOMETIMERS, it's not impossible, but it's really hard. On the positive side, they flash so much potential in front of our eyes. They often come with such great energy. As leaders, we get our hopes up that help has really arrived! But then, after SOMETIMERS work hard for a season, they pull back and disappear. SOMETIMERS often are experts at making excuses for why they couldn't be present or help. Here's one thing I have learned over the years—*any adult can be exactly where they want to be and do exactly what they want to do, if they really want to do it.* Over time, SOMETIMERS take us on an emotional rollercoaster with their on and off commitment.

- SOLDIERS, these people are "all in." They empower a ministry to really grow. The more SOLDIERS you have in your ministry, the stronger and larger it can grow!

Are you starting to think of people in your ministry in these categories? **Here's something that is really important—our goal is not the "label." Actually, labeling some people as SPECTATORS or SOMETIMERS, even though it's true, will frustrate us because we always need more SOLDIERS! Our goal is to try and help move SPECTATORS and SOMETIMERS to become SOLDIERS and to help keep SOLDIERS to continue being STRONG SOLDIERS!**

Only one thing will help people grow into SOLDIERS. It was the very last thing that Peter said in his epistle in 2 Peter 3:9: "... but grow in the grace and knowledge of our Lord Jesus Christ." Growth in our life with the Lord comes only through growth in God's Word. I most often find our three groups are in different spots regarding their thinking about God's Word. SPECTATORS know that strength comes from God's Word. But they don't make consistent time in their lives for God's Word to come into them and strengthen them. SOMETIMERS are like some of us are with taking medicine. When we get sick, the doctor gives us a prescription to get better, but we don't take the medicine consistently. Then we can't figure out why we aren't getting better. SOMETIMERS come in and out of Bible study. They haven't learned that just occasional spiritual injections aren't enough for real life change. SOLDIERS have realized that they can't live without God's Word. They know it gives them life strength to serve and live. They understand the role of God's Word in exactly the same way that Ezekiel did, according to Ezekiel 3:1–3.

Holy Spirit, help me as a leader always to have the right attitude about moving SPECTATORS and SOMETIMERS to SOLDIERS. Keep me from bitterness. Don't let me give up on people, just as God in Christ has never given up on me. Use me as a leader/coach to raise up more precious SOLDIERS for Your work of reaching the world with the Good News of Jesus. Paul told Timothy in 2 Timothy 2:4, "No soldier in active service entangles himself in the affairs of everyday life..." Keep me from this temptation. The verse continues, "...so that he may please the ONE who enlisted him as a soldier." I want to please You, Lord. Amen.

39

PLEASE DON'T TEASE

Many urban ministries bordering on the brink of desperation strongly desire people who are willing to work, especially ones who are gifted and have energy for ministry. I've attended a few installations of pastors at urban churches. On their installation day, that congregation is filled with so much excitement, hope, and belief that this leader whom God has sent is finally "the one" who will lead them back to being the strong congregation they once were! Congregations that are near death's door often try one last time with a brand-new leader and make significant sacrifices to go all in.

When I came to Bethlehem, the remaining 30 longtime members who still worshipped in the 1,100-seat sanctuary took the last $60–70,000 they had in their bank account and "put it out on the table" in hopes that Bethlehem Church would go through a resurrection. I also witnessed how they went along with a lot of new ideas from this new 27-year-old pastor who showed up in 1989 that significantly stretched their comfort zone. Thank God for the commitment to ministry that He worked in those longtime saints. They could have just folded the church, distributed the funds to other ministries, transferred their memberships to other county Lutheran churches, and become another church that abandoned the city.

But they didn't. They stayed and tried one more time to bring aggressive ministry to their community. I honor what the Lord led them to do. Some churches in their shoes do what they did; other churches just close and leave. Still other churches do what is probably just as bad—they remain in the city, but they stay to themselves in their old ways and don't reach out aggressively with the Gospel. That might be the worst option of all!

If you have the opportunity to come to an old urban ministry that wants to see resurrection and is willing to completely commit its resources to do this, PLEASE DON'T TEASE! What I mean by that is you, as a ministry leader, commit also to them.

PLEASE DON'T TEASE urban ministries and take their position while you wait for something better to come along. If you're planning to stay only for a year or two, it would probably be better for you to not even come. You can't really get anything done in an urban community in a year. You will barely get to know the community in one year. They will barely know you in one year. In your mind, sign a five-year contract and decide that for the next five years, you are not even open to listening to another position or call. If the ministry runs out of money, and you have to leave for financial reasons to take care of your family, that's a different circumstance. But to stay only a year or two is not fair to that church. They will have invested much in your coming, with no potential for much return.

Of course, there are always some unforeseen factors like when a family illness necessitates a quick move or when a pastor and the people were forced on each other by an outside party and just aren't a good fit. But for the most part, quick exits from small urban ministries produce so much discouragement among the people. It would be better for you not to go there than to get people's hopes up and then leave.

PLEASE DON'T TEASE by leaving when something with a better salary comes along. I understand you and your family need to be able to pay your bills. But it's a scripturally wrong behavior to base judging a call heavily on the basis of money. It really suggests that your coming and going is about YOU and not about where the Lord places you.

PLEASE DON'T TEASE by coming to a ministry and then claiming that this ministry isn't "going anywhere" after three to six months. This is the "blame it on the church" philosophy. Have you really studied the community? Researched the ministry? Listened to the community? Sought counsel from other ministry leaders about what they did in similar circumstances? Don't fall into spiritual jargon and say, "Well, I just felt that the Lord wanted me to move on." What about having more of a Jeremiah ministry mentality that says, "Yes, Lord, this place is tough. These people are tough. But I am here, Lord, to care for your sheep. Help me love them deeply and lead them effectively, even though it is not easy!" Building trust takes time.

PLEASE DON'T TEASE. Put down your ministry and family "stakes" in this place that the Lord has called you to. Give it your all. Give people something they can invest in.

If you're considering a call to a ministry and you don't believe you can go all in... if you're considering a call to a ministry that you don't think you could spend the rest of your days at... then turn it down. Don't come. That decision will be better for that ministry. PLEASE DON'T TEASE.

40

AN ENTREPRENEURIAL SPIRIT

Acts 18:3–4 says, "...and because Paul was of the same trade (as Aquila and Priscilla), he stayed with them and they were working, for by trade they were tentmakers. And Paul was reasoning in the synagogue every Sabbath and trying to persuade Jews and Greeks." The greatest preacher of the Christian faith, ever, was bi-vocational. Remember something else about the Apostle Paul. It wasn't that he was uneducated, unskilled, and bi-vocational as a tentmaker because he couldn't do much else. No, check Paul's resumé in Philippians 3:4–6 and Acts 22:3. Paul was gifted, connected, and a man of power (even though most of his connections were from his former "Saul" life)! So why work as a tentmaker on the side? Even as an emerging preacher, he could have taken a church. Paul had a following. Being bi-vocational and having an income source beyond his ministry gave Paul some important advantages for ministry. He could bring the Gospel into places that had no money to pay for him. People who didn't like Paul's pure message of the Gospel of Christ couldn't bind him or silence him with the threat of withholding a paycheck. They couldn't say, "Pastor, you need to tone down some of the things you're saying. After all, you know, we do sign your paycheck." More ministry could be done if offerings went mainly toward ministry expansion, not toward paying a ministry leader's salary. Hmmm... sounds like something useful for us to think about regarding urban inner-city ministry in low-income areas.

As we get into this topic, there are some things I need to get off my chest. Although many brother preachers in storefront churches know a bi-vocational ministry life as obvious and commonplace, in the Lutheran experience that I grew up in, it was not so. My grandfather was a Lutheran Church-Missouri Synod pastor. As a child, I saw the pathway to that calling was straightforward—get a bachelor's degree, then go to seminary for four years including a year of internship, then you get a call to be the pastor of a church. At the church where you're called to go, you receive a salary and sometimes you also might receive free housing in a church-owned house next door (a parsonage). You're at that church until another church calls you to their church. That's the way your life goes for the rest of your pastor days—you're a full-time pastor. You won't get rich in this vocation, but the understanding is that your needs will be taken care of by the church that you're called to serve. That was the mode of my grandfather's generation. That was the mode of my father's generation. In my generation, it started to change. In the generation of my kids, it is drastically changing.

If you are led by the Lord to serve in an URBAN MINISTRY, especially in a LOW-INCOME AREA, honestly, most of us church leaders in our third and fourth decade of service are behind the timeline of change concerning how we can support our families. Let me explain this in very unequivocal terms. In almost all urban inner-city areas, the offerings that come in from a small urban congregation or ministry cannot support a full-time minister. For example, in our congregation of about 140 worshippers on a Sunday morning, our annual offerings are about $63–64,000. It isn't that people don't give sacrificially. It's just that their income is very limited. Well, let's say our building costs, utilities, and insurance run about $20,000. Let's say the annual costs for church programs run about another $20,000. And those aren't all the costs of an active ministry! So how does a pastor raise a family on under $25,000? These days, how does even a single pastor live on $25,000? In some cases, most of that would be eaten up in the cost of insurance! Are you getting the picture? From a business perspective, we would say a church business just isn't possible in this area. Yet, from the words of Jesus in Mark 16:15 we hear, "Go into all the world and preach the Gospel to all creation."

So what do we as God's people do? Consider the options:

a) Close ministry wherever it doesn't make financial sense. (We'd be closing a lot of ministries.)

b) Set-up endowments for churches in financially-distressed areas. (That's a possible idea, but where does the endowment principal come from?)

c) Have lots of chicken dinners and fish fry fundraisers. (Yes, that's part of the answer, but we can't have enough fundraisers to raise the kind of funds needed for this matter.)

e) Learn that entrepreneurism and ministry can go together.

While it is great if "b" is possible, and while "c" needs to be part of the solution, I advocate for the "e" approach.

Rev. William Schmelder, a mentor of mine in preaching and who has since gone to be with the Lord, preached my installation sermon at

Bethlehem in 1989. I don't even have to look up the worship folder from that day to tell you his sermon was based on 2 Corinthians 2:17 and was titled, "A Preacher, Not a Peddler." In his message, Rev. Schmelder urged me to give my best focus to bringing the Word of God to people. More than community center programs, more than just social assistance programs, people need the Gospel message that Christ has taken away sin so that again and again we can be right with our Father in heaven. Bill was right that day when he preached it. His message is still right on point today.

In the message, he noted the malady of preachers who have used the ministry as an opportunity for a personal hustle and to build their own kingdom. True then, still true today. However, it may be that in keeping Gospel ministry as the top priority the Lord has called us to make it, we've possibly gone too far and distanced ourselves from Paul's model where entrepreneurism and ministry work together for the sake of people coming to know Christ as Savior. Let me be clear. I totally agree with the mind of Paul: his tentmaking served his ministry. His ministry was first. In entrepreneurism, the goal is to make money. As we combine entrepreneurism with ministry, ministry designates that the money made is for Christ's Kingdom, not for personal gain.

To be sure, there's a danger to be watchful of when combining entrepreneurism and ministry. The danger is to allow successful entrepreneurism to overtake the ministry for which it is intended.

Let me demonstrate this on two levels where entrepreneurism and ministry can work together—a congregational level and a personal level. (I'll more thoroughly define these two levels positively in a minute.) As a congregation, one of the entrepreneurial avenues that the Lord has enabled us to be involved in is to rent space in our building to a charter school. I'll talk more later about the ministry opportunity that this endeavor brings us. Regarding the rent dollars we receive from our charter school... we need them to be able to make our budget. They are essential. If we used all the rental income dollars for our ministry, I could have a healthy salary increase, and parish life could become less of a financial struggle (those aren't bad things).

But our congregation has seen this entrepreneurial opportunity in a different way. From day one of our charter school's opening, while we use a portion of our rental income for our basic ministry bills, we use another *big* portion of our rental income to pay for a free afterschool Christian program for all the kids of our charter school! We REINVEST in ministry what we could have just kept for ourselves. Do you see the balance? Do you see the temptation to get out of balance with the rental income? Will this entrepreneurial opportunity be self-serving or seek to extend Christ's Kingdom? If we can keep that balance straight, entrepreneurism and ministry can work together beautifully.

On a personal level, our congregation would give me any kind of salary raise I wanted. BUT the question I always pose to them is, "If you are giving me an increase, where is that additional income coming from to have a balanced budget?"

Our tithes and offering income has grown, but it is still limited. At the same time, I have four children (they're now grown). Now I have six grandchildren. In raising our kids, I did have income needs that were greater than what the church could pay me. I could have demanded increases from the church, but at the time, this would have cut back our ministry. Here's what worked for me. I combined entrepreneurism and ministry. Through some open doors from the Lord, I created JRS Lawn Service. About eight months of the year, I cut grass (myself and a team of people from the church). It has allowed me to increase my income for my family (and also get some good exercise). It has enabled me to provide some supplemental income part-time jobs for people at our church. It has given me the opportunity to bless some people beyond our regular tithes and offerings.

Yes, it makes for more hours each week. That part I have sometimes let get out of balance. But JRS Lawn Service helped me put my kids through college and provided the basics for my family when my pastor salary fell short. I don't resent the latter. I thank God for the opportunity in the former. I also thank God I have a congregation that knows many mornings, while you can reach me by phone, you won't find me in the office because I'm out cutting grass. Most of all, I thank God for an incredible wife and children who were patient with me through this time. Now here's the temptation I face. As I have the same 24-hour day as anybody else, my temptation is to use it to rack up more money cutting grass, as my church salary is constant. Yet, I need to not let that temptation take hold of me. My first responsibility of my time between business and ministry is to care for God's people in the Hyde Park neighborhood of north St. Louis. Between ministry and entrepreneurism, the discipline to say "no" to the latter, in favor of the former, must prevail. Add that balance to the challenge of keeping a strong personal life with the Lord and a strong family life... all I can say is that it is not easy. I have failed many times, and I live by the mercy and forgiveness of God and my loved ones.

Now let's talk about the two levels of entrepreneurism. What are they? How do they work? How do you figure out what works in your context?

Congregational Entrepreneurism. Actually, many churches have sought to increase supplemental income for their ministries through a variety of efforts. I know of a church who started a restaurant in a community. Many churches have used "human care" as an avenue for making money—both childcare and adult daycare. I would offer a few insights that have shown themselves to be true in our experience.

Good entrepreneurial efforts serve needs of the community. When you can make this happen, it's a "double win" because you are able to gain money for ministry and provide a service that community people need. This opens up another ministry avenue for your church. For us at Bethlehem, affordable family housing was among the top needs of our community. It made sense for us to get into the housing business as we created our housing ministry, Better Living Communities. In creating a new housing community surrounding our church, the Lord has created a brand-new mission field for us right on our doorstep! Bethlehem doesn't presently reap financial profits from Better Living Communities, but one day it will.

Good entrepreneurial efforts are in step with the mission of the

ministry or congregation. This one is sort of obvious. Even though opening up the "Bethlehem Liquor Store" in our neighborhood might be a great financial opportunity, it would be out of step with our mission to help families. In our community, many families suffer from substance abuse. Opening up this kind of business would be counter-productive to our mission of wanting to help people become free of addictions and see their families healed.

Good entrepreneurial efforts capitalize on the ministry's strengths. I believe this is a big one. One thing that Bethlehem does well is ministering to children. So it makes sense that we run our Bethlehem After School (BAS) program to give our charter school parents free, safe, and supervised afterschool care for their children. In running the BAS program, we are helping support our charter school, The Arch Community School. They pay us rent. If they succeed, we succeed. In addition, through our partnership, students have a better chance at succeeding in their education. Most of all, every day we get the opportunity after school to share our Christian faith with the children and with their parents when they come to pick them up.

Good entrepreneurial efforts avail themselves to the experience of others. There is no way we could have started Better Living Communities, or our first charter school named Better Learning Communities Academy, or our second charter school called the Arch Community School, or our More Greater Things mission initiative WITHOUT HAVING MINISTRY FRIENDS and WITHOUT LISTENING to the wisdom and experience of MINISTRY FRIENDS! Over the years, how blessed we have been to be connected to gifted men and women from other Lutheran churches. Friends like businessmen Jack Gerber and Jack Klobnak made Better Living Communities happen. When we started a charter school (which is its own separate corporate entity), gifted friends like Kathleen Mueller and Kirk Mueller made this impossible endeavor possible. Notice the gifted friends the Lord sends your way, and listen carefully to their advice. Again, this is all God's Work.

Good entrepreneurial efforts have a strong accountability system. It is so easy and tempting (when money is short) to use it for a purpose different from which it was given. Never do that! Just as important, when someone funds a particular ministry, report, report, report! Nobody controls results except the Lord, but we can control our faithfulness to doing the ministry we said we would do. Report the victories of what is happening in your entrepreneurial endeavor. Also report what didn't work the way that you thought it would work. If you are the ministry leader, keep your hands off the money. Always leave a clear and thorough paper trail of money received so that you can give an accurate accounting if someone should ask. This is the Lord's ministry. It is His entrepreneurial business, not ours.

There are other kinds of congregational income opportunities that are beyond the Sunday morning offering plate. We'll talk about those in different essays about funding.

Entrepreneurism as a Ministry Worker. When an urban ministry worker considers becoming bi-vocational, some of the same truths regarding congregational entrepreneurism are true for being a bi-vocational pastor.

Your "side job" needs to be in step with your vocation as a pastor. Working a side job as a card dealer in a casino wouldn't be a good job for an urban ministry leader. For sure, you would see some people in need of help with their gambling addiction (and might even see some parishioners at the casino). But as your employer, the casino would want you to urge their patrons to keep on gambling no matter what. You would have a different message as a pastor.

Your "side job" needs to be one that gives you flexibility and availability to be a pastor. This is a big one. Not every job allows this. It would be pretty hard to be both the manager of a restaurant and also be the lead urban ministry person at a church. Turnover is high in the restaurant industry and people are always missing work, which leaves the management to cover many emergency situations. This would be hard for a pastor. Some jobs that provide better flexibility include a nurse, a teacher, sales, etc. My colleague, for example, provides deaf interpretation signing and teaching college classes online as a second job.

It's wonderful when your "side job" can run parallel with your job as a pastor. I cut grass for a housing development near our church. It gives me the opportunity to learn my neighbors and talk to them. It also gives them the chance to see me outside and working hard in a different role than they might normally see me as a pastor. I have had many great ministry conversations with people whose grass I cut.

When you're bi-vocational, balance is difficult, but it is crucial. This is probably the most important point about being bi-vocational. Your ministry job is your first priority, yet your secondary job is still a job. In my case, people pay money for their lawn to look good. I have to provide good and timely service, if I expect to keep their business and collect my wages. Unlike a nurse working a shift, I have to work until the job is done, regardless of how long it takes. At the same time, unlike working a job with a shift, I have the ability to get up earlier or work later if I have to step away for a few hours to take care of some ministry or family business.

Here's another truth—you may only be able to be bi-vocational at certain stages of life. I did not work a second job when my kids were young. (I did still have trouble with balancing time even then.) Still, I haven't always balanced my life well concerning time with my wife. I thank God for her patience. Some people have said to me, "Why bother working the second job? Why not just take a call to a church in another place that can pay you a better salary so that you don't have to be bi-vocational?" The only answer I can give is, "THIS is the place the Lord has called me to. THIS bi-vocational nature is what is best for God's work in this place. Until the Lord tells me something different, THIS is what I believe He wants me to do."

Entrepreneurism on the congregational level or as a bi-vocational urban ministry worker isn't for everyone. As an urban ministry worker, having a supportive spouse and family for this kind of work is vital.

Training is needed for entrepreneurism and ministry to work in harmony.

On the Congregational Level

Congregations need to be very honest about their resources and their ministry expenses. If you have a $500,000 endowment today, but are running a $75,000 annual deficit, your endowment isn't the answer. At a 5% interest return and taking the additional money needed from the principal, the endowment will be gone in less than a decade. If a congregation's regular offerings and offering potential aren't in sync with their normal necessary budget expenses, additional income sources (which may include entrepreneurism) may need to be considered.

Congregations need to understand that some sacrifices must be made in order to have an additional source of income endeavor through entrepreneurism. If you rent part of your building, your congregation must be comfortable with a "tabernacle" view of space. In our case, the classroom in our building is the school's classroom from 8:00 a.m. until 3:15. Bethlehem After School's classroom is from 3:15–5:30 p.m., and Bethlehem Bible Outreach's classroom runs from 5:30–7:30 p.m. I have found that it is possible for multiple groups in a building to work together, but it takes great communication, humility, and teamwork. Sometimes the church has trouble with that idea when it comes to property we think of as "ours."

Congregations need to realize they will need a point person for the activities or business that the congregation is involved in. The pastor or ministry leader will USUALLY have an active role in a small parish or ministry. (It's great if he doesn't have to do so, but that's not usually the case.) If the pastor has to have a leadership hand in the entrepreneurial effort, the congregation will need to realize that he may not be able to do all the other ministry tasks they expect from him. There must be give and take. Some people might say, "This isn't the pastor's calling." I understand. But just as the old "parson" pastor role filled various callings within his community in years past (because he was one of the most educated people in the community), sometimes the pastor today fills leadership spots that might not be in his original calling.

On the Individual Bi-Vocational Ministry Worker Level

In recent years in our denomination, entering the ministry later in life as a second career has become a more popular path to becoming a pastor. These second-career ministry leaders may have a useful advantage in serving in urban low-income areas if the work they did before becoming a pastor is compatible with ministry. A teacher who becomes a pastor, for example, may still teach to supplement his income and take care of his family. The same is true of a nurse, a CPA, an attorney, a deaf interpreter, someone who can fix computers, and other vocations that are compatible with ministry.

Yet, what about young people who begin their post-high school education with their heart responding to God's call into full-time ministry? Perhaps some coaching before someone enters college might be wise. Instead of earning an undergraduate degree in pre-seminary studies or a general ministry degree at a Bible college, why not plan for vocational flexibility in ministry from day one of the freshman year of college? Why not get an undergraduate degree in something that can provide a basic life income, and then go to seminary and prepare for full-time ministry? Such thinking could provide the opportunity for a new ministry worker to serve almost anywhere—in an urban context, a foreign mission field, a large or small parish, etc. By equipping ministry leaders for the possibility of being bi-vocational from the very beginning of their college career, we would help them be available to a much wider bi-vocational context. Further, their bi-vocational second job, if planned well at the beginning of college, would likely provide them a much stronger financial means of support than getting a job in a restaurant or a warehouse.

GET COACHING. Before deciding as a congregation to get into entrepreneurial efforts, find a church that has combined entrepreneurism and ministry. See firsthand how they do it and what kind of pitfalls they've faced. The same is helpful if you're thinking of going bi-vocational as an urban ministry worker. It is not as simple as it may look. Find some brothers or sister urban ministry leaders and discover how they have done it and what it is like.

41

PRODUCING TOMORROW

Have you ever visited another church or ministry and came away saying to yourself, "That's what we need at our church"? "We need music like that at our church, singers like that at our church, a facility like that at our church, leaders like that at our church, and resources like that at our church." I hope that's the attitude you have, if God puts those possibilities on your heart, rather than saying, "No way. That could never happen with our family of believers. Not possible." Now hear me carefully. We should never aim to become the duplication of some other kind of ministry. We need to be the kind of ministry God is calling us to be in the unique place where the Lord has put us. Yet, we can learn new ideas and gain new visions regarding what the Lord wants us to be through seeing what He is doing with others.

Here comes the main question that we all rise or fall upon—"HOW?" How do we move forward toward tomorrow? This is the simple answer: "IT BEGINS TODAY!"

Today! Don't put it off to a month from now. Do something today toward the goal you believe the Holy Spirit is leading you to accomplish. Today! And then do something toward the goal tomorrow, and then do something toward it the next day, and the next day, and the next day. Too many people in ministry, both leaders and workers, are given great ideas by the Lord but fail to act on them. People look at our ministry and ask, "How did you get all that you have in people, programs, and property?" It took 30 years. Today we're working on where we'll be five years from now. In fact, right now at 57 years of age, my work is dedicated to preparing for the day when I am no longer at Bethlehem. When that day comes, I want to leave Bethlehem prepared and provided with needed resources to soar beyond anything that has happened while I've been here! Let me give you some examples of the areas of ministry where it takes time to produce for tomorrow.

FUNDING from new sources doesn't happen overnight. It takes time to cultivate friends, congregational partners, and organizational partners like foundations and businesses who will support your ministry work. Urban areas are full of new not-for-profit entities. There are many more of these organizations than there are funders who are open to funding urban inner-city ministries. There is strong competition for dollars. See the essays about funding to get some specific thoughts on how to develop a funding approach. The point to notice here in this essay is that funding, like other aspects of urban ministry, takes time. Sometimes before funders will seriously look at your organization, they want to see some longevity regarding what you do. Too many organizations, especially urban ministries, go dormant or disappear as quickly as they pop up. Plan for the time it will take to gain new funders.

One of the signature ministries of our church has been our Gospel Choir, especially their vital leadership in our Sunday morning worship. Our choir is also one of the most well-known ambassadors of Bethlehem as we build strong relationships during visits to our sister churches. One thing is true of ministry and life—it always changes. In a span of about two years, our Gospel Choir lost three of our strongest solo/lead voices. (None of the three left Bethlehem because they were mad. Jobs and life changes precipitated their moves.) In our worship tradition, quality music is vital. Lead singers are part of many Gospel Choir songs. Strong lead singers are hard to come by, and these three were also lead singers on our praise team.

But here's the worst part. Prior to that happening, we had neglected developing new lead singers in our current choir. We also got too busy and went about two years without our Jr. Choir program that encourages kids to sing and also feeds our Sr. Choir program with singers and musicians. Guess what happened when our top three solo voices left Bethlehem? That's right, even though we still had some solo voices, our vocal cupboard was relatively bare. Music is an area where you can't fix problems quickly. Music training takes time, whether musicians or singers. We began immediately to make raising up more singers our priority, and I was reminded of an important lesson:

Producing tomorrow's leaders begins today. It is an effort that must be continual and constant because it takes time.

KEEP DEVELOPING PEOPLE who can lead ministries. There are so many areas where this reality can be translated. Who is your next Vacation Bible School leader? Who is your next director of your board of properties that takes care of your church's physical structure? What new people have you raised up for your sound system ministry or your social media ministry? Someone is saying, "But our urban ministry is small. We don't have that many adults." Right now, as I write this essay, I am working on finding some new people who can train to work in these technology ministries that I just mentioned. Guess who I asked? All are under the age of 18! Why not? Don't our kids know technology way better than most of us who are 50+? But it will take time to train them and get them involved. START TODAY to PRODUCE TOMORROW!

VOLUNTEERS. Hear the mantra again about growing more volunteer workers in your ministry—START TODAY to PRODUCE TOMORROW! One of the quickest ways to get a "NO" answer from volunteers is to wait until the last minute to ask them to help. Asking at the last minute often results in "NO" because people have something else planned, or because they don't feel comfortable doing what you're asking because there hasn't been time for training. "Just wing it," you say. Most volunteers don't want to do that, especially in ministry areas where they aren't confident. Nobody wants to be embarrassed. PLAN AHEAD when you're recruiting volunteers for ministry. Give yourself time to RECRUIT THEM. They may want to think about whether or not they will participate. Plan time to TRAIN THEM. Don't just throw them into the deep end of the swimming pool and say, "Swim!" That will be the last you see of most volunteers. Think about ministry in the urban scene. Take a clean-up day at your ministry property as an example. Most of us don't have money to pay people to clean or fix stuff. We have to recruit volunteers, and that will take time. So plan for it in advance. One more thing. Recruit and train more volunteers than you think you'll need, because very likely some of your volunteers will drop off due to other commitments or emergencies. Be covered.

Plan ahead for ministry. Start today. Don't put off recruiting and training the people you will need for ministry tomorrow. Today's training produces tomorrow's skilled ministry serving force.

42

IT TAKES A TEAM

In 1996 when the National Basketball Association (NBA) was 50 years old, the league released a list of their 50 greatest players ever. On the list was Karl Malone, Charles Barkley, and Patrick Ewing. Even if you're not an NBA fan, here is an interesting truth about each of those all-time NBA greats. While they are Hall of Fame players, none of them ever won an NBA championship. You see, basketball is a TEAM sport, not an individual sport, and it takes a TEAM to win a TEAM championship.

In that way, basketball is just like MINISTRY—it's a TEAM sport. A single great pastor doesn't make for an effective great ministry team that reaches and serves people in an effective way. It takes a TEAM. The sooner we urban church workers learn this truth, the better our life will be and the more effective our ministry will be. Without a TEAM, even the strongest and most passionate leaders will burn out. Without a TEAM, we're missing the people who can encourage us, lift us up when we're down, challenge us to do better, and work by our side. Ecclesiastes 4:9–12 is so on point.

For some people, the concept of TEAM is easy. Yet, for others (especially pastors), the concept of TEAM can be hard to embrace. Often, pastors are trained to believe that their level of wisdom is "above" the lay people in the church. It's true that many of us have had more theological training than most of the people in our church. However, especially when we're new in a place, we need to do a lot of listening and sitting at the feet of our people to be taught about how basic life works there.

There's also an "in between" challenge with how a TEAM works. Some ministry leaders pass the baton to the leader of an event or ministry, and then they aren't involved with it any further. Sometimes that person who will lead the activity has everything covered. At other times, passing the baton without any further coaching doesn't turn out so well because that person needed some coaching as they organized the event. Other ministry leaders micromanage every part of the ministry or event without empowering their lay leaders to lead. A wise path of leadership falls between these two extremes. A wise ministry leader knows that a TEAM is vital to the success of the ministry.

Why is it so important for us to regularly pour a significant amount of our ministry time into recruiting, building, and keeping a TEAM?

A ministry team can do more than I can do alone. When I begin a day of cutting grass in my lawn business, if it's just me cutting, I'll finish some lawns. If I'm with one of my guys like Wallace, we'll do a good amount. If we have four mowers going at one time and I'm on the weed whacker, we will do a LOT of lawns in just one day. You can't beat a TEAM. Instead of you making evangelism calls yourself, how much greater is it when there are five or six other members also making calls? A few times a year we go on an "invitations campaign" when we simply urge everybody in the Bethlehem family to participate in inviting four or five people to come to Bethlehem that week for worship. Last year right before Easter, in one week our church of about 140 people worshipers gave over 200 invitations to people to come to worship. How did we do it? It wasn't me alone doing the inviting, or just our board of directors, but a whole army of people. It's the "reach" of a TEAM. Think about it. There are some events, like basketball tournaments and outreach carnivals, where it is impossible to even do the event without a team. You already knew this point. There are days you may get frustrated and think, "If you want something done, you have to do it yourself!" No. Don't do ministry that way. Regardless of the event or ministry, we can do more with a TEAM doing it!

A team helps share the journey with you. Early in my ministry at Bethlehem, after we had built a solid youth choir, we would go on a weeklong choir trip in the summertime to perform concerts at other small, inner-city Lutheran churches. We did this for a period of 10 to 12 years. Our schedule was an intense one. We would be in a different city doing a choir concert/worship evening almost every night we were on the road. We went to New York City, Washington, D.C., Philadelphia, Florida, New Orleans, Dallas, Milwaukee, as well as an assortment of cities on the way.

Some of the same people who went on those trips are among the strongest leaders of our church today. God knit us together on those trips. We have spent so much of our lives together. As a result, we are constantly there for one another today as we do ministry together. That tight-knit Bethlehem culture has translated into new members who have come to our church even after the choir trips. We're the Bethlehem TEAM who works hard in ministry, plays hard, and is there for one another in life. Urban ministry is filled with so many "high highs" and "low lows." Having people around you who can support, strengthen, and pick you up when you're down is so meaningful. But there's another byproduct of being part of a ministry TEAM.

A team sets up longevity even beyond you, the ministry leader. I find this one to be so important. Be careful if you are a ministry leader, especially one who has started an urban ministry or has been part of the infancy stages of the ministry. The enemy will try to create a dependency of the ministry on you. And it feels great to be wanted. It strokes our ego to be the "go to person" nobody can live without, the person who is needed to make every decision! But stop that thinking. Dependence is to be on Christ, not a human leader. Hear the message of Psalm 146:3–6. Moreover, if the ministry is centered around us as leaders, the ministry will be finite just like we are, and it WON'T LIVE BEYOND US! Equipping a TEAM to lead sets up a ministry to keep going even beyond the current leader.

When you think about it, the mark of a great leader is not mainly the gains that happen while that leader is the leader. Rather it is the gains and successes that happen after that leader is gone and someone else takes the baton. Guide people to not be able to live without Jesus, not an individual ministry leader!

You can spend your ministry fixing things and putting out ministry/people fires and get little accomplished, or you can invest in a TEAM and equip and assign them to fix the things that need to be fixed. I wish I could tell you that all this TEAM talk has always been my approach. Nope! I've had to learn it the hard way. I hope you don't have to.

Here's a simple summary:

The sheep of our ministry are better cared for in Jesus when it's not just the ministry leader alone who is doing the care.

I'm convinced that ministry is better when it is done by a TEAM.

Where do you find a TEAM?

When we think about a ministry TEAM, there are a few distinctions we need to make. There are PAID ministry leaders, and there are VOLUNTEER ministry leaders. Since most of us in urban ministry have such limited financial resources, the latter is probably the kind of leadership most of us have in our organizations.

Just as the Word of God in 1 Corinthians 12 speaks about a diversity of gifts a church needs to carry out ministry, all found in the Body of Christ, so it is true that the Lord of the Church has already provided your ministry with the gifted leaders you need right now for this moment. You simply need to discover the gifted people God has placed around you. Here's how you can find the team the Lord has placed before you to help you.

See people for beyond what they ARE and more for what the Lord can RAISE THEM UP TO BE. Few leaders in urban ministries come as a "finished product." Often leaders who are finished products are either already serving somewhere else or coming to us with an agenda they tried to make work at some other ministry and were rejected. More common is our raising up leaders from among people who are already part of our local world.

For example, no one would have given "Doug" a chance. When I first met Doug, he was rarely at church, much less a "soldier." He had just sort of floated into our ministry, helping out and volunteering here and there. He had so much going on in his life with his family. He was well-known among people in our community. But Doug did have an edge about him, sort of a worldly, street edge. Yet, Doug kept showing up to volunteer. I was looking for a leader for a particular program at the time and suggested Doug's name to a few confidants at our church. They initially said, "Hmmm. I don't know about Doug." And, "Uhhhh, Pastor, I honestly can't see that one. But if you think it might be possible..." I'm sure you've heard that kind of answer—it's really a "no," but people are trying not to burst our bubble!

I decided the Lord wanted me to give Doug a shot. Over time, through God the Holy Spirit's work, Doug became more engaged in our church family. Doug definitely had leadership skills. He began to show himself more and more as a potential church leader. He became increasingly regular in worship. I coached Doug, and he became a great leader for a ministry at our church. This was God's work! All I can say is that if I had only focused on who Doug WAS, and not considered who the Lord might enable Doug to BECOME, the church and I would have missed out on a great leader! Finding new leaders can seem risky. But taking the step of faith in trying to develop new leaders is exactly what the Church is called to do.

I have found that the best strong new leaders share three qualities:

1. **They're open to growing in God's Word by becoming involved in regular worship and Bible study.** This is so essential. When we start developing a new leader, the enemy will always begin a counter offensive attack against this new leader. I find that only the promises of God and close proximity to the Lord will provide the strength the new leader needs to stay on the Lord's right course.

2. **Leadership candidates need to have an openness to learning.** Every great leader must have an openness to learning. Learning never ends. Even if a person is very talented, I don't necessarily want a potential leader who thinks they know everything. A friend of mine has an incredible business resumé and has started a few very successful businesses. One time he was having lunch with me and the brand-new principal our charter school was hiring. After lunch, I asked my friend what he thought of the principal. My friend said, "I'm impressed with this guy. He doesn't claim to know everything or have all the answers. Usually the smartest guy in the room doesn't think he's the smartest guy in the room." Humble learners are the best leaders. The Bible would say it this way in Proverbs 29:23, "A man's pride will bring him low, but a humble spirit will obtain honor."

3. **Loyalty. When I'm looking for people for the TEAM I'm leading, loyalty is a must.** Ministry in urban areas is hard. There are many factors that try and battle against us. Division among staff is wasted energy. We must all pull in the same direction. Of course, there are many and different ways to do ministry, and staff collaboration is important. But in the end, each ministry needs ONE MAIN VISION. If a person is not supportive of that vision, a particular ministry may not be right for them.

Once, you've found your TEAM, how do you keep it strong?

COMMUNICATION is essential. Don't assume. Don't leave people on your team guessing. Make sure the vision of what you're trying to do as a ministry is clear to everyone. Make sure each person on your team has bought into this vision and understands their role in it. Regular weekly staff meetings are vital. Keep notes so that no one forgets the matters you've already talked about. Make sure the goals are communicated well and expectations are clear. Revisit your goals often. Continually challenge your team to evaluate their work. Ask, "How are we doing in regard to what we said we were going to do?" The pace of most small ministries is so fast, so intense, and so overwhelming, and it is so easy to slip into doing a lot of stuff and lose focus on the important goals you set.

RECEIVE CONTRIBUTIONS FROM OTHERS, YET THERE MUST BE A SINGULAR VISION. Nobody knows everything. There is great blessing in gaining input from your team. Yet, input must fit into your main goals. Also, disagreements among staff are fine, even natural. But they are to be discussed in private team meetings. When the leadership team comes forward, they need to come with one vision. It is your job as a ministry leader to guide your team to keep the one vision on course.

Financial resources can sometimes be a huge distraction that keeps a ministry from having a focused vision. Some years ago, a local not-for-profit in our neighborhood would change their mission focus every two years. That was also the cycle when most of their grants would run out. Ministries need money to operate, and urban ministries usually are greatly deficient in financial resources. Still, to keep changing the focus of your ministry to "whatever you can get money for" will often result in the same end that occurred with this organization—they closed.

COACH YOUR TEAM. Right now, there are 32 NFL teams, 30 NBA teams, and 30 teams in Major League Baseball. Do you know what they all have in common? When they start their seasons, every one of these teams has a head coach. These are multi-billion-dollar business entities, and many are operated by extremely shrewd businesspeople. If they could find a way to have an efficient championship team without paying coaches millions of dollars each year, they would have figured that out already! Do you understand what they've all learned? Coaching is necessary for success. Jesus said it this way in both Acts 20:23 and 1 Peter 5:2 where He charged, "Be shepherds to God's people."

There are plenty of books that cover Biblical leadership skills for leading ministries. In this space, let me highlight just two coaching activities I consider especially important in urban inner-city ministries.

First, don't expect less or accept less from people who could do

better. Encourage people to be accountable for their skills and gifts. Often people do less because the expectation level is less.

Why can't a church event in the inner-city be attended by crowds of people? Why can't a musical group from an urban church have musical excellence? Why can't our organization be excellent when we run camps and programs? For the Lord's ministry, I don't want us to have a pathetic "it's the best we can do" kind of mindset. If people in the Bethlehem family can have excellence in their 9 to 5 job, why can't they work with excellence also in their ministry? They can. Let not God's Work be something where people think that a second-rate job is okay.

Second, (this is a companion to expecting the best from people): Encourage! Encourage! Encourage! As important as calling people to a higher level is, it is just as vital to encourage them and cheer them on as they move to that place.

Celebrate the victories of ministry. Maybe we didn't make it to 100% this time, but celebrate the 80% you did achieve, while planning for 100% next time. Strengthen people with cards, notes, calls, and texts of encouragement! This life beats us down enough! We have the best news of all to use in our encouragement—the Gospel of Jesus Christ. In our work, even when "we are faithless, He remains faithful, for He cannot deny Himself." (2 Timothy 2:13) When we're anxious about our ministry, the Lord says, "Do not fear for I am with you; do not anxiously look about you, for I am your God. I will strengthen you, surely I will help you. Surely I will uphold you with my righteous right hand." (Isaiah 41:10) What a message for us to share with people working with us in Galatians 6:9, "Let us not lose heart in doing good, for in due time we will reap if we do not grow weary." Ministry is hard. We want to encourage our people with what God has promised in James 1:12, "Blessed is a man who perseveres under trial; for once he has been approved, he will receive the crown of life which the Lord has promised to those who love Him." God has provided us a TEAM. God knits the TEAM together. God will strengthen our TEAM, because in truth, it's His TEAM!

43

THE NECESSITY OF REINVENTION

I t's scary. It seems risky. But it is absolutely necessary. I'm talking about REINVENTION—reinventing how we do ministry in the church, reinventing programs, and reinventing approaches to become even more effective to the people we are trying to reach. Let's be clear about the message of the Gospel—that Christ gave His life on the cross as payment for our sins, and He rose to bring us new life. That message never changes. *How* we bring that message is not only open to change (not change, just for its own sake), but also it often must change for the sake of effectiveness. Our approaches to share the Gospel must regularly be reinvented as people and our world change.

I know, I know. There's the old saying, "If it ain't broke, don't fix it." But in a way, that gets to the heart of the matter of what we often face in ministry. Sometimes the things we think "aren't broke" have actually been declining in their effectiveness for quite some time. Moreover, because of how fast people and our world change, by the time we realize something is broken in its ineffectiveness, we are often so far behind updating what we're doing that we often lose people in the program.

For example, I wrote in an earlier essay about the start of our Bethlehem Bible Outreach (BBO) program that we began in the second week of my ministry at Bethlehem in August of 1989. It was called Wednesday Program back then, and it was one of our strongest evangelistic tools in the community. Our Bible time was simple. Kids aged pre-school to first grade were taught Bible stories using a big flannel graph board. They loved it. For the older kids, second grade to high school, we divided them into groups for a Bible story with a crossword puzzle or a set of questions. After five weeks of these stories, we would have a review week where kids would fill in the answers to questions on sheets of paper. Then in the next week, we would have a Bible tournament. Kids would line up in two teams and answer questions about the previous five weeks of Bible stories. They would compete for pizza gift certificates and other prizes. It was very competitive and the kids enjoyed it.

We taught the Bible to kids in this way for my first 20 years at Bethlehem. In truth, we taught the Bible like this five YEARS TOO LONG.

Kids had changed. Our numbers had declined. We weren't effective doing the nightly Bible lesson sheets and Bible tournaments. Kids were bored. Most of my leaders knew change had come. We needed a more interactive program that would use drama, music, object lessons, and creative teaching to bring the Gospel of Jesus Christ. But there was one person who was fighting the change. There was one person who was against reinventing our Wednesday Program. You know who that person was? It was ME! I didn't want to change how we would teach the Bible.

By this time I had written a three-and-a-half year curriculum of individual Bible story sheets. Each week, all I had to do was throw the next story on the copier, and my preparation was done. I didn't want to reinvent how we would teach kids the Scripture. That would be uncomfortable for me. That would cause more work for me. I would have to go back to writing new weekly lesson plans because we couldn't find curriculum that would meet the educational level of our kids.

But FOR THE SAKE OF THE KIDS, this program needed to be reinvented. A new approach was needed to be effective in communicating God's Word.

Many times, that's the heart of the real challenge when reinvention is needed, isn't it? It's the decision between what is COMFORTABLE to us and what we know will be MORE EFFECTIVE in bringing Christ to people.

That's the issue when a congregation considers changes in worship style. Many years ago, Bethlehem reinvented how our Sunday worship time would communicate the Good News of God's love in Jesus Christ.

The people of our church chewed on this issue. They asked, "Should we continue to worship the Lord in the format we've always used that is COMFORTABLE to us? Or should we consider new worship approaches on Sunday morning (without compromising Biblical integrity) that would be MORE EFFECTIVE at bringing Christ to new people from our community who could come to our Sunday morning worship services?" Our church chose the latter. It has been a blessing to us.

Your ministry may be facing the same questions regarding a multitude of issues like this. "Should we continue to keep this space in our building for this same purpose, or should we reinvent the use of the space? Should we change the structure of how our ministry is governed for MORE missional EFFECTIVENESS? With new generations of people in our churches who have grown up with different experiences, how does this impact how we share the Good News of God's love?"

My children never played an 8-track tape player. The young adults of today have never lived without social media. So should the church keep ignoring that avenue as a way of sharing the Gospel? Life has changed; the days of thinking that all youth ministry occurs mainly through a singular weekly youth activity are over. Now it will take a variety of small group youth ministries to effectively reach and support all the youth of our churches. Two or three years from now, that approach may likely be outdated and in need of reinventing. I think you see the point.

So how did the story of Wednesday Program end? If you read the earlier essay, you already know. When we made the change from Wednesday Program to Bethlehem Bible Outreach, it was more work and it was harder to do in the beginning. But God was faithful. He gave us the creativity and discipline to create new lessons, and the work did pay off. We were much more effective at reaching kids with the Savior. Our numbers began to rebound. That was 10 years ago, and even now we're trying to understand the next way of REINVENTION.

44

THE DECEPTION OF "ITRT"

If you are going to work in low-income urban areas, you need to be crystal clear about what "ITRT" is and how it will affect your ministry. ITRT happens usually about every February and March. ITRT will make people less frequent in worship as they experience a deceptive sense of independence, thinking they can handle their own lives on their own. ITRT will make people spend money in ways you don't see at any other time of the year. ITRT could be a time when people dig themselves out of financial holes, but for most people, ITRT is a time when they spend money they don't have. For example, during ITRT, someone might take on a car note that they won't be able to afford within about two or three months. Okay, what's ITRT? It's **I**ncome **T**ax **R**eturn **T**ime. Someone is saying, "Reverend, you've got to be kidding!" I'm totally serious. In fact, so serious is ITRT that people in the city even make deals to claim other people's kids on their taxes... (I don't know how they do it, but I definitely know that it happens)... in order to increase the amount of their return!

What does this have to do with the ministry of God's people? It is just an "urban low-income flavor" of one of the enemy's most common temptations of all—control and self-reliance because of money and what money can buy.

Many people begin their life with the Lord out of need. Their life has come crashing down because of some kind of tragedy or misfortune, and they turn to the Lord looking for answers. The devastation can be the stronghold of a substance-abuse problem. The pain can be the death of a loved one. The disaster can be losing everything, including a place to live and even food. You've surely experienced how people, in moments like these, turn to the church for help. Even though some of our members have been around our ministry for years, they are babies in their faith life with

God. They remain "spectators" or "sometimers" in their commitment to serve the Lord (see essay on "The Growth Progression"). They make little progress in their lives because they continue to be owned both by what they don't have and, for the short season of ITRT, by the little cash they momentarily do have.

Whether you do have or don't have, regardless of the amounts, Satan tries to use money and possessions to lure every one of us away from keeping our eyes on the Savior.

This temptation isn't just about being rich and loving money and what it buys. It also shows itself in our frustration over what we don't have. It includes our jealousy when we get so fixated on the lives of other people around us. The writer of Ecclesiastes 5:10–11 was so correct. A man in Matthew 19:16–26 also struggled with this very issue. He came to Jesus asking what he must do to inherit eternal life. But that was really just a mask for another issue. When the young man asks Jesus in verse 20, "What am I still lacking?" he is expecting Jesus to say, "Nothing. You're in there. You've got everything." But Jesus uncovers the man's real malady—he loves his money and things more than he loves the Lord. See vs. 21–22. While he goes away from Jesus sad, he came to Jesus incorrectly, confident in himself. That's what money can do to anyone at any income level. If we allow it, it can create a false sense of security where we think we're in control of our lives. That's why ITRT season makes some people disappear from church for a few weeks—they don't need God at that moment. They've got their tax money.

In much the same way that the Lord knocked this young man's financial support out from beneath him, so too, the Lord allows the same thing to happen to many people our urban ministries will encounter.

There may be no truer word on this topic than what Paul spoke to Timothy in 1 Timothy 6:10 when he said, "For the love of money is a root of all sorts of evil..." TRUE! When we give more attention to money/things in our heart than to the Lord, our trouble is only beginning! Paul continues,

"...and some by longing for it have wandered away from the faith..." Yes, this describes how people's closeness to the Lord and His Church disappear at ITRT season. It shows itself in additional "wanderings." Sometimes when people blow their tax money and dig themselves into a deeper financial hole, then they take extra overtime work on Sundays to try and get out of that new hole (and grow further away from the Lord). Sadly, some never make it back to the family of God for a long time. Paul finishes by observing how people who allow themselves to be captured by money and then let it push away their first attention to the Lord have "pierced themselves with many griefs." Unfortunately, yes!

As God's people, the Church, what do we do with people who have the ITRT sickness?

When they go through the ITRT condition and fall, may we be ready to receive them by pointing them back to the Savior who can forgive any kind of wandering away from Him, for all who come with a repentant heart. Then, may we love them enough to help them bow with us before the Word of our God and learn the lesson of Luke 12:15–21. The heart of life is not about money and the possessions we have or don't have, but it is about our relationship with the Lord!

45

YOU NEVER GET USED TO IT

I thought "Jerry" was committed to the Lord and to our Bethlehem ministry. Just weeks ago he had been growing so much in Christ. In fact, he told several other high school young men his age, "You really need to get into Bible study. It will really help you." His life had really turned around. God was opening so many doors for him. While his biological family had seemingly abandoned him, and other areas of his life weren't working out, the Lord showed him the truth of Psalm 27:10—"my father and my mother have forsaken me, but the Lord will take me up."

The Lord does that through His people, the Church, as we step into people's lives and often become the family they never had—dynamically and wholly, not just with "pep talks" but also with time, commitment, finances, and our presence. Maybe I should have seen it coming when Jerry started attending Bible Study less frequently, although he still came to church. And now it's been three Sundays since we've seen him... even though a few times he "promised" he was going to be there... even though when he had needs for a school event that was really important to him, the people of God from our Bethlehem family really stepped up to help him. However, here we are—another Sunday, and no Jerry. No response to texts to Jerry. It happened to me again today: ministry disappointment.

Jerry's story isn't anything special or unusual, considering what most of us Christ followers have faced as we've tried to share with others the joy we have in knowing the Lord. No doubt, you've had ministry disappointment many times when the people you worked with, even gave yourself to, became unresponsive and disappeared from church life. It may simply be people you invited to church, or even your own family members you were hoping so desperately would return to a close life with God. It might be someone you were counting on to help with ministry in a vital way and they were a "no call, no show" when you really needed them. I find this to be true:

You never get used to the pain of ministry disappointment.

Yep, I know—people have told me and I've told myself, "Don't take it personally" when people don't carry through on the promises they make about being involved in ministry or showing up for worship. But you know as well as I do, it's not that simple. Sometimes we can just easily move on. At other times, being let down just hurts!

So today, I'm in that familiar place of ministry disappointment. Maybe you are, too. Maybe you were there last week. Very probably, we'll both be back in this place soon again in the future, if we're seriously committed to Jesus' words in Mark 16:15.

SO HOW DO YOU GET THROUGH DAYS LIKE THIS? I offer you three Biblical thoughts. They won't necessarily bring immediate pain relief to you, but as they come from God's Word, I trust God the Holy Spirit to give you encouragement and recovery strength through them.

God gives free will to people. There is a word from the beginning of time that impacts ministry disappointment moments. Check back to Genesis 2:15–17. As the Lord places Adam into the Garden of Eden to live in it and take care of it, He gives the first man a monumental command. In Genesis 2:16, God says to Adam, "From any tree of the garden you may eat FREELY, but from the tree of knowledge of good and evil you shall not eat, for in the day that you eat from it you will surely die."

God told Adam, as well as all of us, that we are FREE. In this life, we have the free choice to disobey God and do what we want to do. Our Creator won't manipulate us like robots. The devil really preys on this area of our lives. And it plays so well to our egos: "I can do what I want to do. It's my world. Life is my choice." Of course, when I'm in trouble and in situations beyond my control, my favorite two words are, "God, help!" But when life is going better for me, when I've got a little money in my pocket, my two favorite words then are, "God… WHO?"

When you've been disappointed with someone you've reached out to, someone you've prayed and prayed for, asking that this person would know Christ or grow and be more involved in serving Him, keep this truth in mind—each person is F-R-E-E! As president of the "beat yourself up thinking I could have done more" club, I'm here to remind you that every person has free will. Even as we cast the seed of the Gospel upon someone, and our Father would love to have that person come close to Him, each person has the free will to reject the offer of life in Christ.

Sometimes we can't see the bigger picture of God's work from our vantage point. Revisit the story of the prodigal son/the amazing father in Luke 15:11–32. What if the father would have begged the younger son not to leave his house? What if he'd done whatever it took—bribing him, locking him down, all the ways that we parents sometimes deal with difficult kids—to keep him there? What would life have been like for that son then? Would he learn the lessons God the Father actually had for him to learn by leaving his father's house and getting firsthand experience with where some of his foolish choices were going to take him? Probably not. Think about the bigger picture of what happened in that story—the younger son learns about foolish choices, gains humility, and learns about unconditional love from his father. The older son is confronted with his Pharisaic attitude.

We know the truth of Jesus' words in John 15:5, "I am the Vine, you are the branches; he who abides in Me and I in him, he bears much fruit, for apart from Me you can do nothing." We want so desperately for the other person to embrace that truth as well. We want to prevent them from having to go through the pain and heartache of learning difficult life lessons about trying to live without the Lord. Yet, in God's perfect bigger picture, sometimes our Father says this to me:

"John, please don't get discouraged. Don't try to get in My way as I work on this person. In this case, I am going to need to break them before I can build them up into what I want them to be. Their stubborn free will is getting in My way. I won't cross that free will. But I will 'turn up the life heat' for them to see how futile life is without Me."

Am I talking to anybody out there besides myself? Am I talking to any other parents out there who have had to go through that kind of journey with your kids? (Whether they are your biological kids or your spiritual kids in Christ?) Don't beat yourself up, thinking that you've failed because this person hasn't responded the way you hoped. It's true; we NEVER GET USED TO THE PAIN OF MINISTRY DISAPPOINTMENT! But the Lord our God is sometimes working on a bigger picture we just can't see. Speak to us Psalm writer, Psalm 119:67, "Before I was afflicted I went astray, but now I keep Your Word." Speak to us Lord, Isaiah 48:10, "Behold, I have refined you, but not as silver; I have tested you in the furnace of affliction." It's all to bring each of us forward as God's precious jewel!

The Lord is ultimately in charge. We are just the glove of God's Hand. His power is what brings people to faith. His timing is when someone comes to faith. His plans (noted above) are perfect and flawless. As Matthew 10:29–31 says, our Lord never misses even one detail. Of course, ministry disappointment hurts. But bow to the Lord who is totally in charge and whose love for every person is everlasting. He won't step over someone's free will. But His desire is for all people to know Him and His love in Christ!

46

START NEW or TRANSFORM THE OLD?

The picture that best introduces this essay is one I've written about earlier. At one time, our 140-year-old church was one of the largest Lutheran churches in the St. Louis area. But by 1989 when I came to Bethlehem, it had declined as many people fled the city for the suburbs. It was essentially a 17-year vacancy. Were we coming to close Bethlehem or see the Lord bring it back? Only God knew.

In a Bethlehem kind of situation, where a church drops from 2,000 members to only about 30 people worshipping on a Sunday morning, what's the best plan?

Door #1—Let the church die and try to plant a new church in the area.

Door #2—Combine this dying, dysfunctional congregation with some other local dying dysfunctional congregations of the same denomination and hope for something useful and missional to grow out of it.

Door #3—Try to reinvent and transform the old congregation into a new ministry grounded in a Biblical missional spirit.

From my perspective, Door #2 is a useless strategy that simply delays the inevitable death of all the dysfunctional churches. It would be different if the plan was to absorb a dysfunctional ministry into a missional ministry. However, that's not usually what happens on the urban scene. Finding a strong missional urban ministry is usually tough enough, let alone finding one willing to merge with a dysfunctional urban partner. I've actually been down that road of possible partnership a few times myself. In my experience, the dysfunctional ministry we considered partnering with wanted our ministry results—but they weren't ready for the sacrifices and the "stretching" needed to get in a position for the Lord to bless them with those results.

So, in this situation, I see the options as "Door #1" or "Door #3." Much has been written about whether it's better to let old things die and start new in urban ministry or to transition and transform something old into a new mindset and attitude. Each side of this debate can cite examples of how their approach worked and the other one didn't. I want to put before you some things to think about as you look at each situation.

1. Every urban ministry context needs the fair view of being seen in its own way, with its own challenges and possibilities.

Before stepping into this comparison, let's also set forth that urban mission fields do have some pretty consistent commonalities that impact the decision about what to do. Urban mission fields usually lack money. Sure, sometimes a mission agency will sponsor a new worker, guaranteeing two or three years of salary support. But then, after those first years, they're on their own.

2. Most new ministries can't get to a financial place of strength to support a worker that quickly. Most older ministries can't transition that quickly to a place where their new mission approach starts to yield financial support returns.

If the older ministry has an endowment fund, that can be helpful. But often even when older churches have endowments, spending the money for ministry is a battle in itself! Unlike in a suburban mission field, the potential of significant financial support from new members just isn't there in an urban ministry context. The exception is if the new members are "transplants"—people who either commute to the ministry, or people who live in the urban community and are "in" the urban neighborhood but not "of" the urban neighborhood. If the latter group has a missional mindset, it can work. If they have a more selfish mindset of wanting the ministry to serve their needs (especially when they are in the minority), their presence will bring new challenges.

3. Another challenge that urban communities face is that many of the residents of these communities are transient.

They often are inconsistent in their basic lives, so it's not surprising that it often takes a long time before they will be dependable "soldiers" in the ministry. The residents in urban communities also are often temporary until something better comes along—a better place to live, a better job opportunity, maybe a better relationship that leads to the other two things. Who can blame them for wanting a better life? For the ministry, transiency often means losing someone just when they become useful and then having to start over.

4. One more quick challenging truth in this mix of how to start an urban ministry: most people who come to our ministry will need more from our ministry than they are able to give to our ministry.

None of these four truisms of urban work are a reason NOT to start a new ministry or try to bring transition to an old ministry. They are simply realities that every wise urban worker needs to be aware of when going into a new ministry setting.

So now let's evaluate, Starting a New Ministry vs. Reviving an Old Ministry.

Starting a New Ministry

Here are some good things about Starting a New Ministry:

Freedom from Old Traditions. Let's highlight three areas where it is a blessing not to have to comply with old traditions as you start a new ministry: Mission, Business, Worship.

Mission—Some longtime urban ministries are inward focused, instead of outward focused. What an advantage it is to a new ministry when it can see the best way to reach people for the Kingdom and just go and do it, without having to fight battles over the concept that "we've never done it that way before."

Business—New ministries can be nimble in how they operate their business. There are no layers of congregational bureaucracy to overcome in order to move forward into a new program or event. Plan the ministry. Secure the funding. Then, LET'S GO!

Worship—Let's face it, worship is the most identifiable ministry to the greatest number of people who are part of a church fellowship. How worship happens is first on the list of how many people judge a church. Especially among the present newest generations, connectivity in how worship takes place without changing the teaching of the Scriptures is vital. A new ministry might be able to address this matter better than an older established church.

New Things Have an Attraction to Some People. Pretty obvious.

Higher Level of Participation Is Immediately Needed. This is a good thing? Yes. Often times, when people come to a new ministry and see workers are needed, they get involved much quicker and much deeper than they would if they came to a traditional church where there are already people carrying on the basic work of the church. Some people love to be needed. People grow faster into a "soldier" mindset because the ministry isn't old enough or big enough for new people to have the option of being "spectators" or "sometimers."

Freedom Not to Have to Fit into an Existing Structure. Maybe in the place where this new ministry is starting it makes more sense to have Sunday school on Wednesday nights, instead of Sunday mornings before church. Not a problem in a new ministry start-up; maybe it would be traumatizing to an existing congregation. Maybe in a new ministry start-up there will be no Christmas Day worship service. Maybe in the new ministry there will be a drum set, piano, and bass, instead of a pipe organ. Maybe in the new ministry Spanish will be the main language, rather than new Hispanic potential members having to learn English in order to participate. Maybe the pastor or ministry leader is bi-vocational instead of a full-time "on call" pastor every moment of the day or night.

Here are some hard things about Starting a New Ministry:

Location. New ministries sometimes have an inconsistent location, especially for worship or big group events. They often have to rent whatever space they can find at the price they are able to pay. This can be hard for new people to keep up with. Similarly, new urban ministries (because they pay below-average rent) must fit into the availability of the group that owns the location. Sometimes this means that the prime time for events must be adjusted. For example, worship might need to begin at 12 noon or 2:00 p.m. if the congregation that owns the facility worships on Sunday mornings. Often the location that a young urban ministry can afford is inferior to their needs. Of course, renting a facility itself adds another regular cost to the new ministry's already stretched budget.

Logistics of Starting a New Ministry. There is necessary paperwork and organization when a new ministry is created. This includes things like incorporating as an entity, creating by-laws of operation, devising an operating structure, choosing sufficient insurance, and getting not-for-profit tax exempt status. The last item is especially important. Donors want their tax write-off when they give a gift to a ministry. This takes time and can be tedious work to do, but it is vital. Blessed is the new ministry leader who has a lawyer friend who can help them through this or even take care of the matter for them!

Loneliness as a Worker. My wife grew up in the Salvation Army. When the Salvation Army assigns a worker somewhere, they almost always place a two-person team of workers. In the recent years of my ministry, I have personally experienced the wisdom of that approach with my colleague Rev. Gerard Bolling (who just became Dr. Bolling!). It is so strengthening to have someone to talk to about ministry. It is a blessing to have someone with whom you can speak freely when you're frustrated, as well as someone who encourages you when you're down.

A great spouse serves in that role, but using your spouse in that role too much can bring other issues. The matter of having another person around the ministry when you're just beginning is usually prohibited by lack of money. Also add this thought to the topic: getting a break, even taking a vacation, is tough when you're all alone and beginning a ministry. Often times, taking a vacation in these early ministry days means either totally shutting the ministry down for a week or working so hard to prepare the ministry to operate without you while you're gone that you need at least two of your vacation days to recover from your fatigue of doing "double duty" to get out of town! When you're alone in a ministry that is just beginning, before you've built a group of trusted leaders around you, there can be some very lonely days!

No Track Record. You have to HAVE A STORY before you can TELL A STORY to gain support from funders. When you begin a new ministry, you might have a resumé of some amazing ministry achievements that God has done through you in other places. You might very well have every reason for people to call you, "Mr. Ministry Potential" or, "Ms. Ministry Potential." But when you begin new in a place, you have no beginning track record of *that* place. That makes fundraising for the mission hard. Pictures of "ministry going on" aren't there yet. All potential funders have to rest on is your word regarding what you say your ministry is going to do. Even when an established ministry hasn't been doing such a good job of outreach, there is still a story of the past and a story of what is going to change—and that can get people excited. Some funders will invest on the basis of your vision and prospectus. Yet, this is one of those areas that makes a new start-up hard.

Start-up Money... Tick-tock, Tick-tock. Some mission developers of new urban ministries are given start-up money. This may mean a grant, or it can mean that the mission developer is given contacts by a denomination they can use in order to raise start-up money for the new ministry. Any support is helpful. YET, let's recognize the pressure cooker of starting a new urban ministry even with some financial support. In the first place, start-up support is usually for only two or three years. That is a short time to start building relationships in a new community with the intent of beginning an ongoing ministry like a full-blown congregational ministry or street outreach.

It is an even bigger pressure cooker when you are an urban mission worker with a family. Single people can live easier without knowing where next year's dollars are coming from. They can adapt or move on a dime. That kind of nimbleness is harder for a family. Your work includes raising funds for the new ministry, operating the new ministry (it takes time for other leaders to come and be developed to help), and, if you have a family, being a spouse and a parent... all with just 24 hours a day and 168 hours per week. It's not impossible, but it is hard.

Reviving an Older Established Ministry That Has Declined

Here are some good things about Reviving an Established Ministry:

Sometimes It Has a Building That Is an Asset. Established older churches, though small in membership, often have significant building assets. One, they usually have a building that is paid for. Thus, the only building costs are operational and repair costs, not a mortgage. Two, many times established older churches have property with advantages like a gym, a sanctuary, and classrooms. Probably no brand-new ministry start-up could afford to immediately build a gym when they open. Yet, a gym can be very vital to an outreach ministry.

A Heritage of Support. Many times when coming to an older established church, a new leader is greeted with a heritage of support from former members (especially financial support). Even former members who have moved out of the church neighborhood and no longer attend may still continue an interest in what happens with their former church. This can be a wonderful base of consistent financial support and even also some volunteer support for programs.

An Endowment Fund. Some urban older ministries have a significant endowment to fund ministry. Ministry takes money. This can be a big help, as long as the directives of the fund allow it to be used for ministry—and as long as the money coming from the fund is seen as a supplement to fund strong ministry, rather than as a substitute for good stewardship on the part of those at the church. Such a consistent trusted financial boost can remove some of the significant stress of trying to figure out how to fund ministry, while at the same time bringing needed changes to the ministry. One danger is if the current longtime leadership uses the fund as a power instrument to shield the ministry from much-needed change. For example, "If you don't do things our way, we won't fund what you're trying to do from the endowment fund."

Good Community Connections. Let's say your ministry has a parochial school or some other community programs that it has long been known for. This can be a real asset in the revival of an old church that needs to refresh its mission. How so? Such a longtime ministry has natural community connections to draw upon. In Bethlehem's case, I could find many people in 1989 who attended Bethlehem Lutheran School in the past. Today, after 30 years, it is very commonplace for me to be in a store in our community or even in the north side of the metro area and someone will come up to me and say, "Pastor, aren't you from Bethlehem on Salisbury? I used to go there for Wednesday Bible program when I was a kid." Or, "I played for the Bethlehem Bulldogs basketball team." Honestly, rarely does this bring someone immediately back to our Bethlehem ministry to stay, but we do have some people who come back to visit for a few Sundays because they remember their past at Bethlehem. We had about 10 people in that category this past Easter for worship!

Logistics of Starting a New Ministry. This is the "on the other hand" of the challenge of starting a new ministry detailed above. All of the start-up legal procedures are already in place in an existing ministry. It's not that this work is overwhelmingly hard, but it does take time to do.

Sometimes Having a Supportive Core Leadership Group. This is a tricky one. There are two key words here: "sometimes" and "supportive." On the one hand, why did the ministry go into missional dysfunction if it had a strong leadership core? On the other hand, it could be that a strong missional leader died or had to leave because of personal issues. The congregation went off track from its core values and was just waiting for a new strong leader to bring them back to a missional focus. If the leadership of the church is supportive of having the new mission leader refocus them on outreach, then this is a strength. If the leadership of the church is only supportive of a leader who will fall in step with the older ministry's self-serving agenda, then such a leadership group is not a strength. I remember one observation about existing leaders that I experienced early on at Bethlehem. Over half of the leaders that were at Bethlehem when I came, especially the ones who were the most initially thrilled that I had come, turned out to be some of the biggest obstacles toward our church regaining a missional focus.

Already Has Useful Ministry Stuff. Established ministries might already have some existing useful resources for ministry, even though they may not be using it. They may have an operative office copier, a computer, sports equipment, instruments for worship, a portable sound system, etc. These assets reduce the number of things that need to be bought or acquired for outreach ministry to happen.

Here are some hard things about Reviving an Established Ministry:

A Building That Is Not an Asset. Existing buildings can be blessings or curses. We've already noted how they can be blessings. Buildings also can be curses to a ministry:

- When they are in significant disrepair.

- When they cost more to repair than they are worth (often especially true of urban buildings located in historic districts where repairs must be made to historic codes, leading to more expense).

- Where there is too much building for the needs of the current ministry. This means that more funds have to be dedicated toward building repair, upkeep, and operational utilities, thereby reducing the amount of funds earmarked for people ministry.

Truth be told, I cheered the day that our old 1,100-seat Bethlehem sanctuary fell down by an act of nature. It's not that I hate old buildings.

That sanctuary was glorious. My youngest son was baptized in that holy space. But I was glad when we had to move out of it and board it up because we couldn't afford the repairs. I was glad after years of people breaking into it (thinking there were valuable things inside) and being the person who boarded it up and secured it again and again and again. I was glad after catching a group of suburban adults who had broken into it from the back during broad daylight in order to shoot a burlesque video in it with scantily-clothed women. YES, I was glad that on a spring Friday night, for no apparent reason, a corner of the facility caved in, which was the prelude to the entire facility needing to come down.

A Heritage of Former Members Who Resist Needed Change in the Ministry. When I came to Bethlehem, Bethlehem owned a 40-acre cemetery in north St. Louis County. The problem was that the cemetery was badly losing money. Bethlehem no longer had the leadership to operate this business, so we sought to sell it. We were finally able to sell our cemetery (we basically had to give it away!). But the process leading to the sale date was one of the ugliest times of my ministry. Many north St. Louis County Lutherans came forth when they heard we were selling Bethlehem Cemetery. Many were very angry with us. They believed that Bethlehem should hang on to that cemetery, even though we could not take care of it effectively and it was no longer a financial asset to our mission of sharing the Good News of Jesus Christ with people. In the minds of some people, if Bethlehem Church must die, so be it. But don't let Bethlehem Cemetery ever be sold! These individuals were angry, and angry people need a target for their anger. Guess who became their target? Yours truly! As I went through that ordeal, I kept thinking, "Wouldn't it be incredible if all of these people who cared so much about Bethlehem Cemetery could care this much for the ministry of Bethlehem Lutheran Church?" It was not to be. But learn the lesson—a heritage of former members might be an asset, or they might be a detriment toward the mission of reviving an old church ministry.

Community Connections That Are Not Good. Sometimes a church's past comes with bad community connections. For example, there was a local Lutheran congregation located in a predominately African-American community. Back in the 1960s they had a Caucasian pastor who did not have the same passion for reaching African-American people with the Gospel that he had for reaching Caucasian people with the Gospel. This message became well-known in that community. That Lutheran church closed. They could never recover from the bad reputation they had in their community.

Leadership with Old Ideas and an Unwillingness to Change. This is probably the most damaging and difficult challenge in coming to an urban church to bring about missional revival. Honestly, it is a matter that has eaten up young, energetic, passionate ministry leaders. If you studied life in many Lutheran urban churches in need of revival, you would probably observe this in a cyclical fashion of about two years:

- A new pastor comes to a church needing revitalization. He might be assigned there or takes a call there.

- At the very beginning in the courting period, the church leadership is saying, "Yes, we want to grow. We want our church to move forward." Everybody agrees with that.

- Not long after the leader comes and the dysfunctional church sees (sometimes, sees again... they've been through this a few times) the new ideas that a missional mindset needs and the kind of commitment from leaders and members that such a revitalized church direction will take, the leaders themselves get scared to commit to the new missional direction. Instead, they strengthen their grip on what they've always done in ministry.

- The young leader tries to change their mind and lead them into taking faith risks for the sake of new ministry approaches.

- The leadership pushes back with a strong, "No" and, "We call the shots around here."

- The young ministry leader says, "I'm tired. I'm outta here." That ministry leader leaves.

Truthfully, the issue really isn't an adversarial hatred between church leaders and the pastor, although it can start to feel that way. **The issue is the same sly tactic the enemy uses so many times to keep us from going in a new direction the Holy Spirit wants us to go—F-E-A-R!**

It's the fear of failure about trying something new. Many say to themselves, "The safer approach is to stay the course and keep doing what we're doing." The problem in a dysfunctional urban ministry that is declining and dying is just that—the status quo has been a decline-and-death direction. The enemy sows fear in us so we cannot distinguish the desperate circumstance of what things really are from what we'd like things to be.

So what's the answer between choosing Door #1 or Door #3 in an urban context? Even though most of my ministry has been in a Door #3 context, it all depends on the uniqueness of the individual urban place. Sometimes, Door #1 is the wisest choice. I've shared issues for you to think about as you go into your urban ministry calling. Ultimately, aren't you glad for the promise of the Lord Jesus from Matthew 16:18? Jesus said, "I will build My church; and the gates of Hades will not overpower it."

47

FUNDING MINISTRY

In the lifetime and ministry of my late grandfather, Rev. E.T. Schmidtke, funding ministry at a local church was the result of what came in through the offering plate. There were a few exceptions in his case. Since he served in some rural contexts, sometimes the gifts from people in his congregation for the support of his family included food. A ministry team I was with some years ago saw something similar happen when we were ministering in Uganda, East Africa. As people brought their Sunday offering to the altar, in addition to the coins received, I saw someone lay down what looked like a tall stalk. It was sugar cane.

People's firstfruits gifts to the Lord for His work come in all kinds, sizes, and manners. It is important to help God's people know about putting the Lord first with their time, their talents, and their money, no matter what the size of the gift is. We know the Lord is the Provider of all the gifts that HE sees His Church needs in a particular locale. Having said all of that, I believe God's provision for His work also comes from sources beyond what comes in from the people of God in the local offering plate.

It is God's Church at its best when believers in one part of the Kingdom care for one another and help each other in another part of God's Kingdom.

Of course, the Bible speaks about this. It is the very principle behind the Apostle Paul's collection for the church in Jerusalem that was in need. I love Paul's message to the Corinthian Christians in 2 Corinthians 8:1–3 when he said, "Now, brethren, we wish to make known to you the grace of God which has been given (for the Jerusalem church collection) in the churches of Macedonia, that in a great ordeal of affliction their abundance of joy and their deep poverty overflowed in the wealth of their liberality. For I testify that according to their ability, and beyond their ability, they gave of their own accord." There is so much to learn from this. But for the moment, pay attention to these truths. First, one church helped a church different from themselves. Second, helping another church is not dependent on having a surplus yourself. The Macedonians didn't have a surplus; they made a surplus via living sacrificially, and God blessed it.

Most urban ministries in our time will not be able to be self-sufficient only from what is received in the offering plate at a worship service. Most of us in urban ministries will need financial help from sources beyond ourselves. But here is a key that must be noted. My friend, Dr. Frazier Odom, taught me this principle. Especially among lower-income urban churches, Dr. Odom said, "We must not allow a mindset that 'we're just poor people who have nothing to give' to become an opportunity for God's people not to give of their financial resources to the Lord for ministry. It's not that the Lord needs our money to get ministry done. It's that we need to give of what He has given us so that we realize that everything we have comes from Him!"

At the same time, there are places in God's Kingdom that will always need supplemental financial help from the Church at large. If this help is used for Kingdom work, with good stewardship taught and practiced among the people of the local ministry, this is good, right, and pleasing to the Lord. If what others give from outside of that local church is being used as a SUBSTITUTE for putting the Lord first financially in the local church receiving the help, then what is going on is a SINFUL FINANCIAL HUSTLE that the Lord is not going to bless!

For now, let's assume that good stewardship is being practiced by a local urban ministry. Additional funding is needed from the Christian Church at large for a local urban ministry to do a lot of exciting outreach with the Gospel of Jesus Christ. So how does this ministry get funded? How do we find outside funding? What is involved in connecting Godly funders of the Lord's work with places that need funding to do their best ministry? The following is an assortment of mini-essays that are focused on funding ministry.

48

FUNDING TAKES TIME

While we can cook popcorn and boil water in a microwave in a matter of a few moments, there are no quick fixes to finding immediate funding for ministry. Engaging people to invest in ministry begins by cultivating a relationship with them. Relationships take time to develop. There are no ways around that. Having said that, while the best day to start developing a relationship with a potential ministry funder was 10 years ago, the second-best day to start working on relationships with potential funders is today. By the way, did you note the plurality in that last "relationship" word? I can cook corn in my microwave in about three minutes, but cooking a pizza takes about 15 minutes, and cooking a turkey takes a few hours. Developing relationships with potential ministry funders is just like cooking food—different funders will take different amounts of time to begin a relationship and bring that relationship to a point when you can make an "ask." Of course, you can ask in your first meeting with a new funder, if you enjoy rejection. I don't advise it.

To this end, receive these two insights. Your ministry needs vision about funding. You need to plan out the costs in front of you, long-range. Have two budgets. One budget is the bare bones dollars you need to exist. The second budget starts to add some "wishes" and "hopes" that require additional funding but could make your ministry better. As part of this vision, consider the variety of sources where you can build relationships that could help you fund ministry. Some popular funding sources for ministries include: grants from foundations, grants from denominational hierarchy, building sister church relationships, and helping private individuals see God's opportunities in your ministry. It will likely take a variety of sources to provide the funding needed for your ministry, unless you have someone who will write you an unrestricted one million dollar check every year for ministry. Even in that case, while such a check would be awesome (though unlikely), you should be preparing for the day that donor dies or, God forbid, they get upset with you and withdraw their funding. It could even be the case where you feel God is leading you to follow a certain ministry direction and your funder doesn't support that step. You follow the Lord's lead, but in doing so you lose your funder. It's happened before.

49

STORYTELLING

In one sense, raising money for ministry is all about storytelling. The ministry leader tells the story of what the Lord is doing in the ministry where the leader serves. When a funder gets excited about that story, they ask how they can help. The ministry leader responds with the needs, and the potential funder offers their help. It's pretty simple.

The key is THE STORY. Always remember that it's the story of WHAT THE LORD IS DOING through us. As ministry leaders, we might be God's glove, but the glove is nothing without the Hand of the Lord that is in it. The Hand doesn't need the glove, but the glove is nothing without the Hand!

Now for some obvious truths:

You can't tell a story until you have a story to tell. My experience is that if we go to work in ministry and hit the streets with the message of Christ, instead of waiting on people to come to us, the Holy Spirit will provide us with stories to tell. I have never seen this principle fail. Some days I don't feel like going out and making calls on people or walking the streets and engaging people to build relationships. However, those are the days when the Holy Spirit makes the work most fruitful. I've always thought of Him on those days saying, "You see, I told you. If you will just obey and follow Me."

During the COVID-19 pandemic, many churches had to get creative about how to minister to people during lockdown. We taught our small group Bible studies to use Zoom videoconferencing online and restarted the groups online after just the second week of the lockdown. Guess what happened? Our online small group ministry attendance grew to include more people than before COVID-19! We even started a new small group during the lockdown. Another byproduct of our creative efforts in our small group ministry during that unique time led to the chance to develop more leaders who are excited about ministry! Before COVID-19, we did not have this kind of story to tell—and now we do.

While the initial story you tell might be about the need and opportunity for ministry, the "story" can't end there. This is the crazy place that politicians, both Democrats and Republicans, mainly stay in. They focus on talking about the problems—who's at fault with a problem, who does or doesn't understand the problem, etc. They go back and forth. The better "story" is the efforts made toward solving the problem—not just talking about it, but GOING and DOING! This step can be scary for some. Some people hesitate about GOING and DOING because they are afraid to fail. But to do nothing with Jesus' command in Acts 1:8 is failure. Moreover, while everybody wants to be successful in every effort, I find that what funders are most focused on is the story of faithfulness in doing the work of ministry that you promised to do.

The story you tell has to matter. Our story first has to matter to the Lord. This is His work that we're doing. God doesn't bless our own kingdom-building. However, when what we want to do in our story is directly Biblically-tied, that gives it so much more power to Christ followers who may be potential funders.

Also, take time to meditate on the things that matter in ministry. Ministry that touches the lives of people matters and is more easily funded. Building buildings might matter to some who want their name on a building. But my experience has been that most generous Christian ministry funders want to fund "people."

The story you tell also has to matter to the FUNDER YOU'RE TALKING TO. Many foundations are very straightforward about what they fund and what they do not fund. That can help give you some clarity. Whether it's a foundation, a denomination, a sister church, or a private individual, take time to find out what is important to that funder. Then see if there is a match with the ministry you believe the Lord is leading you to do.

An important caution: While sometimes you can "stretch" your core area of ministry to include an area of ministry that a funder might be interested in, be careful. I've seen some urban community organizations change their focus/emphasis of what they do whenever they need funds. In other words, they play to whatever a funder wants to fund. This year, they are about helping kids. Next year, they are about senior care.

It's unwise to lose the identity of who the Lord has called you to be just for the sake of gaining a few dollars in a particular grant. Such behavior will give your ministry little longevity because both your supporters and your "clients" (the people you serve) will be confused about what your organization does.

I think it could even be a "test" from the Lord sometimes to see if we will be faithful to what He has called us to do. Will we TRUST Him to provide the resources or jump to wherever we think the money is? Making sure your story matters will require prayer, studying the context, and studying the Word of God. The next part of telling a story that matters concerns HOW YOU TELL IT.

How you tell your story is as important as the story you tell. When I have the opportunity to tell the story about all the Lord is doing through our Bethlehem ministry, I imagine myself as a lawyer. The good lawyers I have known are usually super organized. They've done their homework about the facts. When they make statements or assertions, they have data to back up what they say. It's like that in telling a ministry story. Don't make general statements like, "We're working hard," or "Our ministry is strong," or "This ministry is important." People already expect that you and I are working hard and giving our best. That's even Biblical. Colossians 3:23 says, "Whatever you do, work at it with all your heart, as working for the Lord." Instead of just using words like "strong" or "important," tell me *why* the work of your ministry is strong and important.

- **Tell your story in a concrete way.** Tell me what events you've held to try and reach the goal you're trying to achieve. Give me numbers, both from your successes and from the events that didn't work out as you planned. I remember the response someone gave me a number of years ago at the anniversary of an old urban church. I asked a church member, "What's the greatest thing going on right now at the church?" The woman responded, "Well, we're still here." That's not really a good answer. If our church doors are open, but we're not reaching out dynamically with the Good News of Jesus, maybe it would be better for the church to close, the members transfer to another church, and some other church to come into this community with passion for reaching the community with the Gospel.

- **Tell your story with timeliness.** If last Easter your church attendance doubled, thank God! But if that's still your best story in September, that story isn't very compelling. What it really says is that over the past few months you didn't do anything with those visitors who came on Easter. You also didn't go out into the community since. News is only news for a short time. The luster of exciting mission news fades fast.

- **Pictures are meaningful.** They help people connect with the emotion of what the ministry is doing. Pictures also give evidence that the ministry being described is actually being accomplished and that the ministry described is really the same as what is really happening. At last year's community Easter egg hunt with 110 people in attendance, we took a panorama photo that showed the crowd size so people could see that when I say "110 people," I mean 110 people! Especially early in your ministry work, building credibility is important.

- **A personal audience is always the best opportunity to tell your story.** For our church ministry, we try to do regular "mission Sundays" at our sister churches who support us. On these Sundays, Pastor Gerard Bolling or I will preach at their worship service, and we often also bring a choir from Bethlehem with us. On the other hand, sometimes we get to tell the story with the head of a foundation at lunch, or we are the speaker at a meeting with men or women from a church society. No matter what kind of personal opportunity you have to tell the story of your ministry, treat that moment like gold! Be organized in what you say and in the visuals you may bring. Be prepared as a speaker—don't read a presentation. Connect with people. Be strategic in what you present. You won't have time to tell the whole story of your ministry. Select parts that are most important for that moment. Not everything is of the same importance. Tailor the telling of your story to the audience. Some audiences want to know about our work with children. Other people I talk to want to know how we are magnifying our ministry by developing new leaders. Still others are mainly interested in pure outreach to new people in events like our street ministry. Some would rather I tell the story about how people who have been part of our ministry for a long time are growing and developing.

Your preparation for the personal presentation that you've been invited to make will help you know what is right for this particular audience. Again, as I have already said above, make sure what you share matters to the people that you are bringing it to. Most of all, preparing to talk about the ministry that we are doing becomes a kind of personal "check" that what we're putting our time into is really the most important thing—particularly in Jesus' eyes!

50

LONGEVITY

For the past 20 years, my wife and I have bought all our automobiles from the same person, a trusted friend of mine named Karen. Buying a car from her is so simple. We tell Karen what we're looking for. Karen finds the car or truck. We buy it. We don't haggle with her about the price, because I know she's found the best price for us. I don't "look under the hood" and scrutinize the car, not only because I wouldn't know what I was doing but also because I don't see any need to do that. I already know Karen has my best interests covered. Simply put, I TRUST HER. I don't want to buy a car from anybody else, because we have a great 20-year relationship. Some day if she ever retires, I will be traumatized. I won't know what to do, unless she connects me with somebody I can TRUST for the next 20 years of my life after she stops finding me cars. Can I say it again? For over 20 years, I have TRUSTED HER.

Longevity is so important in raising funds for ministry.

Longevity is keeping your word over time, particularly when it has to do with resources and funds that you do not possess of your own, but that are entrusted to you by someone else to manage.

That's the idea of stewardship—caring for property or an asset that is owned by somebody else or given to you by somebody else. It's all about TRUST. This whole concept is right out of God's Word. First Corinthians 4:2 says, "...it is required of stewards that one be found trustworthy." This is so true with those who give gifts to the ministry where we are serving. The ministry that has taken place at Bethlehem during my years serving here includes: a new sanctuary (about $250,000), building improvements (about $700,000), Bethlehem After School program ($800,000), More Greater Things Ministry (when the next phase is complete, a total of $1.4 million). The basic annual giving to help us make our ministry budget over the past 25 years totals $4 million. Then there is also our housing ministry, Better Living Communities Salisbury Park development ($70 million). Those numbers are unbelievable, and they are just lowball estimates! I never could have financed ministry costs like that myself. This had to be FROM THE LORD, sending gifts through Godly men and women. MY JOB in this ministry plan is to do my best to ensure that these gifts are used wisely, in step with the Word of God, for His glory, and with great faithfulness to the Lord.

By the way, a quick side comment:

One of the blessings of being in the same ministry place for over 30 years is that God has made my longevity connect with the longevity of incredible donors. This kind of longevity of gifts often doesn't develop when a ministry leader hops from ministry to ministry every three to five years. The longevity of trustworthiness never gets a chance!

Let's always be clear—the connection of donors and ministry leaders is God's Work. However, we can sinfully mess up a relationship that God sets up when we do not faithfully use the gifts He provides through people for our ministry. This not about success. It's not that the more successful you are in ministry, the more people want to sow financial blessings in it (although that's the way things sometimes look).

Rather, you gain trustworthiness among donors not necessarily by always being successful in what you do, but rather by being faithful to do what you said you would do. Many ministry ideas we tried at Bethlehem didn't work the way I thought they would work. But I am honest when I tell you exactly what we tried and how well-prepared we were in planning it, and then why we think it didn't turn out the way we had hoped. I'll say it again—funders aren't looking for perfection when they give dollars. They are looking for wise planning, risk-taking faith, accountability in doing what we said we'd do, and honest reporting on what happened. When these things keep happening, gifts that support ministry continue. AND they often GET BIGGER!

Again, this teaching is right out of the Scripture in Matthew 25:14–30, especially verse 23. "His master said to him, 'Well done, good and faithful slave. You were faithful with a few things, I will put you in charge of many things...'"

Before we close out this word about longevity, it must be noted that how you handle restricted funds can make or break your ministry. Restricted funds are what they say: funds restricted for a particular purpose designated by the donor. That means if Mr. Smith gave $20,000 for the church lighting to always be lit, then that's what you have to use it for, no matter what. You say, "But we're short this month on our offerings, and the staff won't get paid unless we borrow from this fund." NO! DON'T DO IT!

Never use money for a different reason than it was intended, except when you have permission from the donor.

If you touch restricted money and use it for a different purpose, that is wrong. That is deception. Second, if Mr. Smith ever finds out what you did without his permission, you will never get another dollar from Mr. Smith. AND word about your shiftiness will travel to MANY other donors. Instead, if you ASK Mr. Smith if some of that money could be used for a different purpose (giving him the right to make the decision), I have found that the donor almost always says, "Yes."

A long term trust relationship with a donor advances you miles ahead when it's time to ask for money for a ministry project. Of course, you still need to tell your story and make your case when asking for support. But when you have a long term relationship with a donor, often in the midst of the conversation they will interrupt you and say something like, "If you think this is important, I'm behind you. I trust your judgment. You can count on my gift." It's all because of LONGEVITY—because you've been faithful in the past.

51

"YOU SHOULD" follows "I AM"

The words, "You should," are most powerful when they follow the words, "I am." What? Oh, yes! Think about when you were growing up and your family gathered around the table for dinner. Maybe you didn't want to eat the carrots on your plate. Your father told you to eat the carrots. How much more powerful his words were when you looked at the carrots on his plate and then heard him say, "I am eating my carrots. You should eat your carrots." That's much stronger than if he just said, "You should eat your carrots," but he didn't have any on his own plate. This isn't rocket science!

This is simply the concept of LEADING BY EXAMPLE.

It's no different in ministry. Don't tell people in your ministry, "You should make calls on people and get them to come to church" unless you also can say, "I am making calls on people trying to get them to come and worship the Savior." The same is true in giving. As ministry leaders we should be leading the way in giving of our time, talents, and treasure, to the Lord. The same is true when you're seeking to raise funds for ministry.

Don't expect others to invest until you yourself have first invested.

To expect others to give ("You should") funds and time to our ministry, when I am not already giving time and money to our ministry ("I am") feels almost like hustling people for money. Why wouldn't I invest first? Don't I believe in the mission I am fundraising for?

Now, of course, there are people who have the ability to give gifts that are significantly larger than I can ever give in size and amount. That's not the point. The point is a simple call to me and to you as we raise funds. Don't expect others to invest before we have first invested ourselves!

52

IF YOU CAN, INVOLVE YOUR DONORS IN THE STORY

Elizabeth had heard that our Bethlehem After School program did good work with kids. She also heard that the children we work with have significant needs. She had listened to enough stories about how kids growing up in the city were behind in reading and how they sometimes acted out some of the trauma of their home life in school. But it wasn't until she came to Bethlehem After School program to volunteer for a day and work with some of our children that she really began to understand life from their perspective. And it opened her heart.

Tony and Dorothy were in the congregation one Sunday when I preached at a Bethlehem Mission Sunday at their church. They had heard about our Taking Jesus to the Streets (TJTTS) summer outreach ministry. They wondered what it would be like. They decided to come with us to one of our TJTTS outreach nights. This particular one was in one of the low-income housing projects on the north side of St. Louis. It looked like a rough and potentially volatile area as they drove to the site with the rest of the TJTTS team. But then the TJTTS music started and they saw all the children gather. They even noticed some of the intimidating "gang-like" characters were smiling and accepting us. Tony and Dorothy began to feel more comfortable. Later on, when they sat on a sheet on the ground with six children to work on the night's simple craft, this place felt even more like home. The conversations with the children were so easy, so open. The children were excited to do the crafts and were glad to hear about Jesus. Dorothy and Tony's hearts opened, and they became supporters of the TJTTS program.

A youth basketball team from a Lutheran school in Central Illinois came to our Bethlehem seventh- and eighth-grade tournament for the first time a few years back. Looking at the faces of the players and their parents as they entered our small, old-fashioned gym for the first time, it seemed they weren't sure what they had gotten themselves into. A basketball tournament in the inner-city? But once the games got going and the cheering started as the teams went back and forth on the court, everyone soon felt very at home. In fact, they were glad to be part of the Bethlehem tournament. More than that, after the guest team went back home to Illinois, some adults decided to raise money to buy matching socks for our Bethlehem players! How kind! They didn't have to do that. They just wanted to support our ministry to the young men on our basketball team!

I've said it before in earlier essays, but it bears repeating. It's one thing for a potential donor just to hear about ministry, or even see it from afar in some pictures, video, or through a written story. But when potential donors experience ministry for themselves, God the Holy Spirit opens their hearts in a unique way to want to help. So the lesson is, if you can, involve your donors in the story of ministry!

53

BE SURE TO SAY "THANK YOU"

"Does this really even need an essay? It's so obvious," you say. It is. But the answer is, "Yes." Not saying "thank you" can hurt your fundraising. Not saying "thank you" in a timely way can also wound your efforts to raise funds. But more than that, not saying "thank you" is just plain wrong. When people give money, they do it out of joy and excitement. It's just like the Bible says in 2 Corinthians 9:7, "God loves a cheerful giver." Another part of that giving experience is getting a timely letter of thanks. After I give, I love to know that my gift actually made it to the place where I was trying to give it. It's also important to me to know that they were as thrilled to receive it as I was to give it.

Sure, it shouldn't have to be that way. A heart filled with the joy of giving shouldn't even care if they get a letter of thanks, except for the need for a useful tax exemption acknowledgement. However, we are emotional creatures and we want to know somehow that something we did was helpful.

One last comment about letters of thanks. Especially if your ministry is a busy place, especially if you get many gifts at one time, you NEED A SYSTEM. You need a system so that letters containing gifts don't get lost in the office. You need a system so that letters of thanks are actually mailed to donors. You also need a system to track your donors and keep their contact information for the future when you cultivate your relationship with them.

Here is my system:

1. As the ministry leader of Bethlehem, I receive the mail. I then sort it according to wherever in the building it needs to go. I discourage anybody else from touching the mail when it comes into our building. That way, when someone asks whether a letter with a gift got to us or

didn't get to us, I can say with 90% accuracy, "We received that letter" or, "We did not receive that letter." The remaining 10% represents the few times when someone other than me touches the mail first.

2. I open Bethlehem's letters, especially those letters I believe have gifts inside, in my office. Before I deposit the checks into the mailbox of the "money counters," I either *make a copy of the check, or I hold on to the check to write the thank you note.* Yes, this sometimes means I have the check for a couple of days. There are many weeks when I am unable to write daily "thank you" letters. I sometimes save up a group and then do them all at one time for a week. If we had more staff at Bethlehem, I would make this happen sooner. Regardless, I make sure that a letter of thanks is written.

3. I give my written letters of thanks to my office assistant, who makes a copy of the letter and then files it. In this way, we know for an entire year all the people outside of our church who made gifts to Bethlehem's ministry. We know their contact information, and we know how much they gave. A copy of this letter also remains on my computer. Sometimes letters of thanks do get lost in the mail. This system enables us to send a copy of a past letter to let donors know that we did indeed write it.

4. If the donor is new to our ministry, we enter their contact information in our newsletter database. This step enables us to send them our next new mailing and continue to cultivate them as a donor.

5. When I write a thank you letter, in addition to saying, "Thank you," I also try to include a small paragraph with the latest news from our ministry. People appreciate this. This update keeps people even more engaged with what is happening at Bethlehem.

This is my system. You need to figure out one that works for you. Whatever you do, be sure to let donors know how much you appreciate them.

54

KEEP WORKING TO EXPAND YOUR
PRESENT DONOR BASE

There is a lesson in what happened in Flint, Michigan, and also Peoria, Illinois, and Gary, Indiana. In its heyday, Flint was all about General Motors. Just about everybody in Flint was tied to the automobile industry. When cuts were made at GM, it took down the whole city because everything in Flint was tied to GM. Same story in Peoria with Caterpillar Tractor. Even more drastic was what happened in Gary when US Steel's business declined by 90%. The result was devastating. In fact, Gary has never recovered. There's an old phrase that summarizes the plight these three cities faced in their histories, "Don't put all of your eggs in one basket." We could apply the same principle when it comes to funding any not-for-profit organization, but especially funding ministry.

There are various avenues to explore for finding funds for ministry beyond what comes in the weekly church offering plate. Applying for grants is a way to gain income for particular projects. These grants can come from your church denominational hierarchy, as well as private and public foundations. They are usually limited in what the money can be used for, and they are rarely renewable. So you can't fund ministry in an ongoing, long term way through grants. Another avenue for funding ministry, if you have a useable building or property, is through renting a portion of your facility to other groups and businesses. An old church school building can bring significant rental income when rented to a local charter school, not-for-profit group, church ministry, or even a business.

Because not every ministry has useable space to rent, and because grant funding is limited in scope and duration, finding individual donors and cultivating sister church relationships might be the best way to find consistent additional funds you need for an urban ministry. Most important in this area of fundraising is this:

Always keep working to expand your present donor base!

This is an intentional activity. When you meet new people who might be able to help your ministry, add them to your communication list of people that you send your newsletter to and try to involve in your ministry. Be intentional. Seek to grow your contact list by at least 10% each year. Your ministry will need this growth for two reasons. First, you will have donors who age and get to a place in life where they are no longer able to give. In the same way, some donors will lose interest in your ministry. That's just the way it is. Some donors get excited about the "next new thing" they find. They may be with you for two or three years, and then they stop giving to your ministry and move on to the next new ministry.

Second, the more donors you have, the better your opportunity to consistently raise a larger amount of funds. Maybe one year you have a donor who writes a $20,000 check to you, but it's only for that one year. That $20,000 might be attainable again in coming years—it's just that the Lord may choose to fund that $20,000 in a different way. Maybe next time it's via eight donors who each give an average of $2,500.

One more truth about funding urban ministry:

"Hits" usually come BEFORE "home runs."

Don't look for the one million dollar gift. Don't try and schmooze wealthy people. We are not to be spiritual "hustlers" of gifts from people. To be clear, all gifts—big or small—are all the work of the Holy Spirit on the hearts of people. We should receive every gift with gratitude and grace. As urban ministry leaders, our job is simply to tell the story of what the Lord is doing in ministry. Some people you add to your contact list may have given you a gift; others may not yet have given you a gift. Add them, regardless of whether they have given. Add them, regardless of how much they have given. Trust the Lord to move them to give when He sees fit! I've seen this principle work—a growing donor base often means growing funding.

55

KEEP GROWING IN YOUR UNDERSTANDING OF PEOPLE

Someone once said, "Never stop learning, because life never stops teaching." I haven't been able to find the source of that quote. Yet, it sure is true. It is especially true about PEOPLE. Let's plug in the words "about people" to the quote. "Never stop learning ABOUT PEOPLE, because life never stops teaching ABOUT PEOPLE." The day I stop wanting to learn more about people is the day I need to get out of ministry.

If you wanted to do well in the computer market, you would learn everything you could about computers. If you wanted to open a great BBQ restaurant, you would learn everything you could about making great BBQ. For us in the church, people are our clientele. We need to learn everything about them. This starts by recognizing that we will never come to a moment when we know everything about people, because they keep on changing. That's where so many of us church leaders make our mistake—we think after we've been around for a few years that we know people. We know what they like, we know how they operate, and we know what they will invest in and commit to. However, the only way we can get close to this kind of knowledge is when we continue to study people, especially regarding their relationships.

Some time ago, I learned something new from a *Wall Street Journal* story. I might have read the *Wall Street Journal* half a dozen times in my life. But on this Saturday morning, it was the only paper available as I ate breakfast at a hotel. Did you know that, via the Internet, many young adults today have relationships with and even date people they've never physically met before? What does that tell me about ministry to young adults? A bunch of stuff:

- I can't be Internet ignorant, if I'm going to be in ministry to young adults. I need to know how they value online relationships.

- Hmmm... so that might be why, when young adults get together face-to-face, it is often a bit awkward; the forming of relationships in the presence of others doesn't come as easily.

- Just because you don't see someone physically accompanied by a boyfriend or girlfriend, it does not necessarily mean that person ISN'T in a committed relationship with someone. It might be a committed online relationship.

- Might young adults have an inside track with a concept that people in my generation struggle with—that you can have a deep relationship with a person, even though you can't physically touch? Young adults do this over the Internet. Isn't this similar to the relationship we seek to have with our Lord—closeness and intimacy, even though we can't see Him or touch Him?

- If a young man and a young woman come to me for pre-marital counseling, and 80% of their contact with one another in their dating life has been only online, it may inform some of my pre-marital counselling during their engagement process. How different this concept is in today's relationships versus the generation I grew up in!

Keep learning about people. How? By having conversations with people. Reading studies about generational trends is also useful. Likewise, observing pop culture will educate us about people: what they are buying, what they are *not* buying, what they do with their free time, their attitude toward Christ, and their attitude toward Christ's church. How do they see God's Word—is it authoritative to them or more optional? How do they value family? Television tells us a lot about people and so do movies. Notice popular trends like "fantasy" movies, "hero" comic book characters, and mythological topics like the television show *Game of Thrones*. There's so much to learn. This knowledge helps sermons and Bible studies and small groups be effective.

The Bible also is an incredible textbook to teach us about people, for while some aspects of people have changed, some are timeless. For example, death rocks our world—no matter who we are—and this is clearly recorded with Mary, Martha, and Jesus in John 11:20–35. The challenge of living for self is clearly pictured in the foolish man of Luke 12:16–21 and in the life of Cain in Genesis 4:9. The bitterness of the older brother in Luke 15:28–30 is still something that suffocates people today. The desperate suffering of the woman in Mark 5:25–28 is experienced by people still today. The struggle that people have with money and possessions possessing them, like the young man of Matthew 19:16–22, is still something very real today. We all sometimes still want to hide our most embarrassing sins and can identify with the same feelings David experienced in Psalm 32:3–5.

The insight is simple. If we're going to be effective in ministry with people, we need to keep learning about people.

56

GREAT, BUT COMPLEX

Merriam-Webster's dictionary defines the word, "complex," this way: "a whole made up of complicated or interrelated parts." That's a useful description of many of the people we encounter as part of an urban inner-city ministry. In the city, we have great people, committed people, creative people, and loving people, but they are very complex.

In one aspect, we could say that all people are complex. But I find that urban people have more complexity because of many factors that are often outside of their control.

Complex isn't bad; it just "is." I've observed that having more money sometimes masks the complexities of life. For example, while there are some struggles that all single parents face in raising their children, a single parent making a six-figure salary has more resources to address the stressful parts of their life. A single parent with a greater income can afford babysitters and nights out. A single parent with a greater income may be able to work only two-thirds time because their salary is high enough for two-thirds of a salary to be sufficient income. A low-income single parent doesn't have those options. My hope in writing this essay is that, as you read it, you will be encouraged to think about the many people who are part of your ministry and recognize how they are great and most useful to the Master, even though they may be very complex.

What do I mean by complex people? Many in our ministries have complex family situations. A mother who has four children with four different fathers often has four times the drama to deal with in maneuvering life schedules and attending to the children's needs. In the same way, a young man who is a father to several children with different mothers faces child support issues that will be before him for about two decades. It's easy for us to say of these two examples, "That was an unwise move on their part earlier in life." But what do we say when those same men and women come to our ministry and want to go in a new direction and pursue a Godly life with the Lord? Do we tell them their life-mess is just too much trouble? Of course not. That's not what Christ would say.

In the same way, past decisions can also make life more complex. One of my grandfathers never finished high school. He got a job in a factory to help support his family. In those days, that wasn't unusual. He worked in that factory and other factories all his life. In time, he retired and was able to take care of himself and my grandmother financially until he died. Today, that path rarely succeeds. Not finishing high school doesn't mean you're unemployable, but it often does mean that having just one job will not provide sufficient enough income to live. It may mean that you will always work two jobs. That situation affects your availability to serve in a ministry, which may mean you have little time to be with God's people, except coming to worship. It also may mean you will be limited to working in industries like fast food and cleaning, where your work hours will constantly change.

What do we tell someone who comes to our ministry, is filled with Christ's love, and wants to serve but keeps having to deal with an employer who won't give them a consistent schedule to plan their serving life around? Do we say, "Sorry, church doesn't work for you"? No. We still work to help them understand and use the ministry gifts the Lord has given them.

It's not simple to do, yet it's very common in our urban, low-income world.

Add to this the VERY COMMON dynamic that many people we encounter in inner-city areas have untreated mental illness, especially depression (which gets even more accentuated as they often have little hope). Of course, we're glad for the Lord's promise of Philippians 3:20 that "our citizenship (our real home) is in heaven." But we're not there yet. What is our message as Christians to people as they wait for a better home and better life in heaven? Depression can be intense, not simple. Sometimes the complexities of life get woven together. That puts people in an even bigger hole. The unwise past of people's lives connects with the two or three jobs they're working to make ends meet, and then you add in the depression or bi-polar disorder they live with. It can be not only overwhelming for them as they desire to fit in to ministry, but it can also be discouraging to urban ministry leaders who are always looking for more bodies to serve.

People are complex. Some parts of these complexities we can help people sort through; some we cannot. We need God's wisdom to help people see how they can serve, even though their life is loaded.

People are complex in other ways. People don't all learn in the same way. For example, my colleague once met with a ministry leader in charge of a small team. My colleague tried to help this leader understand the areas of ministry he was responsible for. The simple way of doing this would have been to send an email or text as a reminder saying, "This, this, and that area of ministry are your responsibilities." In fact, he actually tried to share the message that way. It wasn't getting through. What my colleague ended up doing was scheduling a one-one-one meeting with this team leader. He wrote each of the assigned tasks on a piece of paper and labeled cups with the names of each person on the leader's team. He then told the team leader to put each of the assigned tasks his team was responsible for into the right cup. One task went in "Tommy's cup." Another task went in "Mikala's cup." The next task went in the cup of another young lady.

Using this more concrete approach, the team leader "got it." Some people would say, "You shouldn't have to do all that for a leader." Maybe so. But here is the essential truth—it all comes down to what your goal is. **My colleague's goal was to get the leader functioning right, not just doing what was most convenient for my colleague.**

The result was mission accomplished. Not everybody learns in the same way. It is our job to keep getting the job done as our main goal, not our own convenience.

The same truth can be said about how people work. You may have already learned in the ministry where you are serving that you can give a task to some people and they get it and run with it. They complete it with excellent work. Yet, we must walk other people through the task almost every step of the way and provide checklists and other accountability help in order to keep them on track and finish the task.

This is one of the big challenges of being a leader in an urban ministry—be committed to doing whatever it takes to understanding your people and drawing the good out of them.

Here's where I think Christ's church does a work that is unique to the rest of the world. Now, it's true, there are some days when I just want to give up and say, "Helping this person fit into ministry because of their schedule, their personality, and their type of giftedness is more work than it's worth." Then the Gospel of how the Lord has been patient and worked with me calls me back to the work of helping coach someone else into what the Holy Spirit wants them to be.

Think about it: the Lord our God has always chosen to work with sinful, complex human beings like us in order to make something great out of us for His purposes. Remember how He used a prostitute to help His people take a key city? The story is in Joshua 2. Her name was Rahab. God also used an adulterer and a murderer to lead His people. The story is in 2 Samuel 11, and his name was David. One of Jesus' own disciples started out as a dishonest, evil tax collector. His story is in Matthew 9:9–13. His name was Matthew. Remember the woman in John 4—the one God used powerfully to reach other Samaritans? Her history with men wasn't so good or Godly, according to John 4:16–19. But God still used her.

I know my life is a story just like these. There are some things in my life that have not been of God and that I regret so much, yet the Lord has used me. I'm certain you have your own story of God's grace and patience with you. So if the Lord has been so kind and patient with us, our assignment is to love others in our ministry in the same way Jesus has loved us! Many of the people of our ministries are complex. But when we think about God's kindness in working with us, we'll keep on working with the people He sends to us.

57

PEOPLE FIRES

If you were an arsonist, and you wanted to make sure a building was going to be destroyed by fire, how would you get that fire started? I know, you're wondering, "What kind of crackpot beginning is this to an essay about ministry?" Keep reading. I'm not talking about using an especially combustible accelerant. Here's what I mean. If you wanted to destroy something with fire, to ensure its destruction you would start multiple fires in multiple places. A fire that is limited to one place can be more easily put out and contained. But a fire in more than one place can quickly become overwhelming and impossible to extinguish.

Now think of ministry. There are almost always people fires in our ministries. Sometimes it's a person who is mad at us church leaders for something we've done. At other times, it's two people in the church who are in conflict with each other and then quickly involve others from the church and insist they choose sides. The result is that the fire grows even bigger and more intense. Often a people-fire breaks out when someone thinks they're not getting enough attention or that they are being treated unfairly in the ministry.

This is the work of the enemy. The devil is an arsonist extraordinaire! He wants to see God's family, the Church, destroyed. What he often does is start multiple people fires at one time among all kinds of people to the extent that leaders can't deal with all of them at the same time. The fire burns, the leaders get worn and tired, and the family of God is wounded and even destroyed.

So how do we deal with people fires like this? Begin by recalling Daniel 3 and one of the most intense human physical and spiritual attacks on God's people ever launched. Notice what happened to the three Hebrew boys— Shadrach, Meshach, and Abed-nego. The attempt to discourage their faith in the Lord by destroying them physically was unsuccessful. Why? Remember what King Nebuchadnezzar observed when he looked into the fiery furnace according to Daniel 3:25? He says, "Look! I see four men loosed and walking about in the midst of the fire without harm, and the appearance of the fourth is like a son of the gods!" Three men were thrown into the fiery furnace, but there was a fourth with them. He appeared to the king to be like the son of a god. You were almost correct, Nebby! It was the Son of God there with His people in the fire—protecting them and keeping them from being burnt or feeling hopeless!

Likewise, consider the fires raging around you and me as ministry leaders. The same Lord is with us in the midst of those fires. "IN THE MIDST." Don't forget that, whenever you have all kinds of people fires around you. Don't panic! The Lord is in control, even though it may take time for these people fires to be handled or burn themselves out!

One other truth—the Scripture also helps us know just HOW IN

CONTROL our Lord really is. Check back to Daniel 3:27. "The fire had no effect on the bodies of these men nor was their hair of their head singed, nor were their trousers damaged, nor had the smell of fire even come upon them." When people fires are burning all around us, it FEELS AS IF everything is out of control. Nope! We need to remind each other that our Lord is in control! These fires aren't too big for Him!

Now for a word about dealing with the fires. When firefighters come on the scene of a fire, they have two targets. Of course, they want to PUT OUT the fire that is burning, but they also want to PREVENT the fire from spreading. Prevention also has to do with PREVENTING future fires from ever starting.

Putting Out People Fires

The most direct way to extinguish people fires is the same prescription for dealing with all conflict—confession and forgiveness. That is, leading a person to confess to another person where they have been wrong in what they've said or done. Or, when the roles are flipped, putting out people fires includes leading a person to forgive someone and let go of a hurt, especially if they don't want to do so. We've all been there. We've all had times when we didn't want to forgive the other person. Those are moments when we lead people to forgive out of obedient gratitude to God. Gratitude, because God forgives us all our sins for the sake of Christ's death on the cross to pay for our sins. Obedience, in the sense that while I may not *want* to forgive the other person, I obediently *must* forgive them, because this is what my Gracious God, who forgives me, wants me to do.

Putting out people fires also TAKES TIME. Sometimes time is needed before a fire is under control. People are much like that. Some of the fires the people are involved in need time to settle down. People sometimes need time to cool off their immediate anger. With people fires, people sometimes need time to come to a place where they will even listen to our sharing God's Word and our leading them to a point where they can put out the flames of relational conflict.

I've found that how you handle people fires is unique. People are different. Some people want to talk everything out. Some people want to apologize and just move on, even if they may still have different perspectives on the same situation that led to the conflict. Some people don't even want to talk much at all but simply want to move forward. Sometimes people won't get back to a good relationship for months, even years.

All we can do is help people see their sin and lead them to confess and forgive. All we can do is help people realize that all of us in the family of God are brothers and sisters in Christ with a basic love and respect for each other. But we can't make people go back to liking each other. That may never happen.

Let me make a confession: I'm still trying to get better at handling people fires.

58

THE JOHN 6:26–27 PEOPLE PROBLEM

Multiple times in this collection of essays you've heard me encourage you to meet people where they are, using all means necessary to build a relationship that leads to your being able to share the Good News of the Savior with them. At Bethlehem, we have an assortment of "entry points" into our ministry, including youth basketball, musical theater camp, Bethlehem After School program, youth fellowship groups, summer pool parties, and carnivals. On the one hand, these are great outreach opportunities in our community, since children and families with a lower income have fewer entertainment options. At the same time, while these approaches can be useful in opening a relationship door into an individual or family, they can't become the "end" of ministry work.

Imagine "Jason." Jason grew up at our church and would spend multiple days of the week at Bethlehem. We became a second home to him. He was certainly a Bethlehem supporter. But here's the sad part. While he was locked into the organization and family called Bethlehem Lutheran Church, he never grew into a strong relationship with Christ.

He deeply loved this family of God, but he never fell deeply in love with the God of this family.

Jason's misguided journey reminds me of the situation Jesus spoke about in John 6:26–27. Earlier in John 6, Jesus did one of His greatest miracles, feeding 5,000 families on only two fish and five loaves of bread. Everybody ate! There was more food left over than what they started with! In John 6:14, John calls the miraculous feeding a "sign." That is, it was not the focal point in and of itself. The feeding of the 5,000 was a sign pointing to the saving truth that Jesus is the Son of God, the "Prophet who is to come into the world." Some people got it. But many people missed this real point of the sign pointing to Jesus as the Savior. Notice what Jesus says to a crowd of people who have continued to follow Him in John 6:26. "Truly, truly, I say to you, you seek Me, not because you saw the signs, but because you ate of the loaves and were filled." Do you follow what Jesus said?

The people's focal point was on the physical miracle of the Lord, not the Lord of the miracle!

Here is a truth to keep in mind as we reach out to people. While we may use all kinds of earthly, attractive programs to draw people, our focal point must always be leading them to know Christ! We want people to see the distinction Jesus made in John 6:27 when He said, "Do not work for the food which perishes, but for the food which endures to eternal life, which the Son of Man will give to you, for on Him, the Father, God, has set His seal." Who cares about the social church activity of a great meal with Jesus one day? What matters is that we get to know the Lord and continue to grow in our life with Him.

That's what Jason never did at Bethlehem. He didn't come to Bible class. He would even float out of the sanctuary many Sundays during the sermon. Why? Because he was committed mainly just to the social organization/ family of Bethlehem, not to the Lord who is the only reason we have a

Bethlehem Lutheran Church. One day, Bethlehem Lutheran Church will be no more, but Jesus Christ—according to Hebrews 13:8—is "the same yesterday, today, and forever." Make it your priority to lead the sheep in your ministry unto the Shepherd who loves them, not just the enjoyment of a "substitute family" called the church!

59

SOLIDIFY & MAGNIFY

*B*uilding LEGO® towers is an activity I have enjoyed with all my grandchildren. Actually, most of the time I'm the one who builds the tower and then they knock it down. However, I have noticed that somewhere between two and three years of age they start wanting to try and build their own tower with "Papa." Watching the grandkids make their attempts at building a tall tower, I see they usually make the same mistake. They try to build something big and tall without a solid, large, strong base.

What a true picture of building in God's Kingdom! Many times we, in the church, focus almost exclusively on the MAGNIFICATION of numbers. Can we reach more people in our weekly ministries? Can we get a bigger crowd coming to Sunday morning worship? Now, hear me correctly. That's not a bad target to keep in front of our eyes. We don't want anyone missing from heaven one day. To aim for adding 20 more new people hearing the Good News of Jesus through our ministries every six months can be a motivating way of doing ministry. Yet, there is another kind of growth that is just as essential as ministry magnification is. It's actually the area of ministry that most leaders in God's family have struggled with. What must accompany "MAGNIFY" is the concept of "SOLIDIFY."

SOLIDIFY has to do with growth. In LEGO® language, it has to do with STRENGTHENING and BROADENING your base all the way up the tower so that you have the CAPACITY to build higher and reach further. Let's think about those two concepts, STRENGTHENING and BROADENING, in people ministry terms.

The people of God need to be CONTINUALLY STRENGTHENED. This only comes through the Word of God. You can't beat what older pastor Paul told younger pastor Timothy in 2 Timothy 3:15–17. "You, however, continue in the things you have learned and become convinced of..." While the rest of this Scripture is gold, just the above words are an entire spiritual meal. Timothy is to stay with, continue in, and grow spiritually in the Word of God. Remember, there are two results that the Holy Spirit gives when we continue in God's Word. He gives instruction to make us "adequate, equipped for every good work." (2 Timothy 3:17) But the Holy Spirit also pours God's power and strength into us as we read God's Word. See Romans 1:16. Let's get specific. STRENGTH from what or for what? The strength God gives us through His Word is strength **to be watchful** against personal temptation and attacks in ministry. It's the **strength to discern voices** that try to sidetrack us from God's plans for us. And it's also **strength in the face of discouragement** when this world tries to encourage us to give up on bringing Christ to people. Aren't those all so real? Let's think about them some more.

If the enemy can attack the leaders, he can significantly wound the ministry "tower" being built! When our ministry team of leaders loses its personal spiritual consistency because the leaders become distracted and start to skip worship, or skip personal time with the Lord, or let an unbalanced life turn their family life into upside-down moments of panic, or wander into some sinfully dangerous behaviors—all of that wounds the ministry! What good is the ministry leader/worker when they are struggling and sick themselves? Likewise, when ministry team leaders aren't growing in God's Word or developing the good discernment needed to sort through deceptive false voices that try and attack the ministry, there will always be a huge number of destructive spiritual wildfires to deal with in the church.

Here's an example. While the Internet is a great blessing for us in ministry, it has also become the match that lit a ton of spiritual mess.

Sometimes people in our ministries surf online for spiritual help on the Internet without a discerning eye. The problem is that a person can find any kind of spiritual teaching online that they want to find, including teaching that is not of God and just plain wrong. What am I talking about? They may be searching online for phrases like, "What is baptism?" or "What is the Lord's Supper?" or "What is God's will for my life?" (Of course our Father wants all of us to be financially prosperous and have a big bank account, right?). They may research online about spiritual legalism and then say, "Look at that new person's behavior and what they wear. They can't be part of our church. Have them come back once they get themselves together!" Then there's always the "anything goes" mentality online (e.g., "It doesn't matter what that person's sexual orientation or sexual practices are; God is love and everything is all good").

The Word of God speaks to everything in our lives. But when ministry workers and leaders aren't growing in God's Word, they become spiritual destructive fire starters in their own lives and among the rest of the people involved in that ministry. The ministry leader then spends all his time handling the multitude of fires, instead of leading the ministry in reaching new people. Solidify, solidify, solidify must accompany magnify, magnify, magnify!

The best way to SOLIDIFY is to have people regularly participate in Bible study. Bible study is the best spiritual pastoral care that any pastor can give to the people he is leading.

SOLIDIFY also has to do with **INTENTIONALLY BROADENING OUR BASE.** Picture a LEGO® tower again. This construction principle says that the higher we build, the broader our base needs to be to support a taller building. In ministry language, that means we must KEEP DEVELOPING LEADERS.

When my grandfather was a pastor in the 1940s-1960s, congregations could have a church that worshiped in the hundreds and even toward 1,000 people a week. And they could take care of the church with maybe two or three pastors and 25 or so church leaders. I didn't live at that time, so I can't say if that's the way it really worked, or if that way really worked at all. But I know this—that kind of leadership model doesn't work anymore today. Today I want a leader/shepherd for every eight to 10 people in our ministry (we're not there yet). Especially in our urban scene, people today have so many needs. With the breakdown of the Christian family, people are much more naïve to the ways of the Lord, and they get discouraged easier. Of course, it's only the Word of God that can take away our discouragement. However, when people are going through a tough time, it's especially needed to both point them to the promises of the Lord while modeling how our confidence is not found in our circumstances, but in our Lord. The prophet Habakkuk nailed that truth at the end of his prophecy. Take a look at it. How would you model what God says through the prophet in Habakkuk 3:17–19?

When people see how the Lord's promises bring hope, even as they go through intense and uncomfortable times in life, that's when people want to buy in to a life of trusting the Lord for everything! How can such intimate ministry care happen in a growing magnifying ministry? Only when the number of leaders is solidified more and more by growth!

Did you notice how I slipped in the word, **"INTENTIONAL"** right before the concept of BROADENING OUR BASE by developing more leaders? INTENTIONAL is an important word. When new people are coming into our ministry, it's easy to get caught up in times of growth and think that the same, smaller leadership base can handle the spiritual care of a growing base of new people. It's easy to forget that all of us are sinful people with a bent toward division, rather than unity and growth in the family of God. It's easy to forget during the good days that our enemy is not in hibernation. The one who wants to destroy Christ's church and any growth is busy plotting, planning, and even doing reconnaissance regarding his next move to pull apart God's people and bring destruction. Remember 1 Peter 5:8? It's easy in the intense flow of "ministry busyness" and all the tasks to accomplish to forget about continuing to develop more shepherding leaders.

We need INTENTIONAL plans to keep developing shepherding people who can stand with God's spiritually young lambs to keep them close to Christ.

I guarantee that the developing of shepherds will not happen automatically. It also won't happen quickly. Thus, developing leaders who point others to our hope in the promises of God must be the kind of work that God's church does all the time. This SOLIDIFY work is vital. After all, MAGNIFY work depends on it!

60

THE DOCTRINE OF CHIPS

Doctrine, the formal term for Scriptural teaching, is so vital in order for the Lord's Church to be the Lord's Church. We treasure the doctrines of justification, sanctification, the doctrine of Church, and what the Bible teaches about the End Times when Christ comes again—as well as all the doctrines of the Christian faith. There is another doctrine that I want to put before you in this essay, but it needs some immediate disclaimers. First, this is not a Scriptural doctrine. But it is a vital life teaching about how to lead people that I am so glad somebody taught me a long time ago. The Doctrine of Chips recognizes that each of us has "chips"—meaning social capital and influence in relationships. We choose how we will spend our chips. An example might be the best way to introduce this concept.

When I first came to Bethlehem, many changes needed to be made, and many needed resources and items were missing for us to do dynamic ministry. I came during the 140th anniversary year of the congregation and, as many churches do for their anniversary, our church had planned several special services and events throughout the year. One part of the anniversary celebration that had not been planned prior to my arrival in July 1989 was the special anniversary offering. Churches will often take a special anniversary offering among their members, former members, and friends to raise funds to purchase something special beyond their regular budget expenses. As Bethlehem's brand-new pastor, I was given the opportunity to weigh in heavily on what our 140th anniversary project would be.

I urged the congregation to raise about $5,000 for a new church sound system ($5,000 would do it back in those days). Some people weren't so thrilled about that idea. They were concerned that we couldn't raise that much money. Others thought we should use whatever money we raised toward our regular ministry budget. I sought to persuade people by reminding them of two things. First, the most vital thing to people (especially a majority of older members) is to be able to hear clearly what is being said and sung in worship. Second, most donors outside of Bethlehem will give stronger anniversary gifts to something special than to helping pay the basic bills (which they believe the church should handle themselves). In the end, because I was the new pastor and I was still on my honeymoon with the congregation, they went along with my request to get a new sound system.

Here's the CHIPS principle in this example. By advocating for the sound system when there were several people who preferred the anniversary offering be used in a different way, I spent my CHIPS with people—meaning, the support that people gave me as their new pastor to go along with something that maybe they weren't really fully supportive of.

So what happened with the anniversary offering? We easily raised all the money for the new sound system. After it was installed and many of our older members realized how much they had not been hearing with the old sound system, they were glad that we made it our 140th anniversary project. Because of how I spent my CHIPS, guess what happened to me in relationship to the congregation? After having made a right leadership decision regarding replacing the sound system, people gave me even MORE CHIPS. That is, they were willing to trust me even more regarding some future decisions.

Relationship CHIPS in a Congregation

CHIPS are gained in a ministry in a multitude of ways:

- Ministry successes often gain a leader CHIPS.

- Longevity at a ministry often gains a leader CHIPS with his people.

- Sometimes when people see how much you, as a leader, are committed and willing to sacrifice for the ministry, this also gains you CHIPS with them.

- Some CHIPS come with age. If I started in a ministry in my mid-50s, the congregation would probably give me more CHIPS than what they gave me in my mid-20s when I started at Bethlehem.

- Sometimes having advanced degrees or additional education can gain a person CHIPS.

How CHIPS are "spent" in ministry:

- To convince people of the ministry to support a ministry that makes them uncomfortable, even though it's a very vital ministry, might cost the leader some CHIPS.

- To get people of the ministry to "stretch" and do ministry that is beyond their comfort zone (for example, making changes in Sunday worship) may cost the leader CHIPS.

- To get people to take risks in ministry (for example, starting a building program) may cost the leader CHIPS.

- Mistakes and failures in ministry programs might not be the leader's fault, but they could cost him CHIPS with the people of the ministry.

- Making changes in an established ministry often costs the leaders CHIPS.

So what are some lessons of the Doctrine of CHIPS?

1. No leader has ultimate power to do anything and everything. (It doesn't matter if you're "The Pastor.") Of course, our first step whenever we're considering a decision is to bring it to the Lord.

2. CHIPS that enable us to have influence toward people are a limited commodity. Realize that truth, and plan appropriately.

3. Use your CHIPS wisely. Don't be shortsighted in how you spend your CHIPS. If there is an important ministry direction worth spending your CHIPS in the future, be more conservative with how you spend your CHIPS today.

61

ACCOUNTABILITY IS A FRIEND, NOT AN ENEMY

I was on the way to BWI airport in Baltimore one early Saturday morning after having spent a few days in the Washington, D.C., area with my son and his family. While I am not a technology kind of person, I have grown to value the GPS system on my phone. I used to be a MapQuest person who would get my directions on the Internet, print them out, and then follow them to my destination. But what I love now about my phone's GPS is that not only do I receive directions but I can also constantly see WHERE I AM in reference to WHERE I am trying to go. I think that is a great picture of ACCOUNTABILITY.

Accountability is the courage and willingness to constantly observe WHERE I AM IN LIFE, in reference to WHERE I AM TRYING TO GO.

If I am in "imagination land" about where I am in life and have no accountability, I am often unwilling to make the changes needed to get to where I am trying to go. If I am in "imagination land" about where I am in life and have no accountability, I might set goals, but rarely ever follow up with the discipline to cross the finish line on those goals. So I often end up lost, not moving toward my destination.

Let me return to my Saturday morning adventure trying to get from my son's house to BWI airport. I followed the GPS directions, BUT after about 15 minutes of following the GPS on some unusual streets instead of a major Interstate, I zoomed out on my phone's GPS map and realized that my GPS was acting crazy. It was not getting me to the BWI airport! I refreshed the GPS direction request, and it then functioned effectively. Without being able to zoom out and SEE WHERE I WAS in reference to WHERE I WAS TRYING TO GO, I never would have made it to BWI airport in time and would have missed my flight.

Accountability is vital in the ministry of our Lord Jesus Christ. In the first place, the Church is His Church. Every ministry resource and gift we have, are given by Him to use to spread His Good News.

Accountability in ministry is essential for us to be good stewards and do everything we can to help as many people as possible know about the Savior who gave His life for them at the cross! Thus, as we do ministry, we RECORD and OBSERVE:

- The number of people in worship and in our ministry programs
- The number of new people who have come to our ministry
- Sheep in our ministry who are growing in their faith and life of service to the Savior (from our outward vantage point; we can't look into the heart) and the sheep who are moving backward or possibly wandering from the Savior
- Growth or decline in stewardship
- The effectiveness of our ministry programs
- How many new people we are reaching out to with the Gospel in programs and personal invitations

The focus isn't just numbers, but the passion to have a sober, true picture of WHERE WE ARE toward our goal that "all people are saved and come to the knowledge of the truth." (1 Timothy 2:4) Accountability takes courage, because sometimes we might not like the true picture of our ministry work. Are we doing the work of the Lord that we think we are doing?

Some people might try to confuse the question by saying, "This is Holy Spirit work." Remember 1 Corinthians 3:7, "...neither the one who plants nor the one who waters is anything, but GOD causes the growth." True! True! True! Any success we have in ministry is all the work of the Lord! I couldn't agree more. But while we have our copy of God's Word open, let's also read the full counsel of God as it records the words of Jesus in Matthew 25:14–30. In this parable, who is praised by Jesus? The faithful and accountable servants who used the talents of money the master gave them. Who does Jesus say should be thrown into the outer darkness? The worthless, unfaithful, unaccountable slave.

In fact, let me suggest to you that ACCOUNTABILITY is our FRIEND in ministry. When I am constantly observing where our church is and what we're doing in ministry, this is helpful in the following ways. Let me help you remember them by using five "E" words.

ACCOUNTABILITY:

...**ENCOURAGES** me to give thanks to God for what He has given me in our ministry. Sometimes we get so rushed in our ministry pace that we miss the many blessings the Lord is giving us (see the essay entitled, "The 3–4 Things"). We need to follow the lead of David on a regular basis in 1 Chronicles 17:16, "Then David the king went in and sat before the Lord and said, 'Who am I, O Lord God, and what is my house that You have brought me this far?'" We can observe that about our own personal lives, as well as in the ministry the Lord has put us in! Especially in an urban inner-city ministry, you need to see the little daily blessings God sends to keep you going!

...Makes me **EVALUATE** who is growing in our ministry, who has been missing from our ministry, and what changes might be needed to make our ministry stronger. To rely only on our memory of who has been around each week for Bible study or worship is a bad idea, particularly in a busy ministry. One of my activities on Sunday afternoon or the following Monday of almost every week is to simply make a list of who was missing from worship Sunday and who was back in worship after being absent for a time. Many times, my memory said so-and-so had just been gone for one Sunday, when in fact I see that she was gone for three Sundays in a row when I look back at my records.

...Challenges me to **ENLARGE** my vision of what could be next for our ministry as we bring the Gospel to people. Observing WHERE OUR MINISTRY IS presently using data that comes through accountability prepares our leaders to dream about what is next regarding how we think about how we bring Christ to people. For example, our church's ability to receive online donations was born out of this principle. What convinced some of the older members to consider having an online giving app for our ministry was the observation that a handful of our members were absent from worship about one Sunday most months. When we checked with them as to why this was so, they shared how their jobs required them to travel more on weekends. They still wanted to give their weekly offering to the Lord, but by the time they returned from their business trips, they had forgotten to render their offering for the Sunday they missed. These members said, "If we had an online giving mechanism so we could give while out of town, we would do it." Our church leadership was willing to give it a try. The yield has been successful with members who are gone some Sundays for work and use the app to still give their weekly offering.

...Is the key to an **EFFECTIVE** team ministry. This is something that our church is working on right now. As our part-time ministry staff has grown and our reach to people has increased to a multitude of new ministries, we have learned that accountability reporting is essential. We want weekly reports from people who are helping us contact people during any given week on: WHO was contacted, HOW (phone, text, visit), and WHAT the result was. Likewise, in our kids programming we want to know on any given night: HOW MANY KIDS were present, if there were

NEW KIDS present, and any CONTACT INFORMATION. If there was a problem with one of the kids, we want an INCIDENT REPORT. It's like when somebody is sick in the hospital and they're connected to many machines that give the medical staff an accountable and accurate picture of the constant state of the patient. Likewise, why not keep our finger on the pulse of something as valuable as the Lord's work in a particular way?

...Is **ESSENTIAL** for any organization that depends on donations. More than ever before, foundations and personal donors want to see accountability to ensure that their donations are being used for the purposes for which they donated funds. This doesn't mean that every program or project works. Rather, it means that to the best of our ability, we have used people's donations for the purposes we set forth when we asked them for those donations.

It is also necessary to note that accountability can be an ENEMY. It's an ENEMY to those who are covering up wrong in ministry, to those who are lazy in ministry, to those who are not giving their best. But accountability is truly a FRIEND to anyone who wants to give their best and do better ministry in the name of the Lord Jesus. What will you do in your ministry to use accountability as your friend?

62

THE 3–4 THINGS

FOR THE TIMES...

When you begin Sunday worship and out of the 140 people who will eventually be at worship, only 30 are presently in the pews...

When you prepared food for 14 at your small group Bible class or ministry activity, and only three have shown up...

When you scheduled four visits with people, and not one of them has been at home and no one called to say they couldn't make the visit...

When you discover the vans you use to transport kids to ministry events have been broken into in your church's gated parking lot, and someone has stolen the batteries...

When one of the strongest members of your choir or one of your deacons tells you that they just got transferred to Atlanta for their job...

When you receive the offering report for last Sunday, and it was two-thirds of the entire church offering...

YOU WILL NEED TO BE WATCHFUL for "THE 3–4 THINGS"!

A couple of months after my 30th anniversary at Bethlehem, I was preaching a mission Sunday at one of our sister churches. The pastor at that church, who was one of my former ministry fieldwork students, asked me, "How have you stayed excited in ministry at Bethlehem for over 30 years?"

"It's The 3–4 Things," I told him.

"What is that?" he asked.

"The 3–4 Things are the little ministry blessings God sends you on a regular basis," I answered and gave him some examples. The 3–4 Things may be:

- Seeing someone back in church on Sunday whom I haven't seen in months

- Opening an envelope to see a huge check to the ministry that we had no idea was coming

- Confirming a youth on Confirmation Day whom I thought would never stay with the church

- Receiving a card from the grandmother of kids who are part of our ministry, thanking us for all we're doing in the life of her grandchildren

- Bad weather that was forecast for our area for Sunday morning dissipating before it ever made it here

- Someone who had been previously unresponsive to my calls over and over unexpectedly calls me

- A member who drops off a meal at our house for no other reason than the fact that they just wanted us to have a night off when we didn't need to cook

You've got the idea! The Lord sends all kinds of little blessings like this into our lives to remind us that He is with us and loves us, even though our ministry days might be hard and we might feel like giving up! Don't you love that "God is faithful and will not let you to be tempted beyond what you are able"? (1 Corinthians 10:13) Don't you love it that God "knows the way I take: when He has tried me, I shall come forth as gold"? (Job 23:10) Keep your eyes open and observant for all of "The 3–4 Things." They are the messages of His love He is sending you to encourage you!

63

SHEPHERDING PEOPLE

Every parent knows that guiding young kids and adult children through life includes a variety of approaches. Parenting is never just one attitude: "It's my way or the highway" or "These are the rules—if you do this, this is what happens to you" or "All law, no grace." Likewise, multi-faceted methods are also needed in leading people, especially the "sheep" of God's flock. It really is an art to know if a hard stand vs. an unexpected outpouring of grace is the best way to get someone back on the right track. Sometimes the sheep who have been lazy will best be encouraged by cheers as they begin to move. Sometimes lethargic sheep need some kind of painful spur to get them in motion.

Also, never lose sight of this truth of God's Church this side of

heaven—it is a volunteer organization!

Leadership in a ministry is not the same as leadership in the workplace. While the church has many business aspects, there is an incentive missing for most sheep in the Lord's Church. In the workplace, if I have a good job that *pays well*, I will put up with a lot of "stuff" to keep that good-paying job. I will even allow people to talk to me in ways that I would normally never otherwise allow, if I'm getting a strong paycheck. I will carry through with more consistent commitment on my job because I NEED that paycheck. Even though we, as believers, know that trusting in Christ and being in His family are vital eternally, the enemy can often diminish and devalue our need to be part of the earthly Christian church. This is especially true when our available time is so short, and our choices to do other things with our time are so available.

Effective shepherding of people really comes down to having strong relationships with them.

Similar to the three most important words in real estate—location, location, location—we might observe that the three most important words in ministry are: relationship, relationship, relationship!

Wise is the ministry leader who understands this. In that spirit, let me put forth four true statements I have learned about ministering to people, especially in urban, low-income areas.

1. We have great people, but they are complex, not simple. Do your homework on people in your ministry. That is, learn their life context. It will personally save you so much disappointment when you understand that their context may not enable them to serve in the ways you would like them to serve. Also, by knowing the complex life context of your sheep, you will be able to realize ways to engage them in ministry that complement and fit the daily life situations they face.

An example is "Ms. Williams." Ms. Williams has such a heart for serving. She really wants to do her part in the ministry of our church. However, she lives far from our church and does not have her own transportation. The metro bus system would be hard for her to use, and it would take her over an hour, one way, to get to our church. On Sunday mornings, she gets a ride to worship. How do you get Ms. Williams involved in serving? Here's one way that has worked for us. Ms. Williams is able to get to church over an hour before worship starts each Sunday. She blesses us by helping to fold and stuff bulletins for worship. What a great fit!

When trying to think creatively about how we can help people find their place in serving the Lord, we always need to see the big picture of people's lives. They may want to serve, but they may need our help in empowering them to serve. Another example includes young moms today. Some want to serve, but they have children with them. They need help with childcare in order to participate in church life. Will the church help them with this need so that they can serve? Another challenge some of our younger members face is that the available jobs require them to work on Sunday mornings. Do we simply write off those people for ministry? Or do we find ways we can involve them in the life of the church at times other than Sunday mornings, until they can get some Sunday mornings off? Another complexity we have experienced with young moms today also has to do with employment. We have simple part-time jobs in our outreach ministries. But even though the young moms are good candidates, they end up being unable to work because if they work, even a part-time job, they lose their government health benefits. These are the real-life circumstances of so many people who want to serve, but their lives are complex!

Our work in ministry is to walk with people through these complex settings, continually point them to the fact that God has not forgotten them, and creatively look for ways they can stay close to the Savior and His Church. It's not easy.

2. Some things that need to be said to people... you really need to have been in a place long term in order to be able to say them.

Every year of my ministry at Bethlehem, we have had fieldworkers from Concordia Seminary. This second principle is one of the lessons our fieldworkers learn early on, especially as they work at our Wednesday Bethlehem Bible Outreach (BBO) kids ministry.

When it comes to moments of discipline regarding the children in our program, often our new fieldworkers will wonder why I (or other long term members of our BBO staff) can say things to kids or give them certain, displeasing looks that never "work" for brand-new fieldworkers. The same principle holds true even in hard conversations with adults. When you minister in a place for a while, you can say some things that other people without that kind of longevity would get significantly attacked for saying. What's the difference? It's the relationship that has been carved out over time! For instance, take the people at our church who grew up with me as their pastor for the past 20 years. If I say something to them that might be hard for them to hear, they know I'm saying it out of love for their ultimate good, almost like a loving parent would say it. It all comes down to the kind of relationship you have built with the people you shepherd.

Permission to talk to people and minister to them in hard moments comes after first having built a strong relationship.

Often that kind of relationship-building takes time. Our focus as ministry leaders isn't on having to wait and be in a ministry for a decade; our focus is on building strong relationships with people in problem-free days so that we have a relationship of love that enables us to care for them in stressful, hard days.

3. Be patient, but pushing, as you coach people to be all that the Lord has called them to be. As I've said, many people we encounter in our ministry have significant challenges. Some come from families where they simply didn't/don't have two great parents who are there for them. Some come from life contexts where behaviors that are addictive and destructive are the norm. Some, for a variety of reasons, constantly struggle financially just to have the basics of life. Some have had significant educational disadvantages, as compared to many other Americans. It is true that some people in life have a harder road than others.

As ministry leaders, our first and primary focus is to bring to the lives of all people the incredible news that God has a better life in store for them because of the death and resurrection of Jesus Christ.

Because of Him we live FREE from the punishment and guilt of our sins—in a right relationship with God the Father. This new life opens up all kinds of advantages and power from the Lord Himself. Our primary work as ministry leaders is to bring this hope in Christ to people.

Behind this Good News, I find that my work as a minister of Christ focuses on leading people to steward their life and use everything God has given them to please Him.

Let me describe this work in a different way. Be PATIENT, but PUSHING, as you coach people to be all that the Lord has called them to be. When you are someone in tough life circumstances or in a church in a hard context, you have only one of two choices in life. You can choose to have a pity party, spending your life blaming everyone else for your struggles. Or you can daily seek to use the gifts and talents God has given you to be all that the Lord has made you to be. I advocate for the latter. I don't want our church to be known as the poor, sad case ministry that can't do anything. Nor do I want what we do to be second-rate or pathetic. NO! Check out the strong words of Ephesians 4:7–16. This promise of gifts that God gave is to the entire holy Christian Church, equipping us to be a "mature man" (verse 13), not constantly rocked by all kinds of false teaching (verse 14), to be a growing and thriving body (verse 16).

However, nowhere do I see where the branches of Christ's Church (churches in low-income, economically depressed, and educationally disadvantaged areas where family brokenness is more common) are missing both the gifts of the Lord and the potential to thrive with those gifts.

While nothing happens overnight, why can't our urban ministries have excellent music ministries? Why can't we use creative worship approaches like dance and drama? Why can't our urban churches be dynamic in our outreach to people who don't know the Savior? Why can't we be among the leading financial givers to God's Work, percentage-wise, based on our income? Why not?

In short, and just a reminder—in the inner-city ministry where you find yourself, while PATIENTLY LOVING people, BE THE VOICE that PUSHES people to be all that the Lord has called them to be! PUSH for the ministry you serve not to be satisfied with just a *handful of new people* gained to the ministry each year. Not when *the community is full of people* who still don't know Jesus. Don't prepare worship services or Bible lessons that you know will easily just "get by." Be thoughtful and be creative. *WRESTLE and STRIVE* at every ministry opportunity to give your best! Encourage your people who work with you in the ministry to do the same!

4. Encouraging people is huge. Do lots of it! The book of Proverbs is an encyclopedia reminding us of the power of our words in the lives of others. Here are three of my favorite proverbs:

Proverbs 12:25, "Anxiety in a man's heart weighs it down, But a good word makes it glad." True!

Proverbs 18:21, "Death and life are in the power of the tongue, And those who love it will eat its fruit." True!

Proverbs 15:4, "A soothing tongue is a tree of life, But perversion in it crushes the spirit." True!

This lesson is especially for me. Life beats people down plenty. Even when they are apparently flying high and acting as if they don't need God, the Bible is totally "100"—their fall is right around the corner. (Proverbs 16:18) One of the most important jobs I have as a ministry leader and one that I don't do enough of is ENCOURAGING PEOPLE! I can do it in notes, in kind words, and through a text, a phone call, or an email. Sometimes my encouragement is thanking them, telling them they did a good job, checking on them, praying for them, cheering them on to not give up, pointing them to the Lord. Sometimes my encouragement is warning them, holding up a mirror to them about some dangerous things in their life. Much of my encouragement needs to be just letting them know that God loves them and I love them! It's easy to forget to do that. Sometimes I get so focused on what people are NOT that I overlook encouraging them about everything they ARE doing that pleases the Lord Jesus! Make it your daily practice to cheer people on in Christ!

Think on these things as you build strong relationships with the people of your ministry.

64

WHAT YOU CAN CONTROL vs. WHAT YOU CAN'T

I believe in the work of God the Holy Spirit, TOTALLY! I have seen Him do amazing, miraculous things in the lives of people that I could never be responsible for doing. In worship, meetings, and during visits with people, I have experienced the power of the Holy Spirit working in me in extraordinary ways for the glory of the Father and the salvation of people—ways that are completely out of my control! And yet, I do not believe God has called us to do ministry without preparation or without doing all that is in our power to forward His Kingdom. There are many aspects of ministry we CANNOT CONTROL. But there are also plenty of parts of ministry WITHIN OUR CONTROL. Success in ministry is OUT OF MY CONTROL. However, faithfulness to serve the Lord to the best of my ability is AN INTENTIONAL DECISION that the Holy Spirit has enabled me to have some control over.

With that in mind, this essay is a plea for us to treat our ministry to people with great care, respect, and responsible preparation. Here's what I mean:

In worship, it may be tempting to think on a carnal side, "I've led hundreds of worship services. I've preached hundreds of times. I'm just going to 'wing it' and go into worship unprepared." It's tempting to try to spiritualize that lazy behavior by saying, "I'm going to let the Holy Spirit have His way." DON'T DO IT. The Holy Spirit BLESSES PREPARATION! Remember what Paul told Timothy, "Be diligent to present yourself approved to God as a workman who does not need to be ashamed, accurately handling the word of truth." (2 Timothy 2:15) You can control the time you put into preparing a thoughtful Biblical message. Out of your control are the potent movements of the Holy Spirit within you, and outside of you, as He uses your preparation to touch God's people in precisely the places where they need to be encouraged!

Also within our control is preparing a plan and ordering how the worship service will take place. Out of our control is how the Holy Spirit sometimes changes that plan and order to His good pleasure! Within our control is preparing the place of worship with Bibles, water for baptism, bread and wine for communion, a comfortable temperature, prayer, and ushering/greeting staff as people enter the worship. Out of our control is how the Holy Spirit draws people close to Christ in this place. Within our control is having done our best to prepare music for worship to the best of our ability prior to Sunday morning. Out of our control is how the Holy Spirit touches souls with the music we have spent time preparing.

The same is true for **training leaders.** We can control teaching new leaders how to lead in a particular ministry. We can control taking time to help them learn how to prepare to teach a lesson or to lead a meeting. We can control checking in with leaders of a Bible study or ministry to see how their group is going. We can be a resource to them and give them encouragement in the ministry work they're doing. This is the opposite of a totally hands-off approach of throwing "bodies" into leadership positions, just hoping that God blesses and everything turns out alright.

You've got the idea. Let me challenge you to think about even more ministry areas:

It is in our control to be **good stewards of the property** the Lord has given to our ministries. We can control giving our best to make sure it is clean and in good repair.

It is in our control to **make follow up calls** with visitors from our Sunday worship and other events. It is in our control to **reach new people and invite them to ministries** at our church. It is in our control to **dedicate time in our schedule** every week to simply reach out to new people with the Good News of Jesus. Can't each of us make a combination of at least seven or eight weekly visits, phone calls, or texts to people who are living apart from Christ? Of course, we can! Out of our control are the results of those calls. The Holy Spirit is the one who brings them to know the Savior and begin in a consistent church home.

It is in our control to have **operating structures for the programs** at our church. We can control having policies for those who lead in these programs. We can control having an operating structure that addresses conflict, injuries, issues, and problems in our programs. We can't control how our leaders conduct themselves in every situation, but we can control the equipping of our leaders with leadership training.

It is in our control to be **financially responsible** and have a budget that outlines the type and amount of ministry we can do. Out of our control is when the Holy Spirit sends unplanned funds to lead us in new additional directions and take ministry steps in faith for the sake of God's Kingdom.

Are there parts of your ministry where you haven't been doing all the preparation you could do, and then are you putting your lack of preparation on the Holy Spirit to "make things work"?

65

BE CAREFUL WHEN YOU WORK IN THE MUD

I was looking at some lists of the most dangerous jobs in the world. High on most lists was loggers who often die in accidents as they harvest lumber. I never thought of that one. There were also some jobs that I totally expected to see on the dangerous jobs list, including stunt people who do amazing stunts in movies, commercial fishermen, and hazardous material workers. Yes, all of those make sense. But curiously missing from this list were pastors or ministry workers.

Stop laughing! If you're a pastor or ministry worker, the calling the Lord has led you into **IS** a dangerous job (even if most people wouldn't recognize it that way)! How so? Well, it's not because some of us ministry leaders work in the dangerous inner-city. Sure, the city has some unique physical dangers associated with it. But this isn't really an inner-city church essay. It's an essay for ministry everywhere. The danger is in THE MUD where we work. Where do those in ministry work? Much of our work is with HURTING people, CONFUSED people, and CAPTURED people.

Let's break those down. HURTING PEOPLE are people who say and do violent and abusive things, even as they are hurting inside. Sometimes hurting people will use sinful stuff to self-medicate themselves and trade long term healthiness for a moment of intense pleasure or relief through an addictive behavior. CONFUSED PEOPLE are like HURTING PEOPLE. They are confused and think they can control the situations and directions of their lives. The Lord really isn't needed. Confused people look for love, belonging, and identity in all the wrong places. CAPTURED PEOPLE, like HURTING and CONFUSED people, get into dangerous and sinful things that they think they can "play" with or manage. But very quickly those sinful, dangerous things CAPTURE them, and they can't get themselves out of that thinking or those behaviors. What's even worse is that sometimes we can be CAPTURED by something sinful and destructive and not realize that it has CAPTURED us! This is the work environment where we spend most of our time. Think about it, the people who believe they have their lives all together (in truth, nobody really does, see Romans 3:10–12) don't usually spend a lot of time with us. The people we typically spend much time with are stuck in THE MUD, and they know they are stuck. Check out the whole scene in Mark 2:14–17 when Jesus called Levi/Matthew to be one of His disciples. The Scribes and Pharisees were so confused about the kind of people Jesus should be close to. Jesus gave great clarity when He said in verse 17, "It is not those who are healthy who need a physician, but those who are sick; I did not come to call the righteous, but sinners." We know what Jesus was saying—EVERYBODY is sick with sin and in need of the Savior. The problem is that some people, in their self-pride, don't realize they're sick with sin and need God's mercy. Like Jesus, so also for us who are His servants—we spend much of our time in THE MUD of hurting people, confused people, and captured people.

That truth leads me to the warning of this essay. The reminder can't be said any better than God Himself says it through the Apostle Paul in Galatians 6:1, "Brethren, even if anyone is caught in any trespass, you who are spiritual should restore such a one in a spirit of gentleness; each one looking to yourself, so that you too will not be tempted." We are called to WORK IN THE MUD. We are called to POINT PEOPLE TO THE ONE WHO CAN RESCUE THEM OUT OF THE MUD. Notice the phrase, "you who are spiritual..." It doesn't say, "you, who are perfect," or "you, who are sin-free yourselves." No, we are dependent on the same Savior as those in THE MUD at this moment.

I love the reminder this Scripture gives us—when you're WORKING in the mud, be careful; it is easy for THE MUD to ALSO GET ON YOU. That's not a reason to avoid working in THE MUD. That's a call to watchfulness! In truth, this entire world is full of THE MUD of sin. The same deceiver who lured the person we're trying to help into THE MUD will also try to tempt us while we are in the same MUD. I've been there. My guess is that if you are "totally 100" with yourself, you'll admit to having been there, too. WE have been in THE MUD ourselves. We've been tempted to STAY in THE MUD of sin.

Now the important part... How do we keep from getting STUCK in the MUD when we are WORKING in the MUD ourselves?

1. **Be AWARE of THE MUD.** First Thessalonians 5:4–11 is such a clear reminder of the difference between light and darkness. We have so much MUD around us; sometimes it is tempting just to merge into it.

2. **Have ACCOUNTABILITY people and markers all around you.** I love the words of 1 Thessalonians 5:11. After the Scripture reminds us of the importance of being watchful as we live in this sinful world,

Paul says to the Thessalonians, "Therefore encourage one another and build each other up..." I have people who do that in my life, and you need the same in yours. We need people to whom we can be accountable and "real" with, as we work in THE MUD of sin.

3. **IMMERSE YOURSELF in GOD'S WORD.** Daily time in God's Word is the strength and sword to deal with the dangers of a spiritual fight. Check out Ephesians 6:11–12, 17.

4. **DEPEND on GOD'S POWER to stay pure, not your own will power.** How meaningful are the words of the Apostle Paul in 1 Timothy 1:12–16. As you read them, pay special attention to the following: a) Verse 16, it was only because of God's mercy that Paul could be forgiven of his failures and be qualified to serve; b) Verse 13, what I WAS is not what I AM, because of Christ; c) Verse 12, Christ strengthened me and put me into ministry... it's all only because of Him!

5. **WHEN YOU FALL and get MUD on yourself (and we all do—we are sinful people needing the Savior), confess your sins, receive God's forgiveness, and live forward out of the MUD to keep serving Him!**

6. **DISCIPLINE YOURSELF FOR GODLINESS.** First Timothy 4:7–8 is a very important Scripture to keep in the forefront of our minds and hearts because we work so much in THE MUD. Thinking about the opposite of this verse helps me especially understand its message. The opposite of disciplining myself for godliness is to live by what I feel. Here is some truth: Many things in THE MUD will MAKE ME FEEL GOOD, but they are NOT GOOD FOR ME and are NOT PLEASING to my Lord. I need to resist and avoid them in the power of the Lord. I can't even "play" with them. They can too easily have much power over me.

7. **Be smart enough to recognize that when people are STUCK IN**

SOME KINDS OF MUD, it will TAKE SOMEONE ELSE to rescue them out of THAT MUD because of the tempting power THAT MUD has over you. Pass the ministry football to somebody else. Christ is the one who saves everybody, not me or you.

Working in THE MUD is a dangerous job. But remember the Lord Jesus, who keeps bringing you and me out of THE MUD ourselves. For us, for those we minister to, and for all of us who GET MUDDY—"The blood of Jesus, God's Son, cleanses us from all sin." (1 John 1:7) Amen! Thank you, Loving Lord!

66

A RIDDLE ABOUT RAISING KIDS & URBAN MINISTRY

How is RAISING CHILDREN like leading an URBAN MINSTRY? Give up? They both need consistency to thrive. One of the great things my wife did as we raised our children is that she was strong about being consistent with our children. Kids need schedules. They need to know what happens when—what time we get up to get ready for school or church, what time to eat, what time is nap time, homework time, bedtime, etc. Kids need consistency also in what they are expected to do, including doing chores around the house. For years, my wife used a weekly schedule board in our kitchen where she wrote everybody's activities so that everybody in the house knew where everybody else would be throughout the week. The board is actually still there in the kitchen, even though our children have grown up and left our home. I guess its purpose now is to keep me in line!

For about 25 out of the first 30 years we lived in St. Louis, we also had people living at our house who were not born into our family. For each of these additional members of our family beyond our four children, my wife wrote a document posted, "How We Roll at Chez Schmidtke." That document basically gave the "do's and don'ts" of living at our house—another example of trying to bring consistency to our home. As a teacher, Sharon will tell you one of the things that really messes up kids today is the lack of consistency in their lives!

The same is true for people who live in inner-city communities.

INCONSISTENCY and CHANGE ARE ALL OVER OUR URBAN NEIGHBORHOODS. If you drive through most urban neighborhoods over time, inconsistency and change are easy to see. And this change is not usually a change for the better.

The building that used to stand on the corner where your friend once lived was first abandoned, and then it was boarded up. After it was broken into several times and all kinds of unsavory criminal activities were going on inside, it started to collapse. Very likely, it was also set on fire a few times. Finally, the building was torn down. Now, all that remains on that site is a vacant lot. The people who used to be there are gone. The home that was there is gone. Any hope of something new happening in that place is also basically gone. The vacant lot feels like a grave. Do you follow me? Nothing stays the same.

Another matter that plagues our urban neighborhoods are the **CYCLICAL VOICES that come into our communities promising BIG CHANGES.** Sometimes these voices are politicians, preachers, community developers, or people who claim God gave them a "vision." They promise new housing, new jobs, the elimination of crime, and programs for our children. Church groups are famous for making these kind of promises. But sadly, in many cases, that ministry or community organization runs out of money four or five years later, its visionary leaders run out of energy because the work is so hard, or the organization finds a new location in greener pastures where the ministry work isn't as tough.

The BIGGEST HOLE of inconsistency in our urban neighborhoods is that **the places where people have traditionally looked for balance and identity in their lives either aren't offering any consistent help, or they**

are on steep declines. I'm talking about places like **FAMILIES,** where you used to be able to find guidance, protection, love, and teamwork. Not today. Many family homes are just places where parents and children sleep after having been out doing their own thing for the entire day (sometimes not even knowing where each other was!). Our communities today don't have **STRONG EDUCATIONAL INSTITUTIONS.** Most young people don't see schools as a place to learn but rather as a required day-care facility where, in order to survive, they need to learn how to fight to avoid getting beat up. In so many of our inner-city communities, there is an **ABSENCE OF SAFE PLACES** for young people to go, rather than hanging out in the streets. **MANY CHURCHES** are mainly open just on Sunday mornings, even though their community cries for them to be a gathering place also Monday through Saturday.

This **COMMUNITY INCONSISTENCY TRIGGERS DISTRUST.** When there aren't consistent places where people know they can find help and love, they begin to feel as if they can't trust anybody. They feel as if it's THEM against the world. They become even more guarded and self-focused. They become suspicious of anyone who tries to come close to them. They become desperate and will even resort to breaking the law in order to take care of themselves. They often give up all hope.

WE AS GOD'S PEOPLE, THE CHURCH, HAVE THE OPPORTUNITY TO BE A DIFFERENT VOICE!

As the children of God, we are to reflect our Father. What did Joshua say to Israel before ending his career as their leader? I love what he said in Joshua 23:14, "...not one word of all the good words which the Lord your God spoke concerning you has failed; all have been fulfilled for you, not one of them has failed." Translation: our God is the very definition of CONSISTENCY—promising something and then fulfilling the promise! That's the consistency found in the coming of Jesus. He was forecast to be born in Bethlehem, and HE WAS. He was forecast to be born of a virgin, and HE WAS. He was called IMMANUEL, God come to be with us, and He WAS and IS! He was forecast to be "wounded for our transgressions and bruised for our iniquities," (Isaiah 53:5) and it came true when Jesus gave His life on the cross for all sin! **Our GOD is the GOD OF CONSISTENCY!**

So now, His children—His onsite AMBASSADORS (2 Corinthians 5:20)—**NEED TO RELFECT HIM. We do this by:**

- **Making promises that can be kept.** Be careful about what we promise to people in our communities. Don't make promises about building a new recreation center until you have the financing in hand. Don't promise a new afterschool program for youth until you have secured the funding and identified the staff. It ruins our credibility as God's people when we make promises that are beyond our capacity to keep. Yes, yes, I hear some of you thinking as you read this, "God is able! He can do anything!" We're not talking about not having faith here. We're talking about this: Why make public announcements until you have seen the Lord open doors that pertain to those announcements? That way, when you make those promises public, God has enabled them to be KEPT.

- **Keeping promises we make.** If you're not intending to keep the promise, don't make it. Stronger than all the rhetorical bravado some leaders and clergy in our urban communities are famous for, is simply making a promise and KEEPING IT. Let the PROMISE KEPT be the fanfare. Keeping your word sets you up with credibility for the future. The second year I was at Bethlehem in 1990, I told our new youth Gospel Choir that I was planning on taking the choir on the road in the summertime for a youth mission trip to Panama City Beach, Florida. Because so many people in the community had heard crazy, empty promises like that before, a few of our youth didn't save their money for the trip. They simply believed it was a lot of talk. But the day we pulled out of the parking lot in the old grey Bethlehem 15-passenger van and headed for Florida, they knew it wasn't talk! (Thankfully, some last-minute angels jumped in with financial assistance enabling those doubtful kids to go.) After that first trip, the word got out about what happens if Bethlehem says they are going to do something in ministry.

- **Being a long term ministry that can be trusted.** Consistency is shown in a track record. A track record is shown over time. When people see the consistent service of a ministry with a track record over time, that is a ministry they will trust. Such trust that grows from consistency can't be cooked on a microwave time schedule. Yet, when a ministry is consistent and people trust it, approval increases dramatically and its impact on people deepens.

- **Living lives of spiritual consistency ourselves.** This is an easy point to make. No leader is perfect. Every one of us lives only by the grace of God. However, if people don't see consistency in us as leaders, they are less likely to buy into it themselves. Two of the "mothers" of our church set this truth before us every Sunday. Rare are the times when you don't find Marge Hoffman and Erma Spivey at Bethlehem Lutheran Church on a Sunday morning at least one hour before worship. It's true they come to prepare the altar for worship. It's true that Marge has her Sunday pick-up ministry for a few people who ride with her to church. But much stronger than those acts of service is their example of spiritual consistency for all of us. They remind me of the consistency of Jesus that Luke 4:16 talks about, "…and as was His custom, Jesus entered the synagogue on the Sabbath, and stood up to read." If you were looking for Jesus on "church day," you would find Him in the synagogue, the Jewish church. If you look for Marge or Erma on church day, you'll find them at Bethlehem… not because they have to be there, but because they choose to be there. They've impacted me. I want to do the same. For me, there is no church family like our Bethlehem church family. I make being at my church home with my church family on church day a priority. Many others in our tight-knit Bethlehem family choose to do the same.

- **Resisting cancelling ministry.** This is a practical tag I added to this essay. I say it only because I think it is vitally important to recognize. Do your best not to cancel ministry that has been scheduled. For example, try to avoid cancelling Sunday morning worship, except for extreme weather. Avoid cancelling ministry events during the week. If you're leading a ministry event and must be away, it is better to find a replacement leader than to cancel the event. It is a matter of CONSISTENCY. It is my experience that when you cancel a ministry event, you suffer for your cancellation both the week that you cancel and also two or three weeks after that. If we cancel our sign fellowship deaf ministry one week, for example, the next week people still wonder whether the event is going on, even though you told people it is! Furthermore, in the future when the weather is even just a bit questionable, the fact that you cancelled once before because of weather makes people wonder if you will cancel again. By the same token, there are times when bad weather simply makes it dangerous for people to be on the road to come to church for a ministry event. When the authorities issue a plea for all residents to please stay off the road because of a serious weather threat, are we respecting the authorities God has placed over us by ignoring that encouragement?

  Do your best to avoid cancelling ministry events. It wounds your consistency. When your consistency is wounded, the trust people have in you is also wounded.

In a world of increasing inconsistency and fewer people/ organizations that people can trust, what a difference the Christian Church can make in people's lives as we model a life of consistency in Christ and point people to the Lord, whose record of consistency in keeping His promises to us is flawless!

67

KEEP TRYING FOR THE WIN!

One of the greatest Christian men in the entire Scripture is the Apostle Paul. However, on one particular day, there was a Christian man greater and more Christlike than Paul. That man's name was Barnabas. Check out the situation in Acts 15:36–41. Here are the highlights. Paul says to Barnabas, "Let's go check on the brothers in some of the places where we started ministries." This is sometimes called the Second Missionary Journey in the book of Acts. As Paul and Barnabas were planning a team to take with them, verse 37 says that Barnabas suggested John Mark should go with them. This was a problem for Paul. Acts 13:13 records what happened on Paul's First Missionary Journey when John Mark deserted Paul and his team on their way to Perga and instead went back to Jerusalem. Now in Acts 15:38, Paul basically says, "Uh uh. Nope. John Mark is a deserter. We can't trust him. He's not going along on my team!" Verse 39 reveals that this was an intense disagreement between Paul and Barnabas. Barnabas wanted John Mark on the team. Paul didn't. What did Barnabas see in John Mark that Paul refused to see? While the Bible doesn't explicitly tell us, follow me in thinking through some interesting possibilities. Many scholars recognize that John Mark was a younger man. Maybe on the First Missionary Journey, John Mark got homesick or scared and just couldn't keep going with Paul. Here's the point. Does one failure or fall mark a person as inadequate from ever again being able to serve on the ministry team? Back to Acts 15. Look what happened. According to verse 39, Barnabas took John Mark with him and sailed to Cyprus. According to verse 40, Paul took a man named Silas as his partner and headed for the churches in Syria. In that moment, Paul had given up on John Mark. But Barnabas didn't give up on John Mark. Barnabas kept TRYING FOR THE WIN with him.

Throughout this series of essays I have continually emphasized the many advantages of staying in the same ministry long term. However, let me now confess one of the hard things about being in a ministry long term. I totally understand Paul's shoes in Acts 15, because I am ashamed to say I have "stood in them" more than once. There have been times... no, there still are times... when someone in our ministry has been inconsistent. They've been off and on with us for a few months, and then disappeared for a few months, and then back and then disappeared, and then returned again. I have played the part of Paul and said, "No, this person has deserted us so many times. They can't be trusted. Let's move on from them." I thank God for my colleague in ministry Rev. Gerard Bolling. Many times, he is my Barnabas, encouraging me to KEEP TRYING FOR THE WIN with that person with whom I've had it. My Barnabas cheers me on to not give up and TRY AGAIN! KEEP TRYING FOR THE WIN! KEEP TRYING FOR THE WIN means to keep trying to reconnect that person to the Lord Jesus in hopes that this time it will "take" and result in a solid faith relationship and a stronger life of following the Savior.

At the heart of all Barnabas work is the truth of how our Lord KEEPS ON TRYING FOR THE WIN with us! That is Jesus' M.O.! He did that with Matthew and Zacchaeus, the crooked tax collectors whom everybody else had given up on. Jesus saw BEYOND WHAT THEY WERE to see what they COULD BE. Wasn't that the same vision Jesus had for the woman caught in adultery in John 8:3–11? While all the church leaders wanted to stone her, Jesus saw her repentant heart and saw her for WHAT SHE COULD BECOME through His forgiveness! Jesus is definitely someone who KEEPS ON TRYING FOR THE WIN! I can't speak about you, but I certainly can speak about my own life. If Jesus wasn't patient and persistent with me, if He didn't KEEP TRYING FOR THE WIN in John Schmidtke's life, and helping me to be right with His Father through His gracious forgiveness, God would have had every right to give up on me long ago.

Incidentally, how did Barnabas' work with John Mark turn out? Look what Paul asks Timothy to do in 2 Timothy 4:11. Paul says, "Pick up Mark (John Mark) and bring him with you, for he is useful to me for service."

So the lesson is clear, as the Apostle John said, "Since God so loved us, we ought to love one another." (1 John 4:11) Of course, it is sometimes hard. Of course, it is sometimes precisely what I don't want to do. But I have no choice when the Lord, who hasn't stopped TRYING FOR THE WIN WITH ME, points to the people I want to give up on and says, "No, KEEP ON TRYING FOR THE WIN!"

68

URBAN

What does that word mean? It might be one of the most misunderstood words in our entire English vocabulary. I mean, I work at an **URBAN** church. If you didn't know me personally, or only met me through these essays, what would you think it meant that I was serving at an **URBAN** church? Would it mean we needed metal detectors to get into the church and a security force outside watching all the parishioners' automobiles during worship? Or would **URBAN** mean I lead a place like the St. Louis Cathedral or St. Patrick's Cathedral in New York? Those are urban churches, right? But **URBAN** in those cases doesn't mean poverty, poor, or "better wear a bullet proof vest" in order to go to Sunday worship. So what does the word, "**URBAN**" mean?

We could define URBAN as a high concentration of people in a place, closely living together and working together.

That would be URBAN, as opposed to neighbors who live adjacent to one another (about a half-mile to a mile), separated by their large farm properties. That's rural, not URBAN. We have other pictures of what URBAN is. **URBAN gardening** is often more "vertical," rather than "horizontal," because space in the city is limited. I remember taking my youngest son, Nat, to look at some colleges. When we visited Concordia University in St. Paul, Minnesota, (where he ended up attending), Nat made the comment, "Dad, this school looks so small, compared to some of the other schools."

I told Nat, "No, it's a good-sized school. It's just located on an **URBAN campus.**" Even though they are larger schools, many URBAN campuses aren't spatially very big. They're not spread out. Their space is concentrated.

You may have also heard of a major at some colleges called **URBAN Studies.** That's the study of how URBAN areas work—their systems, their architecture, and the unique ways that residents in urban areas obtain basic life services like fuel, food, and entertainment. **URBAN architecture** is a particular flavor of architecture. It may include brick houses, rather than wood frame, and houses that are more vertical than horizontal with smaller yards, etc.

Yet, the word, "URBAN" triggers a whole different kind of understanding to other people. When you say to a friend, "I live in an URBAN neighborhood," they might understand that you live in a place "where all the violence and drugs are." To some, URBAN means low economics, low educational level, high crime, a physically decayed landscape of crumbling buildings and empty lots, an AGED place. Take a moment to especially consider that last thought. In America we often think of old, aged URBAN buildings as a declining trend in a community (unless they have been remodeled or restored). However, every year people pay billions to travel to Europe to do what? To tour and look at old, aged buildings. People understand the word, "URBAN" in different ways.

When it comes to ministry, we in the church often understand URBAN in even more diverse ways.

Most of the time, in the church, "URBAN" is a synonym for the words, "MULTI-CULTURAL," or "INNER-CITY," or even "BLACK."

When people don't want to come out and say that Bethlehem is a church that is basically 90% African-American in its racial make-up, they'll say, Bethlehem is an URBAN church. Feels more politically correct, doesn't it? Saying that our Bethlehem Lutheran Church is an URBAN church feels softer than saying we're "inner-city" or "located in the hood," even though that's where we're located!

I'm writing this essay to help you be aware how varied people's understanding is regarding the word, "URBAN."

By the way, some ministries do everything they can not to be branded by people as an URBAN ministry.

It's true. Even in suburban communities where church neighborhoods have changed and become more lower-income and African-American, ministries often live in DENIAL about how their suburban community has become more similar to an inner-city community than a middle-class suburban community. Whether it's actually spoken aloud or just in their heart, they say, "Don't call us URBAN. We might be in a community with lower-income and lower-educational opportunities, a community that's also on the decline and riddled by crime, but don't call us URBAN— because our church is NOT OF THIS COMMUNITY." (They are a commuter church.)

Some URBAN churches don't want that label because the self-picture of their ministry is from years past—when their church's neighborhood had no minority residents, when their church population was huge and growing, and when the community around them was thriving. "Don't call us URBAN" is sort of their lingering, unrealistic passion to be an island of "the old days," uncontaminated by how life has changed around them. Yet the truth is that their community is different; their ministry is declining drastically because they haven't reached out to new people who have come into their community. Instead of having excitement and a passion to minister to these new people that the Lord has brought, they keep focused on what was, what was, what was. "Don't call us URBAN," they say, because they believe URBAN equals death or at least a church life as good as death because it will never be like it used to be.

Please also be aware there is a CULTURAL CONFUSION about "URBAN" for many people, especially among so many of our young people.

Here's the way some of young people think:

I want to dance to an URBAN BEAT.

I want to dress with an URBAN LOOK.

I want to date an URBAN BAD BOY or URBAN BAD GIRL.

I want to be able to sing or rap every word of URBAN SONGS.

I want to hoop with URBAN SWAG.

Sometimes, I want to play in the URBAN ILLEGAL SUBSTANCE GAME. (Why do we often hear of violence among young adults—living in suburban communities almost an hour away—who get in trouble when they come into our inner-city neighborhoods to partake of URBAN "forbidden fruit"? Aren't drugs available in the suburbs? Of course they are, but the call to the URBAN scene is so powerful.)

I want to carry myself with URBAN INTIMIDATION and look URBAN STRONG. (Uh huh... until you meet a "big dog" bigger and badder than you.)

Many young people, and even adults, want this label of URBAN, UNTIL the dangers and effects of the urban scene get too close to them, threaten them, and scare them. Then, they want to retreat to safe places.

You might be thinking, "John, these are good thoughts and true thoughts, but what's the point about the word, 'URBAN'?"

1. **When people use URBAN to describe a community or especially a ministry, LOOK BENEATH what they say and TRY TO DEFINE WHAT THEY MEAN. You'll need to have that awareness as you do ministry.**

2. **Whether URBAN means African-American, Hispanic, multi-cultural ministries, or ministry in a low-income and low-educated**

community, don't let anyone try to imply that your ministry in such an URBAN place is a CURSE! NO! Your ministry in an URBAN place is the EXCITING place where the Holy Spirit has put you to tell others about the Savior, Jesus, and where the Lord promises to be with you as you carry out this work!

By the way, recall Jesus' last words while on earth in Acts 1:8. Jesus said, "...you will receive power when the Holy Spirit has come upon you; and you shall be My witnesses both in Jerusalem, and in all Judea and Samaria, and even to the remotest part of the earth." What was Jerusalem? URBAN. What was Samaria where the disciples would cross cultures to share Christ? By the definition of some today, also URBAN!

69

SHARON'S YEARLY CALENDARS

For almost 15 years, part of the yearly Christmas preparation for my wife, Sharon, has included making photo calendars for our family. She puts together pictures of our family members doing goofy things, or photos from our travels or events like graduations and weddings in the past year. In my office, you can find a pile of these calendars she has made me. Why do I save old calendars? One reason. I love to look at the old pictures of my family on the old calendars. I love to go down memory lane and see how my kids were when they were young, as well as revisit the great times we had as a family in the past. Of course, I love seeing how my four kids are wonderful, Godly adults today. But being able to see "what was" and "what is," I just enjoy that.

When I look back at "what was" and then compare it to "what is," it also transports me to a place of immediate gratitude. As I said earlier, back in Lutheran grade school we had to learn Bible verses and hymn verses from memory (a good practice). Today, I treasure having all of those in my memory! There is an old hymn that captures exactly my feeling about "what was" and "what is." It goes this way: "O God our Help in ages past, Our Hope for years to come!" The Lord is the consistent person back then in the "what was" times of life, as well as today in the "what is" times. I know this thought is nothing new to you. But I want to give it to you as a reminder today.

In the ministry where you serve, take time to remember "what was," and then see the work of the Lord blessing you to the place of "what is." David said it this way in Psalm 103:2, "Bless the Lord, O my soul, and forget not all His benefits."

Going through pictures and looking through old church bulletins and old event programs jogs my memory to help me remember "what was." Remembering "what was" with "what is" speaks to me in a variety of ways:

- Certainly, it moves me to thankfulness to the Lord for the way He has taken care of me and my family.

- Sometimes it reminds me of people who have wandered away from our ministry that I should try and follow up on.

- Sometimes it pricks me and says to me, "Might be time to get back to some ministry priorities that we used to have."

- Reliving the memories of "what was" and "what is" in the lives of people around me (and seeing how they've grown and progressed in Jesus) encourages me in my present ministry with difficult people and hard situations that I might have been about to give up on.

- Thinking about how people and ministry areas developed over a period of time reminds me also to have patience and realize that many changes take time.

- Remembering "what was" with "what is" gives me perspective that my ministry time in a place is just a chapter in a bigger story the Lord keeps telling. It's His work, not mine.

Each of us needs time to zoom out of our present and see the bigger picture of how the Lord guides our lives!

70

HELP FROM ABOVE

On November 1, 1911, Giulio Gavotti, a pilot in the Italian air force, launched the first air bombardment. In doing so, he changed how wars would be fought forever. Simply put, introducing air strikes meant war between countries would no longer be mainly a horizontal battle. From then on, help in fighting a battle could also come "from above." I think you know where I am going.

In most of these writings, I've sought to give you encouragement and strategies for doing ministry and confronting hard situations in ministry. I hope you've found some of these thoughts useful.

Yet, the help we need to win never comes from WITHIN us, but FROM OUTSIDE of us.

How wise was the Psalm writer in Psalm 121 when he captured that very same thought in these words, "I will lift up my eyes to the mountains; From where shall my help come? My help comes from the Lord, Who made heaven and earth." Let me repeat this vital truth again—help and strength for us to do anything profitable and Godly in this life comes from OUTSIDE OF US, NOT FROM WITHIN US. Admittedly, sometimes... no, many times... when I am deeply engaged in the personal battle to live a holy life pleasing to the Lord—or when I'm working with a hard ministry situation that is way beyond me—I get so focused on what I'm doing "horizontally," I forget to call in "help from above." That is the real way to WIN any battle!

If you're like me, trying to handle stuff yourself and failing, don't beat yourself up. You and I are also in the company of Jesus' own disciples. They too needed Jesus to remind them, "In whatever you're facing, look to Me!"

Mark 9:14–29 tells the story of a son who was demon-possessed with a deaf and mute spirit. His father brought him to the disciples, but they couldn't cast the demon out of him (even though Jesus had given the disciples that authority, as they called out to the Father). After Jesus helps the father and son in this story, the disciples ask Jesus why they couldn't cast out the evil spirit. Jesus answers them by reminding them that this spirit cannot come out "by anything but prayer." (Mark 9:29).

The irony is this—any evil spirit can only come out by a power outside of us humans!

As I read it, the disciples had started to believe their own press. They thought they didn't need to fully rely on the Father to cast out spirits every time they were ministering the Gospel. Been there, done that. How about you?

I can't tell you how many times I was dealing with someone in the ministry who was stubborn, didn't want to forgive, didn't want to change, didn't want to work with others, etc. I had used all my best spiritual reasoning and Bible verses to try and get them to turn around, but I was unsuccessful.

Yet, when I baked the situation in prayer, praying for the Lord's will and putting this person totally into God's hands, over time (remember, change rarely comes quickly) I saw movement toward the place where the Father wanted this situation to go.

Also, the right prayer isn't always, "Lord, change them." Sometimes, the right prayer is to begin by adding, "Lord, if there is something in me that isn't right about this situation, change me."

Likewise, HELP FROM ABOVE is vital to call for when facing a situation of incredible need. Small ministries in urban areas live constantly by faith. Rare is an urban mission that has money just laying around. Never forget who controls it all. "'The silver is Mine and the gold is Mine,' declares the Lord of hosts." (Haggai 2:8) It brings me to tears when I open an envelope and find an unexpected, overwhelming check for the ministry. It's not that I'm all about money. No, it's that funding ministry is one area of life that is *completely* out of my control. I personally don't have the ability to write a $10,000 check when I see a big ministry need. I don't have anyone in our immediate Bethlehem Church family I can call up and ask for $10–20,000 to make something happen in our ministry. So when these amazing financial blessings come, it can totally and ONLY be the Lord. It can only be HELP FROM ABOVE when the Holy Spirit moves someone of significant means to obey God's prompting and give in abundant ways.

HELP FROM ABOVE—we can't predict it, we can't prescribe it, we can't force it, but because of the promise of God, as in Philippians 4:19, we can be totally confident in it!

71

TELL THE TRUTH MOMENTS

Scenario One

A staff member of yours used to be terrific. They used to work hard in the area of the ministry where they serve. They were all over it! But recently, they've not been putting in the hours they should. They've been taking shortcuts. They've not been getting the results they should. They haven't been seeking your help with new strategies to try and get things back on track.

Scenario Two

Someone in your church family has been wandering away from regular church family life. They've become inconsistent in worship. They've stopped working in the ministry area where they had done so well. It could also be that the same inconsistency at church has been showing up in their home life. When you've talked to them in passing, they have a Ph.D. in excuse-making. Others in the church family have asked about them. Honestly, you've been covering for them, but now it has come to a place where everybody knows the truth, and something needs to be done.

Scenario Three

A leader in your ministry is out of control. They have stopped attending regular Bible study, where they could hear from the Lord and bow before His Word. Now they have started to spew poison and falsehoods among the people of God at your church. Some less mature Christians in your church family believe what's said. Unrest is growing. It's serious. This well-known church family member has departed from God's Word to follow their own agenda and is trying to pull faithful sheep into their same destructive direction.

Scenario Four

You've been slacking as a leader. You're not preparing to teach/preach like you should. You're accepting mediocrity in the way you've recently carried out your ministry. It's as if your passion is gone, and your heart just isn't in it. Here's the tricky part. You've been at this ministry for a while. Nobody will confront you. But will you heed your own "look" in the mirror? Even when nobody might confront us, the Holy Spirit confronts us through God's Word. Take a look in the mirror of 2 Timothy 2:15. Are you "diligent" and giving "your best" to the ministry the Lord has called you to do? What will you do about what you see?

I hate confrontation. I hate it when I'm the one who needs to be confronted. I especially hate when I'm the one who needs to share a word of correction with somebody else who is doing something wrong. I hate holding people accountable for the jobs they are paid to do or for the voluntary promises that they made. I HATE IT! I would much rather look the other way and hope things get better.

Now, while sometimes being patient and taking more time with people is a good strategy, at other times avoiding telling the truth to someone about something that needs to be shared is just setting up something worse for the future. It is very painful to tell people hard things about themselves. Let me also add that, for my own mental health, I've found I can only have so many of these intense and hard confrontation moments at one time. Do you know what I mean? At any given time, we can only take so much anger, hate, and cruel words pushed back at us from the people to whom we've had to tell the truth.

So what do you do when you are the ministry leader? What do you do when you don't have an executive director or personnel manager you could simply pass this unpleasant task to? Do you just look the other way and ignore it? Do you massage the situation to obtain momentary relief from the pain without really fixing the matter? Or do you confront the situation, sit down, and talk with the person in truth? Of course, the last option is the correct answer. You must do it.

As you do this necessary and hard task, let me encourage you.

First, be sure to bring this to the Father in heaven. Ask the Lord to give you the opportunity to present the matter in a way that will be winsome for the recovery of the sheep who has strayed. Ask God to give you the right words and the right way to say them. Pray for the person's heart to be open to what you say to them.

Second, know that God will go with you; you won't be alone. That's the wonderful promise of our God who is IMMANUEL (God with us). He will be with you as you go into this truth moment.

Third, if you haven't already, get the counsel of a trusted Christian friend. Your friend may be able to help you see insights regarding your meeting with this person that you're not seeing.

Fourth, when you talk to the person, be prepared for the meeting with specific examples of the problem so that you can stay on point and try to avoid getting personal. Language that is full of generalities like, "You are always like this...," usually isn't helpful.

Fifth, keep God's grace always at the forefront of your mind and heart as you talk to this person. The goal is recovery, not trying to put them in their place, not to get your verbal payback in (even though they may have hurt you a lot), not to show them who is boss, not to use them to send a message to other employees and leaders, etc. I know of what I speak. I've wrongly done all those things when I had to confront someone in ministry. I was wrong. It was a bad approach. AND I still don't do it right every time. But here is one important lesson I have learned:

The same God on whose forgiveness, mercy, and grace I DEPEND on every day is the same patience, mercy, and forgiveness I need to show others!

Even when sometimes I don't want to.

Finally, some "real talk" when you are handling conflict in a small urban ministry. **Timing is everything.** Realize that you **can't always confront everything at the very moment it happens or even at the very moment that you'd like to confront it.** Often times, larger ministries have 10 people for every one job. For those of us in smaller ministries, we have 10 jobs for every one person. Here's something to take into consideration. If you think your confrontation may result in that person quitting your ministry, and right now you are not ready or able to replace them, you may have to delay this hard talk. It may not be the right moment to sacrifice the temporary loss in your ministry if you disconnect with that person.

However, if you have to delay the talk, begin immediately to work on raising up other people who could take on their work. Don't decide that the timing is not right and do nothing. Very likely, the problem is NOT going away. Remember, especially in small urban ministries (as well as other ministries and businesses), we are in constant process as we care for people and try to become stronger ministries. There is an ebb and flow regarding how we lead ministries to become stronger. It doesn't happen overnight.

Let me reveal to you what I have found to be the BEST way for "sick" sheep to become well again, as well as "selfish" sheep to learn how to better work with others—**SMALL GROUP BIBLE STUDY!** Small group Bible studies bring the Word of God to people. They are the vehicle for the Holy Spirit to work on hearts. They help people grow in their knowledge of the will of God. God, through His Word, often speaks to them about the destructive things they're doing. (I know that it works that way for me personally!) Bible study in a small group also engages other Christians in the life of the wandering sheep. God uses these other sheep to encourage, strengthen, love, and even turn the fallen sheep back in the Lord's direction.

TELL THE TRUTH with love and great wisdom. RECOVER THOSE WHO ARE WANDERING. The LORD WILL go WITH YOU!

72

ENABLE ME TO REST

"*Pastor, you look so tired. You need to get some rest. Just cancel kids Bible program tonight." "Just cancel choir tonight." "Just cancel the board meeting Saturday."*

Just cancel. Just cancel. Just cancel. Ugh! Of course, everybody needs rest. Everyone needs a break. However, why does A BREAK mean "CANCEL MINISTRY" for some people?

One of the things I sometimes miss about my two years serving in a large parish ministry with multiple staff is the ability to just leave, even leave quickly, because other paid staff members would step up to cover ministry that I wasn't there to cover. While today we have a number of paid and volunteer staff in our ministry at Bethlehem, for many years it was just me. I know where you are, those of you reading this who are Lone Rangers. Sometimes the frustration of being in a small inner-city parish, with basically no paid additional staff, is that it's so hard to take time off. In order to leave town for a few days, you must work twice as hard before you leave and make sure you have people and preparations in place for ministry to flow while you're out of town. Then you work twice as hard when you get back from your break, cleaning up the messes that occurred while you were out of town! It makes you wonder if you would be more rested by just staying home!

Truthfully, everybody does need to get away. Well, why not just CANCEL ministry? As I've said in another essay, the downside of cancelling ministry is that often the ministry "pays" for a cancellation for about two or three weeks afterward. After you cancelled last week, people aren't sure whether the Bible study, practice, youth event, etc. is back on for the coming week. Further, people are creatures of habit. Sometimes when they get out of their weekly habit, even for just a week, they find something else to do.

Back to the reality of a small inner-city parish. You don't have the *paid* staff of a bigger parish to pick up your work. In bigger parishes, the paid staff might not *want* to take on extra work, but there is a motivation that will move them to do it—their paycheck. (Plus, it's also motivating if a senior pastor or supervisor assigns the work!)

So what do you do?

For You, the Ministry Leader

Make it your priority to **always KEEP DEVELOPING PEOPLE** to do as much of your ministry work as possible. Sure, there are some things you do that they may not be equipped to do. But there are other tasks in your typical workweek that others could learn how to do. Make it your priority to spend a little of your time each week empowering others to do your work. Work yourself out of jobs. Don't worry, in the ministry of bringing Christ to people, you will never really be out of work. There will always be more people to reach with the Gospel and new ministry doors that will open! By empowering and equipping people for ministry, however, you both make it easier to take breaks and also make the ministry stronger!

For You, the Congregation

I am a ministry leader who keeps your perspective in mind when you volunteer and work at our church. I know that most of you, when you arrive to donate a few hours in a program, have already worked at least an eight-hour day at your job. I am so grateful for your service. You deeply love Jesus. May I ask you to consider something?

Think of ways you can create "I GOT THIS" nights for your pastor

or ministry leader. Of course, there are some things that he/she needs to take care of. Your pastor needs to be in the pulpit on Sundays. He's been trained for that. But, for example, on a night when your pastor normally picks up people for a ministry event, why not call in advance and say, "Get a break. I GOT THIS for you." When your pastor has served all weekend at the church's basketball tournament and the gym is a mess and it's Saturday night, why not recruit your entire family to stay and help clean up? Tell your pastor, "WE GOT THIS. You go home and spend time with your family." If you want him to rest, give him the opportunity.

Maybe your "I GOT THIS" service is simply going to your pastor and asking, "How can I help you get a break?" You've got the idea. Let's no longer just cancel ministry when the ministry leader is worn and needs a break! Let's do a better job of doing things together as we step up and support ministry leaders! Your ministry leader will be encouraged by your love!

73

A FEW WORDS ABOUT PREACHING

While preaching could be an entire volume in itself, no book about urban ministry (particularly in the African-American community) would be complete without discussing the central role of preaching in effective urban ministry. So many resources already exist regarding the "how to's" of effective, Biblical, Christ-centered preaching, but let me offer a few thoughts about the role of preaching as we bring Christ to people in the inner-city.

There is a great advantage to Christ-centered expositional preaching in an African-American inner-city context.

I am a strong advocate of Christ-centered, expositional preaching.

As I would define it, expositional preaching is taking a portion of the

Word of God and simply "exposing" it to the hearer.

As an expositional preacher, I do the study work of the text ahead of time to help transport my hearer to the place and moment in time of the Biblical text. I want the hearer to hear what those that day heard and to see what they saw. This takes thorough study in order to honor the explanation of God's Word with accuracy. The words of the text that I am exposing, and their meaning in the time when they were spoken, matters. The dialogue context and the cultural context when they were spoken matter. There is a real advantage when a preacher/teacher has the opportunity to go back to the original Hebrew and Greek texts of the Old and New Testaments in their study of Scripture. Many computer Bible programs today can aid in this kind of detailed study. Once a preacher understands what a text is saying, blessed is the preacher who can concisely express that central thought of the studied Scripture in a sentence.

The next task is doing an exposition of the current people and current context you will be preaching to. How does this message from the Scripture still ring true today? Rev. Arthur Schudde, one of my preaching mentors I mentioned in an earlier essay, taught me the value of using a simple, memorable outline of what the Holy Spirit is leading me to share about a particular Bible passage. It is a great didactic tool for revealing the will of God for a hearer's life. Sometimes preachers try to hide what they're saying throughout a message, so they don't give the whole point away until the end of the sermon. In today's world, I believe that is a bad idea.

With attention spans of hearers being shorter than ever, preachers need to lay out the message sooner rather than later.

Be clear. Be unequivocal. After all, we WANT our hearers to GET what we're saying!

But the preparation for preaching isn't finished yet... nowhere near finished. The following principle is especially true in the heritage of the African-American Christian church. While solid, Biblical meat is essential, **I need and want the tasty "gravy" of illustrations within a sermon to help me enjoy the nutritious meat of the Word of God as it applies to**

my daily life!

Not only do useful illustrations help me understand Biblical truth, they also give me a moment to pause and take a breath as I'm listening to a message.

Another vital truth I gained from Art Schudde and the saints at Christ Lutheran Church in Peoria, Illinois, is to say during the sermon, **"Bibles open, please!"** To all of my non-Lutheran readers, some of you might wonder, "Is that really necessary to say?" YES, especially for all of us in "Lutheran world." Sometimes, while we wave the "sola scriptura flag" at everybody, our own Bibles are absent or closed during our study of the Word of God in a sermon.

While I know many fine preachers who, after they have thoroughly studied the text, only form a sermon outline from which to preach, I am NOT one of them. I'm just not that gifted.

I still write out a sermon manuscript every time I preach. I have to. It helps me tighten my thoughts. It keeps me from rambling. It's what works for me.

I don't read my sermon. And sometimes my sermon delivery will bring different emphases in a message. The Holy Spirit always RULES. But I believe the Holy Spirit BLESSES PREPARATION. For me, that includes a manuscript. God bless those of you who can preach well without ever writing one.

Some years ago, at the end of worship while I was greeting people, a man came up to me and said, "I've been stealing your material."

I laughed and asked, "What do you mean?"

"Every Sunday I come here, I take notes on your sermon outline sheet in the bulletin," he said. "During the week, I then preach your message a few times."

He was expecting me to be mad at his sort of "smarty" admission. But my response was, "Great. Use whatever you hear. It's not my material anyway; it's the Lord's Word."

That's my goal every Sunday I step into the pulpit. I hope to be

so clear that someone can take the message I preach and preach it somewhere else. That's the way the message of God's Word magnifies!

Let me quickly add two vital components to that thought:

- This is why whatever we preach must be prepared with diligent scholarship to the best of our ability so that the Word of God we present may be *accurate to what the Bible has said.*

- My task is to accurately understand and prepare a message from God's Word to the best of my ability through thorough examination, prayer, and preparation. However, in the communication of the sermon, the *Holy Spirit is again in total control* to *change* what I say or *adjust* my words to the heart of any hearer.

So you have studied the text. You know what this Scripture is saying. You have an outline. You've written a manuscript. Are you finished? No way. You still have at least one-third more of the way to go. Practice your delivery of that message. Even though people shouldn't judge you this way, the people to whom you are preaching have likely seen and heard television preachers communicate at a very high level!

Advances in media today have raised the bar for all of us in oral communication. Don't ignore it. Don't complain about it. Get to work, and practice delivering your sermon!

In this essay I use the term, "Christ-centered, expositional preaching." Honestly, I just made up that term, although someone has probably said it somewhere before (nothing is new). I have a problem with how some people understand "pure" expositional preaching as preaching only the selected text. In other words, if the message of Christ, the Gospel, is not explicitly in the text—then the death and resurrection of Jesus for our sins isn't preached in that message. I have a single Biblical word for that: "ANATHEMA" (Galatians 1:8), which means, "May it never be!"

Every message needs to point to Christ!

He is the bringer of our salvation! The entire Bible points to Him and

His amazing love for us!

Only the Word of God can free people from spiritual funk and strongholds.

I know you know this. But it's a reminder we all constantly need. Pause from your reading and look in your Bible, Mark 5:1–5. Pay special attention to verses 4–5. Have you ever met someone like the man described? On the surface you might say, "Nope, never experienced anything like that." But think a little deeper. I meet many people in our ministry with strongholds on their life that are out of their control, just like the man Jesus met in Mark 5.

Look at the last phrase of verse 4, "No one was able to subdue him," let alone free him from the evil spirit. Of course, some people with addictive behavior are in this category. But just as powerfully chained by evil is a person who won't forgive, or an individual who is full of themselves and resists ever thinking of others. I'm thinking now of a young woman named "Lisa" who is "spiritually sick," but she thinks she's alright and handling her life. The truth is that she is subtly spiraling down. She's basically on a highway to nowhere in her life, and she doesn't realize it. Lisa is in church pretty regularly. But even when she's in God's House on a Sunday morning, her mind is clearly somewhere else. She is often frustrated that her life doesn't work out the way she wants. But the problem is so simple—she is caught up in herself. She won't let Christ lead her life. And the result is exactly what Jesus said in John 15:5, "He who abides in Me and I in him, he bears much fruit, for apart from Me you can do nothing." How is this a stronghold? Lisa knows better. But Lisa won't trust the Lord and do better by following Him. Friends and family have tried to get through to Lisa, but she has decided to be the captain of her life's journey. I know a lot of people like Lisa. It breaks my heart when they are blind to the strongholds the enemy keeps using to stagnate their life and disconnect them from a real relationship with Jesus.

We **constantly "soak in prayer"** loved ones like Lisa, asking the Father to spiritually awaken them, as well as to keep them from grave danger while they are still in their state of spiritual sleep.

Even stronger than praying to break strongholds is the "sword of the Spirit, which is the Word of God." (Ephesians 6:17)

How does this principle work? It's not some special laying on of hands that breaks strongholds. It's not the "wave" of a charismatic preacher that breaks strongholds. How are strongholds broken again and again in the Scripture? I love how clearly Jesus brings the demons out of the man and breaks the stronghold. Matthew 8:32 says, "And Jesus said to them, 'Go!' And they came out…" Let's be careful to notice what has happened. The command, "Go!" that Jesus uses is not some kind of stronghold-breaking password. The command, "Go!" is powerful because it comes from the Son of God, Jesus, who by His death and resurrection has broken all strongholds for those who trust in Him!

Prove it? Look no further than Colossians 3:13–15. Who has made us alive from the death of our sins, verse 13? JESUS. Who has canceled the debt for our sins to which we should be forever chained, verse 14? JESUS. Where did He do it, verse 14? THE CROSS. Not only did Jesus' death pay for our messed up past, what has Jesus' death done to disarm Satan's stronghold power over us in the present and in our future? See verse 15.

"Okay, okay," you say. "What does this have to do with preaching?" Your Sunday message is the place where stronghold-breaking begins, as you bring the Good News that "greater is Jesus who is in us, than the evil one who is in the world." (1 John 4:4) Your Sunday message is where you reach the most people at one time with this great news. Your Sunday message becomes the prelude to people being able to talk about this power in their lives in a small group Bible study setting. Here, they can open up about the reality of their stronghold and be encouraged by a group of Christ followers about the chain-breaking power of Jesus!

So our sermons need our best time and attention every week. Our sermons need to proclaim the power of Jesus to break strongholds and break every chain of sin in the death and resurrection of Christ—every time we enter the pulpit. Think about the capacity of the Gospel through a Sunday sermon. First, someone hears of freedom in Christ "in real time" from the preacher. Second, if your church is like our church, all the messages are also available on-demand on social media. People in strongholds are only a click away from the power of Christ, whenever their midnight hour of brokenness comes. Third, a multitude of people who are worshipping in the sanctuary when the sermon is preached become equipped with the stronghold-breaking Gospel of Jesus. They can now minister to others within personal, intimate meetings! Relevant, Christ-centered, expositional preaching is so vital in the ministry to people!

As I said before in an earlier essay, relevant, Biblical, Christ-centered preaching covers a multitude of young pastor sins.

Whoa! This is my ministry's life story. I came to Bethlehem at a young age. I've tried to do my best as a pastor, but I've made a lot of pastor mistakes over the years. Especially in my early years, how gracious and patient the people of Bethlehem were with me. Here is the truth of God's amazing faithfulness one of our elderly church matriarchs told me one day:

"Pastor, I don't care for all of the changes with all of these neighborhood kids here. But at my age, you give me a solid sermon every Sunday, and this is the church I want to be buried out of."

As we went through our church transition, we only lost two member families in those early years. So many people, both new and longtime members, judge a ministry by the Sunday sermon. I'm not saying that's right; I'm just saying that is the way it is. Giving your best pulpit ministry will buy you a lot of CHIPS with people, and they'll be patient with you about the new things you introduce that they don't care for. See the essay, "The Doctrine of Chips."

Learning how to preach is like learning how to play jazz music.

I learned so much from one man about music, but I learned even more from him about how to lead people. He was my college professor and a dear friend of mine, the late Fred Sturm. Fred was the Director of Jazz Studies at Lawrence University where I completed my undergraduate college education. For many years, he was also the Director of Jazz Studies at the renowned Eastman School of Music in Rochester, New York.

While educating so many young men and women in the genre of jazz music, of course Fred encouraged us to learn our scales, as well as the music theory of chord structures and chord progressions. But then he would point to the most important work involved in growing as a jazz musician—LISTEN, LISTEN, LISTEN. That is, listen to jazz music. Listen to recordings of the masters like Charlie Parker, Miles Davis, and Duke Ellington. I mean listen for hours. Listen by going to concerts and seeing live jazz musicians. See how they handle a song. Notice the way they phrase it, the way they improvise around the main melody. Is this just copying somebody else? No. When we listen to a bunch of people, we pick up a little something from everybody. However, in the end, who we are always comes forth when we play jazz music.

By the way, have you already recognized that who you are is really a compilation of all the people in your life who have impacted you? None of us is original!

Learning how to preach is just like learning how to play jazz. Many years ago I was working with a seminary student on his first sermon. As we focused on the delivery of the sermon, the student commented, "Pastor Schmidtke, I don't think what you're teaching me is 'my style.'"

"So how many times have you preached so far?" I asked.

"This is my first time preaching ever," the student responded.

"Exactly," I said. "Right now, you have no style. I'm going to show you a style, but trust me, when the anxiety and pressure is on you as you preach, the REAL YOU will always come forth."

And it did! It's the same way for me. In my preaching, I am a compilation of a bunch of people. If you knew the handful of men who impacted my preaching, and you heard enough of my sermons, you could identify them in me at various times—even though it's "me" who comes through in the end.

Also, just like studying jazz music, I have a large collection of sermons in my home that have helped me grow. What is it I look for when I listen to a sermon? I look for how someone handles a particular text. I look for how people deliver messages. I look for illustrations other preachers use. If they tell a personal story, I can't tell that same story because I didn't experience it. Yet, if it's something more general... all preachers use some of the same illustrations. When I listen to sermons, I take note of fresh and creative approaches to preaching without getting gimmicky. There are so many free opportunities to listen to other great preachers today on the Internet. You can learn something from someone else, even if you don't theologically agree with everything they say. The timing also dictates when I listen to other preachers. Early in the week, while I am doing my exegetical work for my sermon and trying to understand the text, I will listen to other preachers. But later in the week, as I form my outline and write my manuscript, I stop listening to any other preachers. At that point, I don't want their impact on me for that particular Sunday.

Like learning how to play jazz music, LISTEN, LISTEN, LISTEN. While you're becoming a great communicator of the Gospel, LISTEN, LISTEN, LISTEN to other excellent preachers and speakers!

The Holy Spirit powerfully uses relevant, Christ-centered expositional preaching to abundantly benefit the entire ministry.

There is never enough time for all the work that needs to be done in leading an inner-city ministry. As I've said in other essays in this book, you have to choose wisely where you will invest your time. Here are some reasons why I believe my weekly sermon needs the top priority of my time:

1. Think about your sermon from a stewardship perspective. In most ministries, the Sunday sermon is where a person reaches the largest amount of people at one time.

2. Sadly, the majority of people who are members of any given church today do not attend a weekly Bible study. Thus, your sermon is your best opportunity to spiritually educate the people of your church.

3. Not only does the Holy Spirit use our Sunday sermons to educate people in the truth of the Lord, but also He gives strength, healing, and encouragement to each of us as God's Word is brought before us.

4. I have personally found the pulpit to be a great place to start introducing needed changes to a congregation. Never do it before you preach/teach it! When we lay out the case of God's Word regarding something our congregation isn't doing—or an area that needs to deepen—the matter becomes inarguable! Who can argue with the Lord in His Word?

5. Right or wrong, here is truth: The most common judgment people will make about your ministry results from what happens on Sunday morning. People will mostly judge your Sunday morning worship by how powerful the sermon is and how meaningful the music is. Make your preaching of God's Word the best it can be!

74

PREACHING "BEEFS"

As someone who is on the high side of his 50s, and has preached for about 35-plus years, I want to get some preaching "beefs" off my chest. If you think I'm starting to sound like a crusty curmudgeon, just turn the page and skip these. However, maybe one or two of them will be helpful for your preaching. I'll put them in the first person because they first certainly apply to me and maybe also to you.

A BEEF: Not every point I make needs to be repeated and illustrated. Some truths are crystal clear precisely by how the Word of God says them.

I must be careful not to fall into a rhythm, thinking I have to bring an interesting story or funny quip to every point in my sermon. Just wondering... wouldn't it be horrible if by my over-illustrating and overly "breaking it down," I unfortunately conditioned hearers to no longer be able to read the Bible on their own and get something out of it? How awful it would be if someone listening to my preaching felt they still needed an applicable story or a sermon alongside part of God's Word—otherwise they wouldn't understand it or would be bored by it. Yikes. I need to be careful of this.

A BEEF: Don't preach mainly looking for response from people.

In the African-American context of preaching, response from the congregation is common. Let me be totally honest. Response encourages and hypes the preacher as well. But I must be careful to not preach FOR the response, as if that is the aim. The aim is that the hearer understands the Word of God before us. Also, remember that terrain that is all mountains is no longer a mountain; it's a plain. Mountains must have valleys. Thunderous mountains of intense preaching include quieter, thoughtful valleys of preaching.

A BEEF: Loudness in preaching is not the only way to emphasize a point.

I preach in a loud voice. That can certainly emphasize a point. But don't forget there are other ways to emphasize something important. One way is to SLOW... YOUR... WORDS... DOWN... ON... THE... POINT you want to emphasize. Another important technique in preaching is SILENCE. Sometimes, Preacher, I need you to stop and let me think about what has been said before you go on.

A BEEF: Keep your preaching fresh. Don't use the same techniques and approaches. Don't be so predictable that we know what you're going to say before you say it every time.

Fresh preaching includes being familiar, but not predictable. I refuse to obey any longer a preacher's request when he says, "Look at your neighbor and say..." Or, "Now tell your other neighbor..." Too overused! When preachers do that, I just sit quietly during those moments of the sermon, wait for the next point, and then tune back in. I know it's an engagement communication technique speakers use with their audience. I get it. But can we become more creative? Do we have to use the same technique every time, even the same words of the same technique? Can't I simply get an occasional, "Repeat after me..." if they really want me to remember something? Of course, if preachers start overusing that mnemonic tool, I will soon refuse to participate in it either.

Preachers, please keep it fresh! Here's some grace—I will give it three sermons a year. I will follow you with the "Look at your neighbor..." bit three times. But after the third time, I am sitting silent in protest of a lack of freshness until you move to your next point.

75

THE COURAGE TO FOCUS ON JESUS

I regret having to write this essay, but the times in which we live and the place of urban ministry compels me to consider this word a "must hear" about life in the inner-city.

Lawrence grew up in your church as a child. Because his mama, Phyllis, went to church every Sunday and was deeply involved in your church, there was no discussion about whether Phyllis' children would join her in going to church every Sunday. That pattern lasted for about the first 16–17 years of Lawrence's life. But then, as he began to wander into some unproductive behaviors—hanging out, doing drugs, dabbling in some gang life (that his mama didn't know about)—Lawrence separated from both God and his family. He did finish high school and graduate. But college? No.

He held little jobs on and off at fast food places, cleaning companies, and some retail shops, but nothing that lasted and nothing that could be a solid career. Although he still had a room and some clothes at his mama's house, he stopped coming home most nights and started "shacking" at his girlfriend's house. You know what's coming next. Yep, she got pregnant with Lawrence's child. The baby was born. But the joy of the baby didn't make life better between the two of them; it only heightened the stress. They weren't ready to be parents and were constantly going at each other.

Lawrence started playing around with other women. His baby mama started playing around with other men. One night, things became very heated at the apartment. The new man with Lawrence's baby mama got into it with Lawrence. The very next night as Lawrence was leaving work, a grey sedan pulled up next to him. The dark tinted window came down, and a gun came out. Lawrence turned to run, but he had no chance. Two bullets in the back took Lawrence down to the ground, and he died in his own blood on the sidewalk.

This fictitious tragic story is all too common in the real life of the communities where urban leaders serve. While sad, we're not surprised by it. In fact, it has become so common that some tragedies like this don't even make it to the 10:00 p.m. newscast anymore.

There is one more matter before us in this story. Phyllis, Lawrence's mama, is one of your strongest members. You know she did her best with Lawrence to "train up a child in the way that he should go…" (Proverbs 22:6) In fact, just a couple of Sundays ago, Lawrence even came to church on Mother's Day. It was his first time at worship in a couple of years. He was at church, but he wasn't really at church. He was in and out of the sanctuary constantly, going outside to talk on his phone. The matter before us is that Phyllis must bury her son. She has asked you if you could take care of the funeral for her.

Of course, you will help. But here's what I feel so compelled to encourage you to think about as an urban ministry leader—at the funeral, what will you say? Please recognize that this funeral moment has even bigger implications for your ministry. At most bigger funerals, the crowds I address far outnumber the people gathered on Sunday for worship at Bethlehem. Don't misunderstand. I'm not saying you should ever look on your funeral message as sort of a commercial for people to come to your church. NO! Yet, it is a significant moment in our African-American community for you and your ministry. So how will you handle it? Be careful.

Will you TRY TO "PREACH LAWRENCE INTO HEAVEN"?

I've heard this one so many times. The preacher at the funeral spends all his time trying to paint the deceased as an angel, but everyone knows he definitely wasn't. Be careful of that. If you spend your time talking about the deceased in ways that everyone present knows aren't true, what has happened to the credibility of your words for this gathering? Even worse, if the preacher hasn't told the truth about the deceased, can people really trust his words as he speaks about the Lord?

Another approach is when the preacher tries to soften the destructive life of the deceased with excuses. The deceased was "confused." The deceased "didn't have a dad around to guide him." The deceased got "caught up with the wrong crowd." Those things may all be true. However, remember the words of Jesus in Matthew 7:13–14, "Enter through the narrow gate; for the gate is wide and the way is broad that leads to destruction, and there are many who enter through it. For the gate is small and the way is narrow that leads to life, and there are a few that find it." Does it sound like Jesus is confused in how He sees the path to life? Furthermore, Jesus has not stuttered about the particular way that leads to life forever with Him. He said in John 3:36, "He who believes in the Son has eternal life; but he who does not obey the Son will not see life, but the wrath of God abides on him."

In trying to "preach someone into heaven," next comes the misrepresentation of the Lord God. "Well, you know the Lord loves everyone! Can I get an 'Amen'?" Or "I'm told that in Lawrence' last breaths, the deceased confessed Christ." Did he really do that, or is this rather what some in the family want everyone to believe? Don't misunderstand me. If I wasn't there to know what the deceased said or didn't say, I cannot speak with confidence as the preacher. By the way, because our God is a God of love, is it accurate to say that He "waves everybody through" the gates of heaven—no matter what they believe or don't believe? No, the wonderful promise of comfort from Romans 10:9, is "...if you confess with your mouth Jesus as Lord, and believe in your heart that God raised Him from the dead, you will be saved."

Here's the point—be careful of focusing on talking about a person you may not have known. Besides, even if you knew the person, the funeral worship is not the time to air their dirty laundry. Even more, the funeral isn't the time to open up a debate in people's hearts about whether the deceased's life merited them going to heaven. After all, remember how any of us are saved according to Ephesians 2:8, "For by grace you have been saved through faith; and that not of yourselves, it is the gift of God; not as a result of works, so that no one may boast" of themselves and their life record. Even more than that, because none of us can look into hearts, can we be sure that what we heard from people's lips was consistent with what was in their heart? Stick to what is sure and true and indisputable—Luke 19:10 says, "The Son of Man has come to seek and to save that which was lost." That's the Good News the Holy Spirit has given us!

INSTEAD, acknowledge Lawrence as a sinner, like you, and POINT EVERYONE TO GOD'S LOVE IN CHRIST, WHO GAVE HIS LIFE FOR ALL!

I love what one of the greatest Christ followers ever had to say about himself and Christ. The person was a man named Paul. If ever there was someone who would make it into heaven by a life FULL of serving Jesus, it would have to be the Apostle Paul. Still, Paul said in 1 Timothy 1:15, "Christ Jesus came into the world to save sinners, among whom I am foremost of all. Yet, for this reason I found mercy, so that in me as the foremost sinner, Jesus Christ might demonstrate His perfect patience as an example for those who would believe in Him for eternal life." This is God's Good News to us, that "while we were still sinners Christ died for us." (Romans 5:8)

Many years ago, a dear friend of mine named Ben Berry was in the last weeks of a fight with cancer. I'll never forget the question my friend asked me as I sat on his bed at his home talking with him during his last two weeks alive. He said, "Pastor, was I good enough?" What he meant was, "Was I good enough in my life to go to heaven?" I can only credit the Holy Spirit for the words that came as I answered Ben. I said, "No, Ben, you weren't good enough. I haven't lived good enough either. But **HE** (Jesus) was good enough for both of us!" He lived the perfect life we can't live and credits it to us through faith. He took on our sinful life and atoned for its punishment at the cross! This is our message as God's servants when we face death. First Peter 3:18 says, "For Christ also died for sins once for all, the just (Jesus) for the unjust (us), so that He might bring us to God." The only message that matters is WHAT CHRIST HAS DONE, not what you, or I, or the deceased has done. It's all about Christ! Christ is our ONLY hope!

Before I conclude this essay, there's one other funeral perspective I need to put before you. It often happens when the family of the deceased are strong people of faith, but the deceased has wandered away from Christ. The question I have for you goes like this:

Will you TRY TO LEAD LAWRENCE'S FAMILY TO "PRAISE THEIR WAY THROUGH THE PAIN"?

The exercise of PRAISE and WORSHIP of our Lord is wonderful. First, it is totally appropriate that we celebrate the great compassion and grace our God has for us. Psalm 147:1 says, "Praise the Lord! It is good to sing praises to our God; for it is pleasant and praise is becoming,"... meaning, praise is appropriate to give to the Lord our God! Praise of the Lord is our glorious response to our amazing Lord who loves us, despite our sinfulness. Praise is our response of joy that even "if we are faithless, He remains faithful, for He cannot deny Himself." (2 Timothy 2:13)

HOWEVER, sometimes praise becomes almost like a kind of "drug" to people. Please don't take offense at my observation, I just want to ask some questions. If what I am asking is off-base and inaccurate to your worship context, then I am wrong and deserve to be ignored. But think about the following, especially in our urban African-American church experience and especially in the context of the painfulness of funerals. First, it is very healthy and a blessing to mourn audibly and animatedly to release grief and let things out. But I have a question about the animation of our praise of God with certain music and with certain rhythmic "whoops" from the preacher, while we're gathered with other animated "praisers."

Can our worship sometimes MISPLACE ITS FOCUS on the ACTS OF MY PRAISE (with loud music and with others joining in), rather than focusing on the HEALING and VICTORY OF OUR GOD amid

the deep painfulness of what has happened to our deceased loved one?

In an instance like the fictitious case of Lawrence, or a father who didn't live a very Godly life, or a little sister who lived a troubled, lonely life and died of an overdose—that pain of loss (even though somewhat expected because of life behavior) is not erased.

Sometimes in an effort to cope with a very hard emotional situation like death, I find that Christians, and even preachers, flip over to the "denial approach." This approach says, "This is a celebration of the life of (the deceased). I don't know what y'all are crying about." I disagree. We're crying about death, about separation from someone we deeply loved. There is also an "unspoken mourning" in that moment—we are mourning our most honest estimate that our beloved loved one did not know Christ and very possibly is in hell. Okay, sorry, I had to say it. Jesus said it in Mark 16:16, "He who has believed and has been baptized shall be saved; but he who has disbelieved shall be condemned." There is a lot of pain and unrest in this reality.

HERE IS MY POINT. There is only one thing that ultimately brings comfort and strength in moments like this. It is not something of US, but something of CHRIST! It is most succinctly said by the Apostle Paul in 1 Corinthians 15:56–57, "The sting of death is sin, and the power of sin is the law..." I need to pause there. Let's not deny how painful the STING of sin and death are. That's what we feel when a situation like Lawrence invades our life. I can't praise my way out of that. Oh, yes, in one moment at a funeral service, I can forget about it via an experiential worship time. But that sting will return like the waves of the sea every time I think about my deceased loved one. Rather, keep reading in 1 Corinthians 15, and you'll find the "peace that passes all understanding." First Corinthians 15:56–57 says, "The sting of death is sin, and the power of sin is the law; but thanks be to God, who gives us the victory through our Lord Jesus Christ." Through Christ's death, our sins have been paid for (no matter the quantity or the kind), and there is a new message in Jesus the Savior. In John 11:25, Jesus says, "I am the Resurrection and the Life; he who believes in Me will live even if he dies; and everyone who lives and believes in Me will never die." What an extraordinary assurance from the Savior. Let's just rest on that— what JESUS has done and what JESUS has promised. Let's not rest on what we think was in the heart of the deceased. Let's not rest on "praising our way" through this pain. The songwriter said it this way many years ago, "My hope is built on nothing less than Jesus' blood and righteousness."

Back to my original question. At the funeral, what will you say? Give the deceased maybe two or three sentences. Then, use the entire rest of your talk to talk about Jesus and what He has done. Have the courage to focus us on Jesus! The Holy Spirit will use these words to bring healing and life!

76

PLAN... PREP... PERSEVERE

There's no reason that small inner-city ministries cannot do great things and offer a buffet of creative opportunities through which people can meet the Savior. But PLANNING is absolutely necessary. You're probably thinking, "Of course, planning is necessary for any successful endeavor." But I suggest to you that planning way ahead of what you want to do is even more important in small urban ministries. Further, let me add the following three components of the planning journey that will encourage successful ministry to happen.

Plan

The following stories illustrate how planning works in a couple of ministry areas.

MUSIC MINISTRY:

At one time in my ministry history at Bethlehem, we did not have a church musician who could play Gospel music exclusively at our church. The best we could do was to share a musician with two or three other churches or sing with pre-recorded tracks. We made sure on a Sunday morning that all our Gospel music fit a narrow window of time before our shared musician had to leave for his other church commitments. If we were running late starting worship, or other parts of worship were running long, that was a problem. We needed to thoroughly plan Sunday mornings and start on time. But even before worship started, we needed a plan because some of our choir members rode the church van. We had to ensure that the morning van driver wasn't late and that all of the pick-ups could happen in the planned amount of time. The van driver couldn't wait at one house for 15 minutes waiting to pick someone up who wasn't quite ready, etc. Advanced planning was also needed for events like choir concerts and for special pieces of music. Planning! Planning! Planning! For the times when we had to sing with pre-recorded tracks, we needed even more planning! Tracks don't forgive musical mistakes or missed entrances. They also don't cover up last-minute changes in the songs because the lead singer was sick. All of this takes much creative planning as well.

We have a Minister of Music today who exclusively plays at our church. She is VERY gifted, but because she works a full-time job as a public school teacher (we can't afford a full-time Minister of Music), we have to PLAN ahead. We don't have 50 people at our church who can sing lead on a song. We have to plan when people are going to be gone from Sunday morning worship. Small inner-city churches can have excellence in their music ministry, but it takes planning. It doesn't happen automatically.

SISTER CHURCH RELATIONSHIPS:

I've written of the wonderful partnership we have with sister churches. Not only are they essential to our ministry existing, but also they make us a better and more effective ministry in bringing the Gospel to people. Planning is vital when you have sister church relationships. Ministry events we do together have to fit their schedule, as well as ours. Also, it takes planning to think about how our sister church friends will participate when they come on campus to serve at a ministry event. If their experience in serving with us is left unplanned, and they're just standing around and not doing anything meaningful, guess what will happen the next time they come to serve at our church? Uh uh. There will probably not be a next time.

Sometimes Pastor Bolling or I are invited with one of our choirs or dance ministry groups to a sister church to do a Mission Sunday. Talk about the need for planning. Now the planning doubles! Not only do we need to get ready for us to be at that sister church on a given Sunday, but we also have to plan for how ministry at Bethlehem still takes place in an excellent way! Planning also happens with the group we take along to the sister church—especially because many in our traveling groups are kids and youth. We make sure everyone is ready with their song or dance. We make sure we secure transportation to the sister church. We make certain everyone wakes up early that morning (yes, even that is not left to chance), etc. There's a lot on the line when we travel to sister churches. For people to simply oversleep and leave us without a worship group is not good for our ministry relationship!

Prep

While I know "plan" and "prep" are often seen as synonyms, I want to use the idea of "prep" in a distinct way here. (Maybe I'm even stretching the definition of it.) While planning has to do with how something is going to go and needs to be done way ahead of time, "prepping" is more of a reminder right before the event. Prepping can be a last-minute check that everything needed for the event has been acquired and set up. Prepping is also about people. I know, some of you are thinking, "Do I really have to remind people, especially grown adults, where they need to be? They volunteered with their own mouths to be there!" While there are some people who don't need to be reminded, and while we want to keep developing people to a point where they become very conscious of the commitments they make and carry through on their own, the reality is that if you want a strong event with good participation, a reminder text, email, or phone call is a good idea! People's lives are busy. Remember, unlike a job where people are paid to come to work and paid to complete assignments, the church is still a volunteer organization. Do you want a better shot at having ministry success and stronger numbers? Then, PREP!

Persevere

Every person I know who has worked in urban ministry—and has had challenges with people keeping their commitments and showing up for ministry events—has sometimes said, "I feel like I'm herding cats." Or, "I'm not going through all of that. I'll do some basic planning and if the ministry happens, it happens. If it doesn't, it doesn't." Or, "I don't need to stay here and serve. There are a multitude of other ministries that would have me as their leader, and I wouldn't have to work this hard."

I totally understand what you're saying. Think about a few things with me:

- If the Lord called me to this place to serve, then, like it or not, easy or exasperating, this is the place He wants me until He calls me to a different place.

- Take a break. We all need breaks. We all need to step away and recharge our batteries. Don't make important decisions when you're angry, tired, or worn down.

- Reflect on what Jesus would say. I'm thinking especially of Luke 15:3–7. Remember what Jesus does? He puts such a high premium on each sheep that He will leave 99 in order to go find a single lost sheep! From my vantage point, that's a "do whatever it takes to reach the lost" mindset. I already know your pushbacks. You may argue, "But if I am spoon-feeding the sheep all the time, they will never learn or gain personal investment in their faith." I'm not saying this is about spoon-feeding forever.

Let's take a different Bible picture—Proverbs 22:6. May I apply this verse in a bit of a different way? Let me remind you of the verse, "Train up a child in the way he should go, Even when he is old he will not depart from it." The heart of this Scripture is both an assignment and a truth. The *assignment* is for us to "train" young people in the Christian faith. The *truth* is that, by the Holy Spirit's power, when we have trained up a child to know the Lord and His Word, God's Word has been implanted in them forever. Sadly, they can choose not to trust Christ as their Savior and not enjoy life in Him. But, at the very least, the Gospel and God's Word have been imparted into them! And we believe in the power of God's Word—see Isaiah 55:10–11—according to His way and His timeframe. That person may be away from the Lord and the Church, but when we have trained them up in Jesus' Good News, they can always return to the Gospel implanted within them.

Over the 30-plus years of my ministry at Bethlehem, we have reached thousands. Not a high percentage have stayed in their faith at Bethlehem. But I do know that the Good News has been implanted in them. We have seen evidence of this fact many times in the life of a child who was trained, wandered, but then returned to faith because they remembered what was placed in them through Bethlehem Lutheran Church. Now take this Proverbs 22:6 picture and apply it to those who are adult in age, but children in the faith. Do you see our role in continuing to persevere and engage "babes in the faith" in ministry? We're serving as spiritual parents! Just like good biological parents, spiritual parents are consistent and continual in their training of spiritual children to know the Lord and become involved in ministry. So don't give up. Yes, this is tough work, messy work, exhausting work! But never forget God's promise to us in 1 Corinthians 15:58 to "be steadfast, immovable, always abounding in the work of the Lord, knowing that your toil is not in vain in the Lord."

77

SOMETIMES YOU HAVE TO BE THE CHRISTIAN PARENT

Throughout this collection of essays, I have suggested that one of the strongest ways to reach more people with the Good News of Jesus Christ in inner-city areas is through children. I believe this is the most effective way to gain entrée into families. At the same time, it is also often a hard, time-consuming, and even exasperating ministry road that takes much energy and patience. One of the reasons it is difficult is because beginning a new ministry often requires the pastor/ministry leader to take on a plurality of roles. Yes, you are a spiritual leader—that should always be the heart of what you do. But those of us in urban churches must wear other "hats" in a ministry while it is still smaller and just beginning. Very likely, we will wear the hat of program administrator—organizing and often being the lead planner on most ministry activities. Another hat is that of fundraiser/ director of development because few urban emerging ministries are self-supporting from offerings. They need a significant third source income to exist. At times, we also wear the hats of janitor and bus driver.

There are many other hats to wear in a new inner-city ministry. I'm not saying for you to plan on wearing all of them forever. No, keep developing people! But the reality is that, early on in your ministry, you may have to be more than only a pastor/spiritual leader.

In this essay, I want to focus on wearing the hat of a CHRISTIAN PARENT. Sometimes a ministry leader has to play that role, not just with the kids of your ministry, but also with adults who are still growing into Christian maturity.

The following examples will give you the best picture of what I mean:
CHRISTMAS – I grew up with Christmas traditions that included Wednesday night Advent worship every December, along with special church music rehearsals, Christmas caroling to shut-ins, special Christmas

programs/plays, and worship on Christmas Eve before any presents were ever exchanged or opened. All these things were aimed at recognizing the fact that there is no Christmas without the coming of Christ.

That is not the traditional upbringing everybody experiences today. In fact, fewer and fewer people experience it. **MY ROLE AS A CHRISTIAN PARENT to children and adults in my church** is to urge them to see how Christmas starts with CHRIST. There is no real Christmas without Him. Even though additional spiritual activities in the days before Christmas make an already full schedule even more so, carving out a place for the One who makes Christmas possible and saying "no" to some of the non-Christ-focused things the world connects with Christmas is the only right thing to do! At the beginning of this book, I talked about my 30th Christmas Eve Worship at Bethlehem where only 11 people attend. But that will not keep me from having Christmas worship on my 31st Christmas Eve at Bethlehem and beyond. It is my duty to lead the people of God in this place to set apart time to worship Christ on Christmas! As my colleague Pastor Gerard Bolling has well said, "We must not let go of doing Christmas worship and Christmas programs, plays, and preparation that remind us this time of the year is special, holy, and vital to our lives!" Even though it would make life so much easier to give in and not do these events, sometimes you have to be a CHRISTIAN PARENT and train people how to set time aside to worship the Newborn King in ways beyond their usual routine.

CONDUCT IN WORSHIP – If your church is going to grow (and especially grow with new people who don't know Christ), you will continually have people come to worship who have little experience in a Christian worship service and are trying to figure out how to act. So how will you handle that? In some churches, this matter is managed by a militaristic usher staff (often smartly dressed in black, wearing white gloves). If you misbehave, are talking, or are on your phone in worship, the usher motions you to leave worship. And it's usually not done too gently! What does that result in? These days, will someone new return to worship after something like that happens? Probably not. However, having order in worship is important for the sake of maintaining an atmosphere where people are not distracted during an intimate time with the Lord.

One of those intimate times in our Sunday morning worship is when we celebrate Holy Communion. For those who come before the altar, this is a very personal and intimate time with the Lord when we receive His forgiveness and strength in a powerful way. It is disturbed by those who remain seated in the congregation and use the time to visit, almost like half-time in a football game. Honestly, we have this challenge with not only children but also adults. It's a problem not only with new people (who may not know any better) but also longtime church members. What is to be done?

In our church, my first desire is that our mature members gently and quietly encourage people who are talking to instead sit silently, pray, or participate in the worship songs we sometimes sing during communion so people at the altar have undisturbed time with the Lord. This is something leaders can coach mature worshippers to do in a winsome way. Sometimes it takes Pastor Bolling or myself to say over the microphone, "I call the church to a time of order." You know what that is? That's one of us taking on the role of a CHRISTIAN PARENT. It's sort of like "daddy" saying, "Shh! Let's respect the worship of others." It's not what we enjoy doing, but it's a role we sometimes need to play. It's all about teaching people to grow in Christ and be mindful of the rest of the worshipping family around them!

Getting the idea? **The following are some other moments when ministry leaders must play the role of CHRISTIAN PARENTS.**

At ministry budget time, if nobody else will say it, we as CHRISTIAN PARENTS have to say, "How do you propose paying for what you want to spend? We can't spend more than we have." For example, somebody says, "We should have a Thanksgiving dinner after worship." Or, "We should have Christmas cookie decorating." Or, "Let's have better technology and start livestreaming our sermons on Sunday morning." The ideas are exciting. But when people just put out the ideas only, a CHRISTIAN PARENT sometimes needs to say, "Those are all great ideas! We can do them! But if you want these things, you need to invest in making them happen in the ministry. Who will take leadership to put a plan together to make this happen and then follow through on the plan to completion?"

There are also times when, as a CHRISTIAN PARENT, you have to say hard things.

For example, a person talks a lot and makes promises to help, but never carries through on keeping the promises they make. A CHRISTIAN PARENT sometimes has to have a private, gentle, but firm conversation with them following the theme, "If your actions aren't in step with what you say, nobody will believe or respect what you say."

For example, someone in the family wants help from the church. They want the perks of being part of the church family, but they aren't consistently present for worship when the family gathers and won't volunteer to serve in the ministry projects the family does. A CHRISTIAN PARENT sometimes needs to have a private, loving conversation and say, "In this church family, you can't be family only when it suits you. Family is not just about what we 'get' from the family, but more about what we 'give' to the family."

Being a CHRISTIAN PARENT to people (both children and adults) who are growing up in the faith isn't always an enjoyable role. At times it calls on us to say and do things to help people grow that may be uncomfortable for them.

But this role of CHRISTIAN PARENT is vital for a young and growing church that is young in age and young in Christian maturity.

Over the years, I've watched so many Bethlehem members serve as Christian parents to the children of our church, especially as we gather for worship. One of those Bethlehem "mothers" in recent years continues to be Shanta Henderson. Shanta is well-known in our community. She lives within a block of Bethlehem and works on the Bethlehem ministry team in our Bethlehem After School program. At Sunday morning worship, she uses her relationships with the many children who attend Bethlehem programs to help parent them during worship. It would be easy for her to come to worship and ignore the need for raising up children in the ways of the Lord. However, she purposely chooses to lovingly give a disappointed look to those playing on their phones, a parent-like "Shh!" to young people who are talking when they should be listening, and sometimes even an after-worship reminder to young people about God's goodness to each one of us and why the Lord is worthy of our respect and praise. Sometimes you just have to be the Christian parent to those outside of your own biological children.

Our goal is not to be CHRISTIAN PARENTS forever. We want people to grow up and seize their own Christian responsibility for their faith and their service to Christ.

What we really want is duplication—we want young people in the faith to grow up into Christian adulthood so that they can be CHRISTIAN PARENTS to the next new young ones to come through the front doors of our ministry. I think that is what David had in mind when he said in Psalm 145:4, "One generation shall praise Your works to another, And shall declare Your mighty acts."

78

THE OTHER SIDE OF VISION

Walt Disney would have to be on my list of the most visionary people who ever walked the face of this earth. When he would take his kids to parks and zoos, his out-of-the-box thinking enabled him to "envision beyond" and create places like Disneyland, Disney World, and all of the Disney theme parks where parents and children could have fun together. I love to study people of great vision like J.C. Penney, Milton Hershey, Henry Ford, Sam Walton, Madame CJ Walker, Bill Gates, Oprah Winfrey, Robert L. Johnson, and even Tyler Perry. They were able to see future opportunities in business, science, and entertainment years in advance. They were also willing to take the risks necessary to make their dreams become reality.

Although the Good News of the Gospel of Jesus Christ is timeless and never changes, how we bring that message in our ever-changing world takes great vision so that the church can stay effective in its proclamation of Christ. As an urban ministry leader, you either need to have that creative vision yourself, or you need to know where to tap into that vision to help your ministry be as effective as it can be and help people come to know the Savior.

Vision is two-sided. There is a side of vision that involves being able to consider new programs and ministry approaches with the Gospel. This side of vision is sometimes being able to picture new models of ministry. This side of vision also includes being able to imagine new places for ministry— sometimes in creating facilities and sometimes in finding facilities that can be rented/used instead of owned.

Let's be clear—all vision is God-given and not from a person. I've been told I have a gift of ministry vision in the urban ministry scene. Maybe so. Yet, I want to reveal to you that there's another side of vision.

Accompanying the side of vision that enables some people to see possibilities is the same vision gift that enables us to see problems in advance. Both kinds of vision are needed in an urban ministry.

The two-sided nature of vision makes me think of Joseph in the Old Testament in Genesis 41:14–36. Through Pharaoh's dream, God enabled Joseph to see that seven years of famine were coming, but Joseph also saw the provision of God in the seven good years to sustain the people through the time of famine.

In ministry, here's what the "other side" of vision is like:

- It's seeing how we need to reach new people with the Gospel when our church community has begun to change and new people are moving into the neighborhood.

- It's seeing when the adult children of the members who grew up at our church are missing Sunday morning worship for various reasons and even going to other churches. In this case, our congregation is actually losing a generation we will need in our ministry.

- It's seeing that if we don't handle repairs to our property today, these repairs will be way more costly for us tomorrow.

- It's seeing that if we don't keep raising up and training people for ministry today, especially leaders, we will be in trouble in the near future when we lose people or grow beyond the capacity of our current leadership.

I must tell you that when we share this kind of vision within our churches, people may acknowledge it, but they often won't be very anxious to embrace doing something about it. Sharing this other side of ministry vision won't make you the most popular voice in the church. But it is necessary. Remember in the story of Joseph and Pharaoh that the seven years of famine became an OPPORTUNITY for everybody to trust God and for His leader Joseph to take care of the people in the seven years of plenty! The point is this:

Help God's people see the full picture of ministry life before them. We often only see what we WANT to see, not FULLY WHAT REALLY "IS." But when you share the other side of vision, connect it with a GREAT OPPORTUNITY for the Church to LOOK TO THE LORD WHO PROVIDES FOR US, even when overwhelming mountains are before us on our path.

After all, that is our God. He is ever faithful! We can have confidence in Him! Psalm 34:8–10 expresses this confidence well that we have in the Lord, "O taste and see that the Lord is good; How blessed is the man who takes refuge in Him! O fear the Lord, you His saints; For to those who fear Him there is no want. The young lions do lack and suffer hunger; But they who seek the Lord shall not be in want of any good thing." No matter what the vision before us is!

79

THE OTHER SIDE OF VISION
Part 2: The Hard Part

How are urban churches and post-high school youth alike? Consider the following two stories about the "other side" of vision that enables us to see problems in advance.

You could start to see changes in the neighborhood of First Immanuel Church. Some people had moved out in the past five years. Some businesses decided to relocate when crime became much more frequent. More and more neighborhood residents replaced their screen doors with wrought iron security screen front doors. But First Immanuel Church and School remained strong. The church still had more than 400 people in worship on Sunday mornings. Their school was still a fine place to get a good education.

The new people moving into the First Immanuel's neighborhood were of Hispanic descent. Most of the new residents were young Hispanic families—perfect for the mission of First Immanuel Church and School! At their monthly church council meeting in May, a visitor spoke to the First Immanuel leadership. He was a pastor with First Immanuel's regional church judicatory. The visiting pastor official came to First Immanuel with a load of data and a proposal. The data projected continued changes to the community where First Immanuel was located. In short, the projections were that as their larger metro area expanded in other places, the community around First Immanuel would become more populated with young Hispanic families. The data was solid and credible. The official wasn't there to spread panic. Rather, there was great excitement in his voice about the mission opportunity that was coming right to First Immanuel's doorstep.

For First Immanuel's leaders, however, this news brought much anxiety. They knew life would change for this strong church that was 99% Caucasian and of European descent. But honestly, they didn't want it to change. The leadership was fair and agreed to allow the church official to share this information in a series of congregational forums. There was even more nervousness about the future among the people of First Immanuel when they heard the church official's findings. He explained that he wanted to see First Immanuel continue in its ministry to its current membership. But he also wanted First Immanuel to begin reaching out to the new Hispanic families in the community. He further suggested that to do this outreach effectively, First Immanuel would need to consider new ministry approaches and create additional ministries especially targeted to their new neighbors.

To many at First Immanuel, it felt like a lot of work. It also seemed as if the First Immanuel where they grew up and loved was changing. Some of the needed changes would stretch people at First Immanuel beyond the kind of church life they had become accustomed to. In truth, they didn't like it because their eyes were on themselves. The church official warned that if they did nothing to create a new outreach to these new families, within the next 10 years First Immanuel could decline by 50%.

First Immanuel decided to do nothing to reach out to their new Hispanic neighbors. Just six years later, the church had declined by half when many members moved out of the neighborhood and found new church homes. The decline at First Immanuel's school wasn't as drastic. Some of the Hispanic families sent their kids to the school, but they never felt comfortable or welcome at First Immanuel Church. In time, as the church membership shrunk, their financial resources also declined, which meant less money to support their school, which then led to the school's decline.

The church official saw this coming. He did his best to warn First Immanuel. If only they had acted on the church official's recommendations six years earlier, maybe things would have been different?

Jericka and her parents had really been going at it, beginning in her senior year of high school. Jericka wanted to go to college. Jericka's parents wanted her to go to college. So they pushed her to apply for college scholarships. But Jericka was stubborn and a procrastinator. She kept saying to herself and her parents, "I'll do this next week. I've got too many things going on this week." Jericka had a LOT of fun in her senior year of high school. Her parents were on Jericka almost weekly about filling out applications and seeking out scholarship money. They reminded her that they didn't have the money to pay for Jericka to go to college. They could help a little, but they couldn't underwrite half of the cost. But Jericka's promise to "do this next week" never happened in time.

In the spring of her senior year, when she finally got around to taking care of her college financial business, it was too late to receive scholarship money. There would be no going away to college in the fall. So Jericka and her parents regrouped. The new plan was that Jericka would start at a local community college and then transfer to a four-year school after her first two years. While at the community college, Jericka would work part-time to pay for a car. Jericka had the plan all laid out—she would take classes until 3:00 p.m., then work 4:00–10:00 p.m. at a local chicken restaurant. She and her parents seemed to be on the same page and headed in a good direction! That schedule worked for about six weeks.

BUT THEN Jericka started coming home at 1:00 a.m. after work because she started going out with a girlfriend from the restaurant. Her grades started suffering. She ended up being put on academic probation at school. Her parents were on her about her choices, but Jericka's famous words were, "Don't worry! I got this!" Shortly thereafter, she went out with her girlfriend Toni one night and met DeMarcus. Jericka threw herself at DeMarcus. Honestly, DeMarcus wasn't going anywhere in life. Most of the time he hung out on the street. Occasionally, he would work with his uncle who had a carpet business. Jericka's mother and father kept telling Jericka that Demarcus was bad news and not a good thing in her life. But Jericka continued to "know better" herself.

Soon she stopped coming home at night, often spending overnights with DeMarcus or Toni. Do I have to finish this story? No, you know how it ends. While there may be various endings—flunking out of school, pregnancy, getting fired, having no job and not being employable—the ending is not good.

Jericka's parents saw this coming. They did their best to warn Jericka about where some of her choices would land her life. But Jericka wasn't listening.

Of course, "First Immanuel" and "Jericka" are fictional stories. And yet, I've known hundreds of First Immanuels and Jerickas. So have you. Sometimes, people will listen to the other side of vision—a vision God gives people, like church officials and parents. But sometimes they won't listen. It *IS* frustrating to see how different things could have been for First Immanuel if only they had listened. It's the same way with Jericka—how much pain could have been avoided and how many more open doors she would have had in life.

But timing is EVERYTHING! We all know stories of First Immanuel churches who started listening and reaching their community later, after the church had already declined drastically. We all know Jerickas who turned their lives around later, after they experienced some serious deep pits of pain and heartache.

So here's the hard side of "The Other Side of Vision"—even though we would love to save churches or people from going through the pain of being humbled by life, sometimes that's the only way toward rising and becoming what the Lord wants them to be.

It's hard for those who saw it coming to watch, but this really comes down to having faith in the Lord at the end of the day. Stay with me as we walk through the following truths to keep in mind when you're praying over churches or people that seem a bit stubborn and won't do what they should do:

God won't step over human will. He will do everything He can, sometimes including pain, to change our minds and humble us. Remember how the Lord did that to His prophet Jonah in Jonah 1:4? He wants us to turn to Him and do what is right. But just as in the Garden of Eden, the words of Genesis 2:16–17 still ring true today. Disobedience and sin are not God's fault. They are our unwise choices. Sometimes it takes us a while to realize the foolishness of our decisions, even though wise voices were trying to guide us in the right way.

This world is not all there is. Maybe someone could have been a doctor but because of unwise life choices they ended up being a paramedic or a medical office staff person. That doesn't mean life is over! What is most important is their RELATIONSHIP WITH THE SAVIOR! That's because this world isn't all there is for those of us who are in Christ! "Our citizenship is in heaven," says Philippians 3:20. That's our real home!

God is famous for making lemonade out of life's "lemon" situations. You've heard that before. It is so true—even in hard times, times of disobedience, times when we are tested. What Job said about God in Job 23:10 still stands true, "But He knows the way I take; When He has tried me, I shall come forth as gold." What confidence that gives us as we go through life. Even when we've been disobedient toward the Lord, when we confess our sins, God forgives us for Jesus' sake and makes us new again. "...if anyone is in Christ, he is a new creature, the old thing passed away; behold, new things have come." (2 Corinthians 5:17)

So if you're in the role of the church official or Jericka's parents, don't panic. Don't panic, even when you've seen trouble coming and the person or organization remains unresponsive. Commend the person or the organization to the Lord's care. If they are away from the Lord, keep planting the seed of God's Word in them and keep on praying for them. In faith, rest, because you have put them in God's Hands!

After you have warned the church or the person about the danger in front of them, after you have prayed and put them in the hands of the

Lord, practice what David says in Psalm 4:8, "In peace I will both lie down and sleep, For You alone, O Lord, make me dwell in safety."

80

ESPECIALLY

Every day as I drive to Bethlehem Church, I see an elderly man standing in the street at one of the major intersections I cross—his hand out, begging for assistance. In most inner-city neighborhoods, particularly at intersections with high-volume traffic, it's common to see people holding signs like, "Homeless, please help" or "Out of work, please help." The term most people use for this in a legal sense is "panhandling." There is both legitimate begging for help and people who scam and hustle to get people to give them money and other assistance. You may have encountered people who sometimes ask, "Could you give me a few dollars so I can get something to eat?" But if you say, "Tell you what... instead of giving you a few dollars for food, I'll go into McDonald's on the corner and buy you a sandwich," then they don't want your assistance, and they suddenly disappear. I'm not saying everybody is like this. There are people who have real needs who ask for help. There are also people who hustle for a living. There are other people who ask for help for food but then turn around and feed their habit of abusing substances with the money they receive.

People come to our church door asking for assistance all the time. It can range from people wanting to sell us tools and other items (usually stolen goods), to people looking for food, to people looking for help paying their rent or utility bills.

There is great need among people today. There is also great confusion about this topic. Sometimes when people come to the church asking for help they will even try to shame people of faith into helping. They say things like, "You say you're God's people. You're supposed to help others."

What they mean by that is, "Give us whatever we ask for." No, that's not Biblically accurate.

There is also confusion about the church's place in even helping those in need in society. For example, we're not a United Way funded agency. In St. Louis, the United Way funds 160-plus agencies that help people. Among this group are agencies like Catholic Charities, Salvation Army, Urban League, Grace Hill, and St. Patrick Center. Agencies like these receive funding in the hundreds of thousands of dollars annually to help people. Churches are dependent only on individual donations from people. We have nowhere near the resources that publicly-funded agencies receive.

So what does the Lord want us to do when people in need come to us asking for assistance?

Among Christians, there is a wide variety of understanding about social ministry. Some churches see taking care of people's physical needs as their primary mission. If a person in need comes to faith, well, that's alright, too. Other churches see their mission as only spiritual. They say, "Come to us for faith matters. Go to those other agencies for food and life matters."

I think there are some Scriptures to wrestle with to gain an understanding of how to care for people with the mercy of the Lord.

Is showing mercy and helping others the mark of a follower of Christ? Yes, without question! Remember what the King says in Matthew 25:34–40.

The Bible is also clear as to the motivation for our showing mercy to others. Jesus said in Luke 6:36, "Be merciful, just as your Father is merciful." Where would any of us be without the unconditional kindness of our Father God to us in Christ Jesus?

At the same time, the Lord gives us some perspective on helping others in their physical worldly needs.

In John 6:26–27, after Jesus fed 5,000 families in the miraculous feeding with two fish and five loaves of bread, He turned to the crowds following Him and said, "Truly, truly, I say to you (Jesus' formula for saying something of ultimate seriousness), you seek Me, not because you saw signs, but because you ate of the loaves and were filled. Do not work for the food that perishes, but for the food which endures to eternal life, which the Son of Man will give to you." Think about those words. Among the gifts Jesus gives the people (food and signs of who He is as the Savior), there is a PRIORITY, and there is an ESPECIALLY. Isn't the lesson clear?

Spiritual provision is superior to physical provision.

That wasn't the only time Jesus reminded people not to settle for just physical blessings of the Lord but to seek God's real gift of life through His Son. Jesus said in **Mark 8:36,** "For what does it profit a man to gain the whole world, and forfeit his soul?"

I find that Galatians 6:10 puts all of this together—both God's desire for us to help others, but also the "ESPECIALLY" regarding those who are in the Christian faith, as well as those who also seek the Christian faith with their physical needs. Paul wrote, "So then..." Stop. Let's observe what the Word of God just said in Galatians 6:9. It says, "Let us not lose heart in doing good, for in due time we will reap if we do not grow weary." Got it, Holy Spirit. You want us to be vigilant in good works toward others. Now continuing with Galatians 6:10, "So then, while we have opportunity, let us do good to all people..." Pause a moment. Yes, we want to use our material resources and our physical abilities to reach all people. Now here comes an important word. The next part of 6:10 continues, "and ESPECIALLY to those who are of the household of faith."

There is a priority placed on our help—ESPECIALLY toward those who know Jesus or want to know Him!

For Bethlehem, this verse frames our approach in social ministry.

1. We do seek to do good to all people. We give aid and help to all people who are in need.

But there is an ESPECIALLY.

2. We ESPECIALLY stand with and help those who know Christ or want to know Christ! What does that mean, since we cannot see into a person's heart? We judge in the only way we can. Are you responsive toward Jesus Christ being brought to you through the Word of God? Specifically:

- Will you come and hear the Word of God in worship?

- Will you come and hear the Word of God in a Bible study?

- Will you allow us to share the Good News of Christ with you one-on-one?

- Will you allow your children to hear of the Word of God in one of our children's ministries? We've found that bringing Christ into the home through kids is an opportunity for Christ to come to their parents.

This really boils down to being clear about who the Lord has called us to be. While we help people with their needs, that is only secondary to our desire to bring the Word of Life in Jesus to people as Christ's Church. While we use sports in our ministry, we are not a Boys or Girls Club, or a YMCA, or a basketball academy. As Christ's Church, our first desire is to bring the Word of Life in Jesus to people. While we have an afterschool program for kids, and we want to provide a safe-haven for them during afterschool hours, if we were not allowed to teach about the Savior in this program, we wouldn't operate it as Christ's Church. For this reason, we take no public dollars for our afterschool program.

For those who seek to know the Savior, I've seen people of God help other Christ followers get jobs. I've seen people of God even open their homes to people in need of a place to stay. I've known people of God who GAVE automobiles to Christ followers who needed one. I've witnessed people of God babysit others' kids for free when they need help... and I've seen a whole host of other acts of service, help, and mercy. Just like Galatians 6:10 says—we seek to help all people, but there is an ESPECIALLY!

81

BE A FOUNTAIN, NOT A DRAIN

While on vacation in Oregon, we drove past a small, wood frame church with these words on its front sign: "Be a FOUNTAIN, not a DRAIN." Isn't that good? In case you didn't quite catch what that means, the sign urges us to be a FOUNTAIN of God's love and grace (it comes to us and then passes through us to others), not just a DRAIN (only a receiver/consumer and not a giver). Proverbs 11:25, especially the end of the verse, gives a great picture of this principle. God pours into us so that we can "water" others! People who live as DRAINS only want to BE SERVED. Philippians 2:3–4 has some very straightforward words about living like a DRAIN. A man who understood living as a FOUNTAIN of God's grace was Barnabas. See what he does in Acts 4:36–37 and Acts 9:26–27 (with Saul/Paul). Also, I love the promises the Lord gives to people who live like FOUNTAINS in Isaiah 58:10–11.

So why put this truth in a collection of essays about ministry in urban areas? Isn't it a lesson for all ministry, no matter where that ministry is located? Absolutely! I want to remind you, however, that this malady of living as a DRAIN is especially true in low-income communities. How so? It's really a faith issue.

In low-income areas where many of us don't have the opportunity or ability to easily make significant dollar amounts when we need them, the enemy comes at us with the temptation to be just a drain that takes and stores up everything we can get, whenever we can get it.

Here are a couple of fictional portraits that illustrate this truth:

Jerry has a car that isn't the most reliable. He works consistently but barely makes above minimum wage. Jerry doesn't have the opportunity to make a quick $1,000 or $2,000 by taking on an extra project or working a little overtime at his job like some people with more education and opportunity do. Jerry's car breaks down, and the damage is around $1,500. In this immediate situation, Jerry sells his family's food stamps to try and get his car fixed. He hustles food from multiple food pantries and then resells the food. When the local church is giving out coats, Jerry finds a way to get six coats, and then he resells five of them for cash. Jerry is tight with his money. He's not a bad person. He's just trying to make it. But as far as giving or helping others, Jerry is always a "NO." He's got to look out for himself. So like a drain, everything that comes to Jerry STAYS with Jerry!

On the other hand, Ms. Sadie Jenkins has lived on Trumble St. for 40 years. Ms. Sadie doesn't have much—just a small pension from her deceased husband and a few investments that she saved for retirement. Ms. Sadie has, however, decided to live her life to be as thrifty as she can so that she can be abundant in her help to everyone who needs it. She has a deep faith in the Lord and trusts that God will provide everything she needs and then some! Ms. Sadie is always helping people out with meals and paying a little something on the electric bill of someone who really needs it. Blessings seem to just keep coming her way. The more she gives, the more the Lord blesses her in ways that never could have been predicted! She is the perfect picture of a fountain of blessings—God keeps pouring into her, she keeps giving God's blessings away, and the Lord keeps pouring more into her.

Do you see the contrast?

It's really all about SELF and FAITH.

If we live our lives dependent on ourselves, we will think we never have enough. We will be drains. This is the stronghold the enemy leads many people in low-income areas into. And it doesn't just stop with being a selfish DRAIN of blessings. People who live for themselves are blinded to the love God has for them. Second Corinthians 4:4 is a Word worth looking up in your Bible. People full of self also have trouble with good relationships. They often live with a chip on their shoulder and are gripped with a spirit of entitlement. Believing they've been "wronged" or that "everybody in life owes them" is the kind of thinking that becomes an almost impenetrable barrier and keeps them from enjoying a joyous life with God. But there are those who live in the pathway of Proverbs 3:5, "Trust in the Lord with all your heart and do not lean on your own understanding, in all your ways acknowledge Him, and He will make your paths straight." They enjoy a peace that is unending. After all, who can take better care of us—ourselves or our Father in heaven? A DRAIN says, "It's up to me." A FOUNTAIN says, "The Lord's got me!"

FOUNTAIN or DRAIN. How have you been living? All of us sometimes live as DRAINS. Over time, we even get spiritually "clogged." But thank God the Lord doesn't give up on us! Jesus also gave His life at the cross for sins of selfishness. They are all paid for. In Christ, we are free to live new lives and live "no longer for ourselves but for Him who died and rose for us" (2 Corinthians 5:15).

Let's bring this truth to THIS DAY. How can you live this day as a FOUNTAIN of God's grace and love for others, instead of a DRAIN focused only on yourself?

One final thought: **who takes time to look at a DRAIN? Many people, however, watch FOUNTAINS. Maybe your FOUNTAIN life might be used by the Holy Spirit to show someone else the blessings of being a FOUNTAIN.**

82

NEST

One of the best places to eat in St. Louis is a cafeteria-like steakhouse on Grand Avenue, right across from the Fox Theatre. It's even called, "The Best Steakhouse." As you stand waiting to begin your journey through the food line, the grill master of the day keeps yelling to everybody in the line, "Next! Next!" He wants to know what meat entrée you want so that he can put it on the grill, get it going, and have it ready for you by the time you get to the end of the line at the cash register.

You need to pay attention as a customer because the "Next!" calls come pretty quickly! Somehow, the staff at The Best Steakhouse are able to keep everybody's order straight and give you exactly what you ordered. There is a useful metaphor about ministry regarding the way the staff at The Best Steakhouse takes your order. They don't know your name. They don't care who you are. They're just interested in "Who's NEXT?" as they keep the operation moving.

In urban parishes, we would do well to adopt this thought as we approach ministry. No, I'm not talking about the impersonal part of "Next!" I'm talking about the concept. In other words, "Who's next up to serve?" It pushes the issue—have we found and developed a "NEXT!" for every part of our ministry? Sometimes life teaches us and God pushes us to consider "Who's next?" in various positions of leadership in our ministry. Yes, I know that we're often just relieved to find anybody to do a job that we no longer need to do as the leader of the ministry. But one thing is certain, ESPECIALLY IN URBAN MINISTRIES. Considering the transiency of people, the dependency of most urban ministries on outside funding that can change on a yearly basis, and the instability of most inner-city communities, some annual change is almost certain. Usually part of that change includes people in the ministry moving from the area because of a job or the opportunity for better housing and then relapsing into destructive lifestyles. Sometimes it's just simple life-burnout. For the ministry of Jesus Christ, it is so vital to be able to have an answer to the call, "Next!"

I know I have already written similar essays on the concept of "Next!" for urban ministries, but it is so crucial for urban ministries to keep developing people, especially ministry leaders, in order to simply survive as well as thrive!

What does it take to have the "Next!" spot filled? First, remember that few people come to our ministries pre-trained and ready to walk right into the places where we need their help. So after we identify who could be the "Next!" in a given area and after we recruit them to help the Lord's work, there is still a need for training and mentoring. Training and mentoring in ministry *take time.* For example, even a Christian leader who comes from another church with skills for teaching children and who might even be a teacher by profession will greatly benefit from some training and mentoring in ministering to the children in "your hood." In addition to showing new leaders the particular "how to's" of our ministry context, our best training can be helping new people build relationships with others in our ministry. Training is also vital in established, more internal parts of our churches.

Who are your next leaders in music ministry?

Who are you raising up to be your next church musicians?

Who will be your next coaches for your sports ministry?

Who are your next teachers in your kids Bible program?

Can you raise up an assistant treasurer to be ready when your current treasurer retires?

Have you identified your next elder or deacon?

Who will be your newest small group leader?

It's easy to live only for today and not even think about the "Next!" of tomorrow. DON'T DO IT!

Tomorrow will come before you know it. If you didn't prepare people to be the "Next!" person ready in ministry, not only will it be a harder road for you, but also the ministry of Jesus will suffer! Can I suggest a few things for you to write down, either in a computer file or "old school" in a notebook? Take time every week to:

- list potential new people who could serve in your ministry.

- consider the ones you can help grow into a greater position in the ministry as you look at this list each week

- commit to training them and using them in ministry to give them experience

Don't put off this important work of developing the "Next!" leader or let it slide to the side in your ministry work. It will hurt your ministry before you know it!

The early Christian church held developing whoever is "Next!" as a priority for ministry. Remember in Acts 15:36–41, Barnabas was passionate about not giving up on John Mark but developing him. Check out 1 Timothy 1:2, 18, and 2 Timothy 1:2, 2:1. In these verses, Paul calls Timothy his "son" in the faith. He spends much of these letters pouring into Timothy the truth of God, mentoring and developing him in ministry. Timothy is Paul's "Next!" See also in Acts 18:24–28 how Priscilla and Aquila invest in developing a gifted young man named Apollos.

Who is "Next!" in your ministry?

83

WHAT'S GREAT ABOUT MINISTERING IN AN URBAN PLACE

Throughout this book, I've shared many of the real-life challenges of ministering in a small inner-city ministry. It is hard ministry sometimes. But it is also very JOYOUS ministry. I wouldn't want to be anywhere else! So what's especially great about ministering in an urban place?

Here are some of the top benefits of urban ministry based on experiences from my life:

Permission To Have Creativity in Sharing Christ

Travel across the United States of America, and you will see low-income urban area after low-income urban area where the Christian church struggles. There isn't one approach that has worked for every place. I don't think there ever will be one approach for all, even though some ministry principles are true for most places. To me, THAT OPENS THE DOOR FOR CREATIVITY—not for creativity's sake, but for the sake of the Gospel! One of the great things I love about our church is that PERMISSION IS GRANTED to do whatever it takes to bring the message of Jesus to people.

Sports can be a ministry tool to reach people for Christ. We go into the low-income housing projects of St. Louis to tell people about the Savior with our Taking Jesus to the Streets ministry. We offer free summer community carnivals to make connections to new neighborhood people we can begin ministering to. In a recent Christmas play, an angel entered the scene to the R&B hit, "I'm Every Woman." Sounds crazy? It was. But it locked in some visitors who normally don't go to church so that later in the play we could communicate some very serious issues about God's care and love for us. We reach people through our kids summer Musical Theatre Camp doing secular shows like *Willie Wonka* and *The Lion King*. Our music department creates fresh Gospel music with solid Biblical lyrics and "bumpin' beats."

Our mode of ministry wouldn't be accepted in every church. It doesn't have to be. But for us, we do whatever needs to be done to bring Jesus to people and people to His Church. I love the opportunity for creativity in ministry that serves the Gospel!

Work Schedule Freedom

Of course, the downside of being a pastor is that weekends and holidays when everybody else is usually off from work and school are among my busiest times. But there's another side of the coin! I was able to BE THERE for my kids at school activities my wife could never make because of her work schedule. When the school called and one of my kids was sick, I could almost always leave work, pick them up, and take them home—and then go back into the office later to finish my work. If I had a project at home that I needed to finish during daylight hours, I could adjust my schedule to do it. If somebody in my family needed me during the week, I could leave town and go help that person. Of course, I had to get all my work done and be sure that the worship and program plans were covered. But in a small urban ministry, the work schedule freedom is awesome! *The blessing of such freedom can be a curse if you're not self-motivated and self-disciplined to complete your work. Many a church worker has experienced periods when they picked up their paycheck without having finished the work they should have finished that week.* But for me, I love the freedom to know the work I need to accomplish and then work on it in my own way, on my own schedule, and at my own pace!

You Can Do Ministry with Your Family

My kids had seen half of the entire United States before graduating from high school. But it wasn't because I had the finances to afford so many family vacations. I didn't. Still don't. But we took ministry mission trips with our Gospel Choir for about 12 years, and I took my family with me on the road! Together, we saw Times Square and Niagara Falls and ran the "Rocky" steps in Philadelphia; we saw the sites in Washington, D.C., and ate crawfish in Louisiana; we went to the Louisville Slugger baseball bat factory in Louisville and visited the National Civil Rights Museum at the old Lorraine Hotel in Memphis.

When our Bethlehem Bulldogs basketball team went out of town, my family also came along. On Sunday afternoons in the summer when we do our Taking Jesus to the Streets ministry, the next generation—my grandchildren—come with us as we share the Gospel and have fun in local housing projects. It's true that PKs (Pastor's Kids) are special kids. They put up with a lot when their dad is away doing church work. But if you plan things right, your family can be right by your side ministering to people. Isn't that also an exciting activity through which faith in Christ and a serving heart can be passed to your children?

Proximity

While there are always some relationship parameters that must be remembered, one of the best things about being at Bethlehem Lutheran Church is that this church family has become our family! We work together in ministry. We play together. We cry together. We celebrate together. We're raising our families together. We care for each other and support one another. Yes, of course, sometimes we get mad and fight with each other.

But because of the mercy of God won by Christ on the cross, that same forgiveness that has been implanted in us by the Holy Spirit is the same forgiveness that moves us to forgive each other and resolve our differences. A small inner-city parish is a place where people open their lives to each other, even with all their warts and shortcomings. How moving it is to see Christ turn around the lives of people who have been struggling. The proximity to His work isn't limited to just among our local Bethlehem family. As has been noted many times already, Bethlehem is part of a larger network of suburban sister churches. After two decades of these relationships, we also have other Christians who have become part of our family. That's what a small inner-city ministry can be like!

People Are Often More Open to Risk-Taking

I love the words of Matthew 14:28–29 when the disciples were out in a boat on the Sea of Galilee. A terrifying storm arose, and the disciples feared their boat would capsize and they would drown. Jesus came to the disciples' rescue by walking on top of the water. Remember Peter? He was an impulsive, risk-taking disciple. He said to Jesus, "Lord, if it is You, command me to come to You on the water." When Jesus invited Peter to come to Him walking on the water, the middle of verse 29 says, "And Peter got out of the boat, and walked on the water, and came toward Jesus." Stepping out of the boat to walk on the water was a RISK! Peter could have sunk into the waves. Many people would never take that risk! But because Jesus invited Peter, it was a completely sure bet!

Doing ministry is filled with risks! Often when I write grant applications to foundations and congregations, their questions sometimes make me chuckle. Some funders want every part of a plan so spelled out and every piece of due diligence completed. I sometimes think they want a statement that just about says, "This ministry is a sure thing. There is no risk to it. It has a 100% chance of total success!" I'm sure by now that you are chuckling, too. Of course, we want to do our best in planning ministry. We want to try and have answers for every possible question or hole in a ministry plan. But think about it—there is no sure thing in a private business deal, a government funding plan, a ministry endeavor, or anything else in life! There is risk to everything!

When churches have people in their pews and sufficient tithes and offerings coming in to have the kind of ministry that they want to have, sometimes they become comfortable and complacent in their approach to ministry. They hesitate in trying to reach people who are beyond what they currently are as an organization. Even when the community mission field around them has changed, they maintain a mindset that says, "We'll just stay how we are. If those people want to come to us and become like us, then wonderful. If they don't want to come, then we'll just exist as we are as long as we have people and money to remain how we are."

Since urban communities change at such a fast pace, this thinking is often the prescription for the rapid death of that ministry. Yet, there are instances when urban churches realize that doing "the same things the same way" in ministry will likely spell a quick death to their ministry. While churches that realize this and are willing to try and address it are rare, being open to new risk-taking approaches that can reach people with the Gospel in new ways is exciting. I am the kind of person who says, "Sure, this ministry plan has risks to it, but we have put it before the Lord in prayer. He is nudging us to go in this direction. Okay, LET'S GO!" Finally, I find that working with a group of people whose faith is in the Lord of All who enables them to take risks is another reason why it's great to be part of a small inner-city ministry!

84

CHURCH or BUSINESS, WHICH ONE IS IT?

To have a dynamic outreach ministry in an urban community, you will need help as a pastor/ministry leader. That's an understatement, right?

Where will your help come from? I've already pointed to the fact that as ministries with very limited funding, we have to be strong in developing volunteer staffs for our work. At the same time, there are some jobs that will benefit from having a paid person—a person who will be accountably present and whose leadership is vital for the success of the program.

WHERE do you find such a person? That is an especially challenging question for the specialized work of an inner-city ministry.

My church body has professionally trained church workers who can be called to become professional ministry leaders in parishes. They have titles like Director of Christian Education, Deaconess, Director of Evangelism, Director of Children's Ministries, etc. Here are three challenge we face in the inner-city:

1. We usually don't have the finances to pay the full-time salary that such candidates like this need to serve in our contexts. Most people in these positions in the Lutheran Church-Missouri Synod are not bi-vocational.

2. Even if we had the money to pay them, it is rare to find a professional church worker with the skill set to walk into an urban outreach and be effective. Such individuals, though experienced and wise about general ministry, often don't have the first idea about how inner-city communities work. They almost need a "full plate" of training to even begin to become effective in an urban or multi-cultural context.

3. In addition, there is often a very real fear factor. If you didn't grow up in an urban, high-crime context, and if you've never lived in such a community or had any experience ministering in such a place, your comfort level will often keep you from doing the kind of community work that is needed. You won't feel comfortable calling and visiting at night when most people are home. Workers like this spend more time in their office, when they need to spend most of their time on the street. They know they need to be on the street, but they're not really comfortable with it. I'm just being REAL about how it is! In the

exceptional case where you might learn of an urban church worker who is excellent at ministering in an inner-city community, they are often sought after by others and not affordable to you. Or they are already leading their own urban ministry and aren't really interested in working on a staff led by somebody other than themselves.

In the long run, I think our national church body needs to do a better job of raising up ministry professionals for urban city ministries (that's a realm that I can't directly control) for our immediate ministry needs. However, I've discovered that the best way to find strong staff for our urban outreach is to raise them up from within our own congregational context.

I first saw this idea in action from my very creative colleague Pastor John Brunette. Pastor Brunette is the lead pastor of Faith Lutheran Church in Oakville, Missouri, (a suburb of St. Louis). They have a huge staff today, but when John first came to Faith, the staff was basically just him. He began employing capable wives and moms within the congregation who had paused their work life to have children. When they were ready to get back into the working world, Pastor Brunette brought them on staff part-time. As they grew in their work and the church grew, the jobs grew. Many became excellent full-time staff members.

One of my first experiences using this concept was about 20 years ago with one of our Bethlehem family members. "Ruby" was looking to pick up some extra hours at a second job in a clothing store to supplement her family's income. I asked her if she would want to lead our Jr. Youth on a part-time basis instead. She was excited about it and did a great job with them for a number of years until her son grew out of that age group. At Bethlehem, we've repeated that strategy several times. Today, we employ many part-time people in our programs. Most of the time it has worked well both for the workers and the church's ministry.

HOWEVER, through it all, there is one hard understanding we've often had to keep clarifying:

Bethlehem is your CHURCH HOME, but also your PLACE OF

EMPLOYMENT. What is life like when the CHURCH is both your FAITH FAMILY and your PLACE OF EMPLOYMENT? What is life like when the PASTOR is both your SHEPHERD/PASTOR and your BOSS/SUPERVISOR? What is life like when you are in a place where you are both a SHEEP and an EMPLOYEE?

Pause a moment and think about this dual position. Some people are able to keep it crystal clear. For many other people, the situation often becomes cloudy, sometimes causes hurt, and needs continual clarification. Maybe some fictional examples will help this problem become more real:

Tony has been working for you as an outreach worker. His job is to contact people—both new contacts and follow-up contacts. You meet with him every week to talk about his contacts. You have made it clear that you expect 10 hours each week of calling on people. You ask for documentation. He has given you some documentation, but it's not 10 hours' worth of calling. When you ask him if he has been doing 10 full hours of calls, he says, "No, not really. Sorry." While you appreciate his honesty, what do you do? What would happen if Tony worked for the "Smith Company"? Would Tony receive his full paycheck for that work period?

Jason works in your afterschool program for kids and is supposed to be present every day at 3:00 p.m. However, at least two days each week for the past two weeks he hasn't shown up until 3:15 p.m. for work. What do you do? What would happen if Jason worked for the Smith Company?

Carmen works as a receptionist at your church. Her job is to be in the office, on-site, from 8:00 a.m. until 1:00 p.m. every weekday. She is an hourly worker and has other office duties besides just being present. Carmen has small kids and has been leaving two or three days a month for doctor's appointments for her children. However, she claims her full five hours each day (even when she has missed a couple of hours for the doctor appointments) because she thinks she should be paid more. Some days Carmen also brings her kids to work with her. What do you do? What would happen if Carmen worked for the Smith Company?

Do you sense the tension? Some people know work, is work, is work.

Other people, while they expect real money from the church for the work they render, see "church jobs" as not real jobs. They sometimes think fair and true basic work protocol and decorum should be relaxed in the name of the church being "the family of God and a place of love and unlimited forgiveness."

There is an additional tension from the church/employer perspective. It's a matter of stewardship. Jesus Himself has said in Luke 10:7, "The laborer is worthy of his wages." The same is said in 1 Timothy 5:18. This principle of "a fair day's wage for a fair day's work" is both true for the worker to do *and the employer to expect.*

So is it okay for a worker to leverage their way to not doing the job they were hired to do, while claiming the church should be loving and understanding, even to the point of making special work allowances?

Think about the funds that were given to pay a certain staff person in a particular ministry project. We know it is common business practice for a company's money to bear its best return by each employee working in a fair and upright manner. Isn't that same principle God-pleasing when it is the church's money funding the employed position?

Consider also the following two points:

The church is a business. Some would say that it's the "biggest business in the world." We need good business practices. We need to keep good records. We need to have accurate accounting practices for the funds we receive. Likewise, we also need a good employment structure and practices. Workers need to know job expectations so they can succeed. Having good business practices, especially in the area of personnel, can save a lot of wasted time and energy dealing with personnel matters.

For example, our ministry has grown and we've hired a number of part-time employees. As far as getting your paycheck early, don't even ask. The answer is, "No." Pay day is pay day. That is our policy and, like any policy, it is useless if it is not adhered to. For us, the intent is not to be unfeeling, but it's a stewardship issue. We have a wonderful treasurer who is a VOLUNTEER! If we allow one employee to get their check early for their emergency, every other employee will expect their turn for their emergency. What happens when you have a VOLUNTEER or even a paid treasurer who has to deal with 20–25 employee "emergencies?" That treasurer gets worn down. The energy they could use toward their regular treasurer work gets sidetracked to deal with people's emergencies. (Of course, we have a social ministry arm of our church that can sometimes partially help with occasional emergencies among Bethlehem family members, but this is a separate and different issue from the business procedural practice of our church.)

The church needs to not lose sight that it is also a ministry. Picture a good worker on your ministry team who has already used all their personal and vacation days. Then comes the news that this worker's mother must be put into hospice care. The worker needs a few extra days to make that transition for her mother. Add to that reality the fact that this worker can't afford to lose pay for those three or four days. This is an opportunity for the church to show compassionate love for a worker who has been faithful and productive, even though by the letter of the law, the church is not legally responsible to grant such paid time off to help this worker. *But it is the church's compassionate call, not something the employee should feel is owed to them!* Consider another example. A worker needs to take a couple of weeks of leave to handle personal business. They are a part-time, hourly worker. The church would have every right to let the employee go and move on with someone new. As a ministry, however, they could choose to hold the job open for the employee who needs an unpaid break, even though they are not legally bound to do so.

The challenge is defining both aspects of this in wise ways. How do you navigate and ensure an employee is not taking advantage of the church ministry? At the same time, how does the church know when to show compassion?

One of the great thematic distinctions of God's Word is Law and Gospel. In its purest sense, the Law of God tells us what we are to do for God. When we fail to do it, it is called sin. The Law outlines that all wrong and shortcoming has a consequence. The Law operates by saying, "When I do 'this,' 'this' is what happens to me. I get what I deserve." The Gospel of the Lord is just the opposite. The heart of God's Good News to us is the wonderful news expressed in 2 Corinthians 5:21. While we should suffer for our own offenses and wrongs and get what we deserve, "God made Jesus who had no sin to be sin for us, so that in Him, we are the righteousness of God." God is compassionate unto us on account of the work of Christ at the cross. The Gospel is that God doesn't give us what we deserve, but graciously gives us BETTER than what we deserve through the sacrificial work of Christ.

What does that have to do with handling people? It's precisely the wise roadmap toward handling people. Let's say there is a person full of pride who wants to try and "get something over" on their employer (the church) by not giving a fair day's work for a fair day's pay. That person needs to receive the law! They need to know that what you do, or don't do, is in direct connection to what you receive in life. If you've not been a good employee, if you've been lazy, if you have not been honest and not given your best at your job, then you will get your just wages for your behavior. There's no break or mercy for you! On the other hand, for an individual who is humble, grateful, and recognizes what their behavior and situation deserve, this individual is primed and ready to receive the undeserved kindness of gracious favor from their employer. Such treatment by a ministry of Christ can remind them of the greater grace of how God makes each of us right for the sake of Christ.

So are we CHRIST'S CHURCH or just a BUSINESS? Yes, in fact, **BOTH!**

85

RAISING UP 21ST CENTURY URBAN MINISTRY WORKERS—A FOLLOW UP TO "CHURCH or BUSINESS, WHICH ONE IS IT?"

At one time in the history of occupations, if you wanted to serve in the medical field, you went to medical school to be a doctor. Or you went to nursing school to be a nurse. If you wanted to be a plumber, you went to trade school to be a plumber. If you wanted to help people physically recover from injury, you went to college to get a physical therapy degree. If you wanted to work in ministry, you went to seminary to get a Master of Divinity degree. Our world has changed. To serve in the medical field today, you might go to a shorter training program and become a paramedic. Instead of becoming a full-blown plumber, you might undertake training to work for a national company like Roto Rooter. Instead of getting a doctorate in physical therapy, you might go to a two-year technical school and become a physical therapy assistant.

In the area of ministry, there are so many people who are very GIFTED BY THE LORD for ministry and who can be INVALUABLE MINISTRY LEADERS in an urban ministry—even though formal seminary training may not be for them.

We so desperately need more urban ministry workers in the 21st century. How do we equip and empower more workers to reach people with the Good News of Jesus for urban mission fields? Let me suggest a few theses to chew on regarding this topic.

1. If we want to be serious about bringing the Gospel to people in low-income urban areas, as national church bodies, let's intentionally train more professional church workers who feel called to the mission field of the inner-city. Let's also **develop creative ways for them to be supported** as full-time workers in urban mission fields. This is a call to my national church body and to the excellent institutions we have to train professional church workers.

IF WE, AS A CHURCH BODY, WANT TO AGGRESSIVELY REACH THE CITY FOR CHRIST, LET'S INTENTIONALLY TRAIN WORKERS FOR THIS MISSION FIELD.

IF WE, AS A CHURCH BODY, WANT TO AGGRESSIVELY REACH THE CITY FOR CHRIST, LET'S ENGAGE SOME OF OUR MOST CREATIVE MINDS NATIONALLY TO DEVELOP A WAY FOR SUCH URBAN WORKERS TO BE FUNDED. To continue to put the development of that funding strategy **on the individual worker** or **the individual urban congregation** will simply continue to yield the result we've been seeing—some workers work in the city until they can't financially handle it any longer; other workers gifted for urban work never even try because the pressure of making ends meet for their families is so difficult to handle. The bottom line is that this strategy results in fewer and fewer ministry professionals in urban low-income areas.

IF WE, AS A CHURCH BODY, AREN'T COMFORTABLE WORKING IN URBAN AREAS and DON'T WANT TO INVEST IN INTENTIONAL MINISTRY FOR THESE AREAS, let's just be honest about who we are and publicly declare that we are a denomination mainly for the suburbs and that urban work just isn't cost effective. And let's no longer pretend that the Acts 1:8 mandate of Jesus "to the remotest parts of the earth" applies to us, but rather to the worldwide Christian Church at large.

2. Let's recognize that a full master's-level seminary education or even a bachelor's-level Bible college degree is not for everyone to pursue. There is MUCH GIFTEDNESS BY GOD to HIS CHURCH in people who will never be able to enter a seminary academic or Bible college program.

Here's some REAL TALK:

Some people who can be powerfully used as leaders in urban ministry contexts won't be able to handle the academic rigor of a seminary or

Bible college education. Some can't financially afford to pay to go to seminary and suspend their family income for the years necessary to do this.

Regarding these servants of Jesus—we can't afford to lose their giftedness from God to His Church in low-income, urban, cross-cultural settings. For some of our essential ministry jobs in dynamic urban ministries, a more formal academic theological education (though a blessing) isn't needed. **Does an evangelist** whose main job is to lead the church in reaching children and families with the Gospel and inviting others to church programs need a college-level academic theological training? **Does a team leader who supervises meaningful activities in an afterschool program** and teaches basic Bible stories and the truths of our Christian faith need a college-level academic theological training? Especially if we've empowered them with a strong Christian curriculum? **Does a church worker who assimilates new people into the life of the church family** through small group fellowship events and simple small group Bible studies need a college-level academic theological training to do this kind of work well? **Does a church worker who leads a social help arm of a ministry** that receives donations from friends and then distributes items to families in need really need a college-level academic theological training to do this well?

I think you see my point. I am not against excellent formal and rigorous seminary and Bible college training for ministry. We need trained theologians in parishes. I am grateful for the opportunity I had to study at Concordia Seminary in St. Louis. I am simply advocating for us to raise up and develop "another level" of employed church workers. They are VITAL team members to any urban outreach. If we are to effectively reach the vast multitude of spiritually lost people in the city, we will never make even a dent in the work if it's left only to professional, seminary-trained church workers.

Currently, we have few ministry training options beyond an entire formal seminary education, and even fewer ministry training options specially tuned to working in low-income, urban, cross-cultural settings.

3. While we still need the excellent theological development a seminary education affords, pragmatic virtual online training can be a valuable resource to those who are gifted to work on a ministry team (but for whom a regular seminary residential program is not workable). Here's the good news. Already, many fine theological institutions are making use of this excellent training medium.

It is such a benefit for people to be able to grow in their ministry skills and deepen in their knowledge of Christ, while not having to leave their life context. So we are headed in the right direction.

Let me make three final pleas regarding this avenue of urban ministry training:

- Let's keep it affordable. How excellent a product is is somewhat immaterial if it is priced beyond what the people who need it can afford.

- Let's keep urban ministry training accessible on an academic level that is especially tuned to people who may not have had much academic training beyond their high school education.

- Let's keep urban ministry training current and true to ministry life by using teachers who are still currently on the ministry scene to teach this mid-level training. This is so essential because the landscape of urban ministry is in constant change. This training will be so much more effective if led by those who are in the midst of the urban ministry scene every day and who can see how the context of ministry and the people being reached continually changes.

86

THE BETHLEHEM EMPLOYMENT AGENCY

It is one of the most rewarding parts of our ministry—and one of the most frustrating and time-consuming parts at the same time—when we serve as, "The Bethlehem Employment Agency." First, let me say from the outset that my colleague Pastor Gerard Bolling is an extraordinarily gifted partner, especially in this area. He has taken our ministry of developing people to a whole other level! That means more effective workers for the Kingdom of Jesus! But it hasn't been easy.

Let me recount what kind of church employment I'm referring to. Some programs at Bethlehem operate using volunteer leaders. This includes programs like our weekly kids Bible outreach ministry, our basketball teams in our athletic ministry, Vacation Bible School, our Taking Jesus to the Streets ministry, staff for events like our four annual weekend basketball tournaments, etc. Other Bethlehem programs are operated by some part-time paid staff members. These include programs like our nightly Bethlehem After School (BAS) program, our Ephratha Activity Center ministries to the children of Ferguson, the lead organizers of our Sr. and Jr. Youth programs, etc. Why not staff these with volunteers? Most of these programs meet on multiple weeknights and serve children. Part-time paid staff are more dependable than volunteer staff for programs that meet with greater frequency (because of the paycheck incentive).

Here is our thinking: We can't have a program where children show up and there is no adult leadership to take care of them. We also can't have a program where children show up and there is not a large enough group of adult leaders to take care of them (that sets up our effort for failure). As I have said in other essays, we have found that our best staff for our kids programs are leaders who are already within our ministry. They understand both the message of Christ we're trying to communicate and the life context of the people to whom we're trying to communicate it. Yet, in our urban ministry context, raising up part-time paid leaders and workers for our program is not simple and has some different components to it than other ministry contexts.

To illustrate the complexity of this issue, I will present the rest of this essay in a point-counterpoint format.

POINT: It is so encouraging to see someone grow in basic life-work skills—especially as they become a better servant of Christ and are used in the work of Christ's Church.

COUNTERPOINT: It is very emotionally taxing and time-consuming to coach people into an understanding of basic work practices. You must cover things like being on time, not calling off work when they don't feel like coming in, keeping a good personal and team attitude at work, understanding basic work decorum, understanding how pay day works, etc.) so that they can be assets to a church ministry staff.

POINT: We find that our urban context is full of extremely gifted and skilled people who could be excellent potential church ministry staff members.

COUNTERPOINT: Many of the people we encounter for church work lack basic work disciplines and the ability to not only gain a job but also keep a job.

POINT: We would love every person God puts into our path to develop to their fullest as a servant of Jesus. We especially need strong ministry leaders and workers who understand how to work in an urban context and extend the pastoral ministry God has called us to do. Otherwise, the outreach to others who don't know the Gospel will be significantly limited.

COUNTERPOINT: Because ministry leaders have such limited time and are not called to be employment counselors, we have to exercise great wisdom and know how much employment coaching we can really afford to give someone. We must know when it's time to move on from a particular person in a certain ministry job because it just isn't a good fit.

POINT: For the sake of good stewardship of the Lord's ministry funds,

A PLACE NOT FORGOTTEN

I must often take on the role of an EFFECTIVE MANAGER of employees and seek to get the best work from them.

COUNTERPOINT: Because we don't have the money to hire a church human resources person or a business manager, I have to remember I am still their PASTOR. I should have a deeper level of understanding than most managers. Being their pastor also means I need to be sensitive about not allowing a messy job situation to disturb my line of communication with them to bring them the Gospel of Jesus Christ.

POINT: Many people we encounter are unemployed and in need of a job.

COUNTERPOINT: Our first mission is not simply to provide people a part-time job, but to help them know the Savior. Furthermore, not every person is right for the jobs we have at the church. Working in a church ministry in a paid capacity is not a good fit for every person.

POINT: Some people who work for the church see their church work as "not real" work.

COUNTERPOINT: Yet, these same people expect real money.

POINT: The pace of our urban ministry work and the complexity and intensity of people we often work with often makes for a hard job for ministry workers. A number of people have recognized this and have chosen not to work in the jobs we offer. Or they have attempted to work in the jobs we currently have available and have not lasted.

COUNTERPOINT: Because these are hard jobs, our work as trainers and coaches in developing good, part-time paid ministry workers is challenging. Sometimes it is also exasperating and discouraging. Yet, it is needed for the sake of aggressively bringing Christ to people.

POINT: In most jobs, the LAW rules. "Here are the rules of this job and work context... follow them or you're fired."

COUNTERPOINT: In our work perspective, LAW and GOSPEL must constantly be practiced. Yes, there must be structure and order—the LAW—you can't continually be late for work or call to say you're not coming in. You can't continually have bad days at your job, etc. But there also must be GOSPEL—even when we've had to fire someone. A person may have been away from a job for a while, but when a person has wanted to try and start over, we have given them another chance to succeed as a part-time paid urban ministry worker.

POINT: Often my friends in the business world have offered many great tips on how a business should run, even in a ministry.

COUNTERPOINT: There will be very few people who understand the context of developing and managing urban ministry workers. Why? The work is hard. The hours are often long. The pay rate is usually at the bottom. The "disrespect factor" is often abundant. Most managers in regular business contexts, after one week in an urban ministry context, might very well fire everybody! Find other urban ministry mangers who face what you face so that you can continue to be encouraged and not give up.

POINT: When people you've been trying to coach and manage get upset—even though you've been the kind person who gave them a chance at this job—you will very possibly be labeled the "devil."

COUNTERPOINT: Don't take it personally. Think about God's amazing patience with you and all of us!

I want to offer a few closing thoughts about "The Bethlehem Employment Agency." **Our ministry didn't start this way.** In the beginning, there were no grants to help us with these expanded ministries, and we also had no money of our own. In the beginning, there were only volunteers. Paid part-time ministry positions only occurred over time as our ministry expanded.

Remember that leading and managing volunteer workers and leaders is even harder, since there is no financial incentive for them to work consistently. Sometimes when the urban ministry work gets hard or exhausting, volunteer workers are quick to call off. This happens even in the times they had committed to because they just don't feel like doing it. When that person is a volunteer, there is much less you can do to get them to be consistent about serving.

When your funding is dependent on grants, the conditions of jobs, pay rates of jobs, and even duration of jobs are often stipulated

by the grant or gift arrangement and are out of your control. This can become frustrating for workers. Understanding how to effectively develop and manage employees is another important "toolbox skill" for an urban ministry leader.

87

INJUSTICE

Some people would say it is impossible to write on the topic of "things urban" or "urban ministry" without saying something about the topic of INJUSTICE. That is a fair and true statement. However, what I will share below will very likely disappoint some and anger others. Some people may say, "You side-stepped a key and vital issue to ministry in our society today." Let me say a few things in advance. First, this isn't a book about social injustice. That would be a work unto itself. Second, the hard part of talking about INJUSTICE is that everybody has their own definition about what INJUSTICE is... even what is REAL INJUSTICE vs. INJUSTICE that is just people being "overly sensitive." The phrase, "overly sensitive," isn't mine. It's one I hear from people all the time when another person has something that, in their view, is "unjust" and they feel very passionate and upset about it—but someone else doesn't think this unjust matter is that serious. So they label it as merely being "over sensitive." Everybody has their opinion on what is true INJUSTICE and what is just being "overly sensitive."

It's like the urban phrase that has been quoted in many speeches and sermons, as well as sung in many songs—"You don't know my story." It's hard to even track down a source for that quote, or versions of that quote, because it has been used in so many different ways. Pause and think about the quote for a moment. Of course, I don't know YOUR story because I'm not YOU. Likewise, because YOU are not in MY SKIN, there's no way you can know EXACTLY ABOUT ME. This is the context in which we need to think respectfully about that word, "INJUSTICE." None of us can know exactly about another person—what they feel, what they value, how hurt they are about issues. But what is vital is that we RESPECT and UNDERSTAND people from all walks of life and levels of life and understand INJUSTICE in their life differently. (I'll get to the source of this principle in a moment.) One other preliminary comment. If we are ever to understand each other and empathize with what each other faces in life regarding INJUSTICE, we need to get past the INJUSTICE COMPETITION. In other words, thinking my lot in life is far worse than your lot—and not only that but my horrible lot in life can be my lifelong excuse (more about that in a moment).

What is Injustice?

It is factual that there has been and continues to be INJUSTICE in our world regarding life opportunity based on ethnicity and gender. It's true that skin color and ethnicity have been barriers for many regarding financial and career/job/life upward mobility. The same could be said for unequal pay among men and women who do the same job. True! True! True!

But people's individual stories reveal that the matter of INJUSTICE in everyday life pervades so many more areas. Consider these examples:

It's NOT JUST when someone in their 50s faces a tough time getting a similar paying job when the company they worked for downsizes and lays them off because of their age.

It's NOT JUST that our society keeps saying that we value our children so much. We pass so many laws to guarantee the safety of our kids. However, a teacher like my wife who spends the most daily time with a family's kids during the school year, makes so much less than some of the kids' parents with corporate jobs and significant incomes. The profession of teaching is so devalued salary-wise, yet so much is expected job-wise from a teacher (e.g., "Make my kids great and successful, even though I spend less and less time with my kids").

It's NOT JUST when one person talks in all kinds of vile ways "motherxxxxxx this" and "Bixxh, come over here..." or blares their music with that kind of language through mega-speakers in public places. Of course, freedom of speech in this country allows someone to say or play what they want. But where is my freedom not to have that blasting in my ears in public places, or worse, in the ears of my grandkids?

It's **NOT JUST** when people gather in public places, some reeking so strongly of weed, and I almost get "high" just being in the same room. They have the right to be who they are and smell like they smell. Where's my right to have fresh air and share that same public space? INJUSTICE again.

In a public place or even in the workplace, what gives one person the right to dress provocatively, yet another person can't uphold their standard for a more modest public dress environment? Of course, one person says, "You don't have to look at them." That's true. **That's NOT JUST.**

What is JUST about the fact that two people today can commit the same crime, yet receive very different penalties because one person can afford a better lawyer than the other? That's NOT JUST.

In the same way, you demand that I be ACCEPTING of YOUR GENDER PREFERENCES, but you won't respect my "story" that has a TOTAL DIFFERENT PERSPECTIVE on GENDER PREFERENCES. Who decides who is right/wrong or insensitive? **Is it INJUSTICE when one person ends up always having to adapt to the other person?**

It's **NOT JUST** when someone doesn't work a fair day's work for a fair day's pay, and thinks that is okay because they're not getting paid what they think they should be paid.

UNDOUBTEDLY, INJUSTICE THAT RESULTS IN LOSS OF LIFE COMMANDS OUR ATTENTION. That is inarguable.

Yet, there are so many other cases of INJUSTICE IN LIFE that significantly affect the lives of people and also bring real hurt and frustration. For example, what about the individual whose car is stolen and our local administration decides the police are not to chase the suspects who stole the vehicle? Some would say, "Just report it to your insurance." What about the cost of the deductible and other associated replacement costs for the crime victim who was barely making ends meet to begin with? What about lost wages for the time they spend handling that situation? Isn't there some INJUSTICE for them as a taxpayer who pays for law enforcement when that law enforcement has been instructed not to serve in that situation? Is the wrong done and the loss experienced by this person simply to be dismissed as not that important? **Who decides what is real INJUSTICE that should be dealt with and what INJUSTICE isn't that important?**

There's another follow-up truth we need to think about, especially as Christians. **What is the standard for what is JUST and RIGHT? We would say that the Lord God Almighty, through His Word, decides what is JUST and RIGHT. Yet, not everybody else who lives on this planet would agree with that absolute standard.** Let me picture this concept in a very brief and Biblical way. Hear the Word of the Lord.

Proverbs 28:5, "Evil men do not understand justice, but those who seek the Lord understand all things." How true! God has His standard of what is just and right. It is often a totally different standard from what our world has decided is right and wrong. We're facing that dichotomy in the world right now. For example, God defines marriage as only between a man and a woman, but our world labels that truth as insensitive and unjust. **Romans 1:26-28** makes clear that homosexuality is not right in God's sight. In **1 Corinthians 6:19-20**, the Lord also reminds those who believe in Christ as our Savior that "our body is the temple of God the Holy Spirit... you are not your own... you have been bought with a price; therefore glorify God in your body." Many today would reject that idea as not right and even unjust. They would say a person's body is their property. So, they would argue, it is a woman's choice to do with her body what she wants, even if it means aborting a child in her womb.

One of the most famous words regarding justice in God's Word is **Micah 6:8, "...what does the Lord require of you? But to do justice, to love kindness, and to walk humbly with your God."** That is an interesting Scripture to chew on. For some people, only the first phrase matters—"DO JUSTICE" as they define it, and they ignore the latter two phrases. Others believe life is mainly about being a good person, so they espouse, "DO JUSTICE... LOVE KINDNESS... but that 'walking with God' business? Uh uh. Don't really have time for that!" Still others would say, "I walk with God... MY god (whatever I conceive him to be)."

Whether we like it or not, the Lord spoke these truths through his prophet Micah:

- JUSTICE is what the Lord our God determines is right and correct (as revealed in His Word); it's not open to our opinion or decision.

- For us, the work and living out of justice and kindness proceed out of a right relationship with the one true God, the Lord.

Without first having a right relationship with the Lord our God, through Jesus Christ and His reconnecting us to God through His sacrifice on the cross, there is no way we can DO TRUE JUSTICE in His sight. God said through His prophet Isaiah in Isaiah 64:6 that, on our own, "all our righteous deeds are like a filthy garment."

To be sure, there is CIVIL JUSTICE—acting just as our world would define justice (though even that definition keeps being open to interpretation, as noted above). But the justice we seek to do is GOD'S JUSTICE, as defined by God's Word. As we've already observed, many times these two perspectives on WHAT JUSTICE IS are vastly different and often come in conflict.

Let's get back to the basics. Let's go back to the Creator who brought forth this world that we live in. HE sets the definition for what is RIGHT and JUST. As servants of the Most High God, the only God who truly IS GOD, we must never forget one thing:

The LORD OUR GOD is the arbiter of JUSTICE through His Word!

With that truth clear, let's be clear about something else:

THE ROOT OF ALL INJUSTICE IS SIN. And THE ROOT OF ALL SIN IS SELF.

So what's the way to LIVING as GOD'S PEOPLE who CHAMPION HIS JUSTICE? **Each of us needs to BECOME RIGHT before we can BE RIGHT toward others.**

I find the first chapter of Isaiah to be a very useful guide toward DOING JUSTICE TOWARD OTHERS. Before we get to the call in verse 17, "Seek justice, Reprove the ruthless, Defend the orphan, Plead for the widow," come back with me to the beginning of the chapter and see where we need to start regarding ourselves. Follow me through a quick study of this precious word:

Verse 3 – God's people are focused on themselves (always a prescription for failure) "An ox... a donkey... But Israel does not know..."

Verse 4 – When we ARE sinful, how do we act?

Verses 10–15 – I love this part. It is so true. In verse 11 God says, "I have had enough of burnt offerings..." In verse 13, God says, "Bring your worthless offerings no longer..." In verse 15, God says, "So when you spread your hands in prayer, I will hide My eyes from you... your hands are covered with blood." "Worship, having church, giving offerings, is NO SUBSTITUTE for BEING RIGHT WITH ME," says the Lord (which is the PRELUDE for DOING RIGHT TOWARD OTHERS).

So Where Does Doing Justice Begin?

In verse 16, God says to His people, "Wash yourselves, make yourselves clean..." In verse 18, the Lord even reminds us that HE will do the purifying of us if we want Him to do so. "Though your sins are as scarlet, they will be as white as snow; though they are red like crimson, they will be like wool." That's what God did for us when He put His Son, Jesus, on the cross for our sins. For every INJUSTICE of our lives that we HAVE EXPERIENCED or HAVE DONE toward somebody else, at the cross JESUS "was pierced for our transgressions, He was crushed for our iniquities..." (Isaiah 53:5) Think about those words, "transgressions" and "iniquities." They are simply synonyms for SIN, synonyms for INJUSTICE done. That verse from Isaiah 53:5 concludes, "...and by His scourging we are healed."

Back to Isaiah 1. When we are RIGHT and JUST with God because of the work of Jesus on our behalf, we are ready and able to "Seek justice, Reprove the ruthless, Defend the orphan, Plead for the widow," like the Lord says in Isaiah 1:17.

So what does it mean for us to SEEK JUSTICE as urban ministry leaders? I've known some pastors who have felt their ministry calling was to carry a sign at every protest and show up for every march or press conference when injustice is receiving attention. You could spend almost all your ministry time speaking out and working against every example of injustice—unjust housing practices and corrupt landlords, racial injustice, gender discrimination, abortion, the need for reform in our penal system, etc.

Let me call it the way that I see things:

While all of these are worthy causes, from my perspective as I serve as a pastor/urban ministry leader, I have to use my time and resources in a balanced way that supports my calling as a minister of the Gospel in a congregational setting.

A Justice Balance

My first focus is that people know Jesus as their Savior, that they know He gave His life for their sins on the cross, and that they have a faith relationship with Him. Whatever I am going to invest ministry time in, it has to be connected to bringing about this goal. "For what does it profit a man to gain the whole world, and forfeit his soul?" (Mark 8:36)

My second focus is that I'm not expecting this world to be a JUST and RIGHT place. I don't expect the United States government to respect life in the same way I uphold life as valuable because I am a follower of Christ. While I wish that they would do so, and I'll vote for those who do, I don't expect lawmakers to make decisions with a Biblical mindset that is not of this country or of this world. While I want life on Earth to be in step with the values of the Lord our God, I keep remembering what my "play" sister, Annette Silver-Betts, says, "Jesus is coming!" This world isn't our end. We're looking forward to the next world. Philippians 3:20 says of our real home, "Our citizenship is in heaven." We should never lose sight of that fact as Christians. Our search for JUSTICE in this world is limited.

My third focus is that I believe I can be the most effective by working with people one-on-one. If my calling was to be a community organizer, I might act differently. If I led a social service agency, I might act differently. If I had a large staff of people, I might be able to do more in the area of advocacy. But I don't. For example, in the area of valuing life, I'm against abortion. I find my best work in valuing life happens when I work with a young pregnant woman in my congregation one-on-one and encourage her not to have the abortion. *AND* then, after she chooses life and has the baby, I am THERE for that child, and I call on our church to BE THERE to help her raise this new child in Christ. Don't miss that last sentence about presence and action.

I respect that everybody has their own calling and role to play in justice work. Some people's work includes being part of loud voices and demonstrations calling on our nation to stop the unjust treatment of people on the basis of their skin color. After having lived through the Mike Brown incident and the accompanying riots in Ferguson in 2014, let me share what the Holy Spirit has shown me to be our role in our congregation.

As I mentioned earlier, news media came to our city from throughout the world during those riots. Big time preachers and even large local ministries made their presence very visibly known. But when all the lights and the cameras packed up, and the low-income housing developments of Canfield Green and Northwinds Apartments were no longer inhabited with a national media presence, guess what else happened? For the most part, the CHURCH of Jesus Christ seemed to leave as well. I can't forget the families who asked us, "Are you coming back? Or are you gonna be like the other church folks who were here, but then left and have hardly ever come back to help us since?"

Christ's Church needs to be dynamic and active, not just in moments of tragedy and emergency, but also after those moments to try and keep those moments from happening again. Rhetoric is important to inspire people and expose sinful behavior. However, there is no substitute for ongoing Christlike Servanthood to make a difference in people's lives day in and day out—even when there is no immediate incident on a national stage.

You will need to determine what your social justice role is for you and your ministry. But our role at Bethlehem is helping families in low-income urban communities by providing strong programs so that kids have safe places to go, creating new affordable housing in the community so families have good places to live, and starting new educational opportunities so that there is a good place for children to go to school. Those are some of the components of building a strong and safe community where families can thrive! That's the kind of JUSTICE WORK that proceeds forward after God's initial work of making us RIGHT WITH HIM.

INJUSTICE IS EVERYWHERE, and it comes in ALL KINDS OF PACKAGES! No one has the market cornered on injustice. I want to use my life to help people first know Christ. Then they will be perfectly RIGHT with God. Then, I want to use my time and energy to come alongside people in need of help with all the resources I can muster.

88

INCARNATION

I enjoy watching Guy Fieri's television show, *Diners, Drive-ins, and Dives*. Because I enjoy cooking and love eating, I love to see the demonstrations of various dishes. The cooking inspires me to be creative in the kitchen and try new things. What the show really makes me want to do is VISIT the places to try the food myself. That's how business works. When you offer a great meal for people to eat and word gets out, people will flock to you!

So why doesn't that work for us in the Church of Jesus Christ? We have the greatest meal to serve people that exists in this world. Remember what Jesus said in John 6:35, "I am the Bread of Life, he who comes to Me will not hunger, and he who believes in Me will never thirst." A "meal" of Jesus that satisfies a person so that they hunger and thirst for nothing more—what else would anyone need? So why aren't people flocking to the church to know their sins are forgiven and that God is on their side in life? That's easy. Turn to 2 Corinthians 4:4 in your Bible. I love how Paul says, "The god of this world has blinded the minds of the unbelieving so that they might not see the gospel of the glory of Christ." Now for a more difficult question. What is the church to do when it has the MEAL that EVERYBODY NEEDS, the MEAL that TAKES CARE of EVERYTHING, but people often aren't attracted to it? The answer is... drum roll, please... **INCARNATE!**

Usually, what we first think of when we run across that word is Christmas and the INCARNATION of Christ. Of all the ways the Lord could have chosen to love us and save us, the Son of God chooses to do it by actually coming into our world to live with us. No wonder the Father named the Savior, "IMMANUEL, God come to be with us." (Matthew 1:23) INCARNATE! And that was Jesus during His 33 years on this Earth. He never cared for us from a distance. His M.O. was always to come up close into the lives of broken people.

One of my favorite memories of this truth is found in Mark 1:40–41. Do you remember it? A man with leprosy "CAME to Jesus." (Mark 1:40) Most people would have run away or not allowed such a man to come close to them because of the false belief in that day that leprosy was contagious. But look at how the next verse takes the INCARNATION of Jesus into people's lives to a whole other level. It says, "Moved with compassion, Jesus stretched out His Hand and TOUCHED the leper, and said to him, 'I am willing; be cleansed.'" Why not stay at a distance, Jesus, and sort of command him from 50 yards away, "Dude you've come close enough. Be cleaned and go your way!"? That's not Jesus' way.

In doing so, Jesus shows us that love for people and compassionate ministry best happen as we INCARNATE people's lives. Of course, it might get messy. Of course, it might bring danger to us, cost us time, and include sacrifice on our part. But INCARNATING people's lives is the location where vital ministry happens.

In years past, many congregations encouraged the INCARNATION of their pastor by having a parsonage. Some might not be familiar with that term. The parsonage was a house owned by the congregation that was often located right next to the church property. When a pastor came to serve the church, he and his family moved into the parsonage. When that pastor left to serve a different congregation, they would leave the parsonage, and the parsonage would then become the home of the new pastor. One downside was that many pastors who spent their ministry moving from one parsonage to the next never built up any home equity. For some, that became a significant problem when they retired. On the upside, parsonages enabled pastors and their families to live directly in the community where they served. It encouraged them to be able to live INCARNATIONAL in their community, especially at a time when most congregations were made up of people from their surrounding neighborhood. An added benefit of parsonages that we could benefit from today is that in certain communities where housing costs are through the roof, a parsonage would enable pastors to afford to live in the community they serve. I'm thinking about places like Manhattan or Los Angeles where rent is extremely high and the thought of purchasing even a modest home is over half a million dollars (usually outside the budget of most inner-city pastor families). Wouldn't the option of living in a church parsonage be an advantageous option?

Yet, INCARNATIONAL MINISTRY means so much more than just living in the community where you serve.

In reality, this is not even an option for most urban ministry leaders today, especially families with young children. Further, some pastors have missed the real heart of INCARNATIONAL ministry by confusing simply being on-site at the church all day and being available to whomever might stop in with their problem or concern with INCARNATIONAL ministry. NO. Let me be clear. Even in our day of technological instant access via cell phones, every urban ministry leader needs to have some consistent times when people know he will be on-site at the church, in his office, and available to them. Of course, we have to set aside time to get away from people and be alone with the Lord studying His Word, both for our own personal growth and to prepare Bible studies and sermons. Even so, people need to know there are times when they can "drop in" on us to talk. Some might push back, "People can reach me on my phone whenever they want. They can schedule a time for me to meet with them." Sometimes that works, but at other times it does not. Consider the following example:

"David" is a youth at our church. He had been playing basketball one day with some friends he brought to our gym. I just happened to walk through the gym on my way to the bathroom. The gym reeked of marijuana. When I asked who had been smoking weed, even though David hadn't been smoking it, David started talking smart toward me, trying to justify that smoking weed and coming into God's House was no big deal. He and I exchanged some heated words. I wasn't going to force them to leave the gym. I just wanted to make a point, so I said, "Next time, please respect God's House by not getting high and then coming up here to hoop." Then David took the whole thing to another level and began cursing and threatening me!

Here's my point about INCARNATION. A few days later, there was a knock on my office door. It was David, the David I have always known. Humbly he said, "Pastor, sorry about the other day. I shouldn't have said what I said."

"No problem," I said. "I forgive you."

Why did David's apology happen this way? I can't look into David's heart and decisively answer that. But my best guess is that David felt embarrassed. He didn't want to call me because he wanted to see my face and see how I would react to his humble apology. He knew he could catch me most mornings before 1:00 p.m. at my office. For privacy, he also chose a time right before lunch when he thought nobody else might be around.

INCARNATIONAL. Having some consistent known times when people can know that we will be on-site at the church, in our office, and available is important.

But our most valuable INCARNATION in ministry to our people is something more.

Real INCARNATIONAL ministry is LIVING and ACTIVE. It GOES to where people are and then MINISTERS to people in the CONTEXTS where they need our Gospel presence.

Here are some other examples:

Pastor Gerard Bolling is one of those people who could do anything in life and be excellent at it. One of the things he does so well in our ministry is coaching people in developing basic job skills. But he doesn't do this in a scheduled seminar. He does it as he supervises some of our kids outreach programs. When he needs to correct, or as he says "recalibrate," a worker who has gotten off-task or isn't hitting the outcome targets we have set for our individual programs, he is very INCARNATIONAL. He meets with the worker in their job context. Sometimes in this process, he ends up listening to them express some personal matters that have taken the worker off track. He gets to minister to that person about those issues. Sometimes, the worker has gone off track in their work because their life has wandered out of balance. In those moments, it's almost always a spiritual imbalance that is part of the work problem. This is another opportunity for ministry because he was INCARNATE in that person's work life with the church.

My son, Dan Schmidtke, along with Darrell Rogers and Arlando Bolden of our Bethlehem family, are better known as "Coach Dan," "Coach Darrell, and "Coach P." They have led our 4–6th grade, 7–8th grade, and high school basketball ministries for years. And it is, in every way, ministry. Over time, they have INCARNATED significantly into the lives of a few hundred boys using the place that is among the most important places to males of all ages in our community—the basketball court. Coaching basketball has given them opportunity to share Christ as Savior and help kids find a church home at Bethlehem. But it has also been an opportunity to INCARNATE to the boys important lessons, including how forgiveness works when you've lost your cool and being selfless and thinking of others ahead of yourself (just like Christ did for us). These men have also taught the boys that there is a caring among God's people who can support us, even when our biological families let us down. This family love is simply a mirror of what David said about the Lord in Psalm 27:10, "Though my mother and father have forsaken me, the Lord will take me up." Without INCARNATING through basketball (that is so important to our boys and men), I'm not sure that Coach Dan, Coach Darrell, and Coach P, would be able to do such effective ministry to so many young people.

How important ministry to women is today! How do you get it started? How do you draw women together where ministry can occur? Find a common ground and then INCARNATE! Cherelle Hamilton and my daughter, Tequila Pruitt, have done that so well with our dance ministry where women and girls meet weekly to put meaningful coordinated dance movements to Gospel songs with strong, powerful messages. It is truly beautiful to watch and it's most meaningful in Sunday worship. While I enjoy what dance ministry brings to our Sunday worship, to me, the most important ministry among the women of this group happens in their weekly rehearsals. As the ladies (and often their kids) come together to enjoy rehearsal, leaders Cherelle and Tequila have INCARNATED in their lives. Actually, because this group has been together for a while and has grown deeply close, they all have INCARNATED into each other's lives. Thus, before they get into a serious rehearsal, they share about their lives, pray with one another, and minister to each other. They have INCARNATED into each other's lives also by doing a small group Bible study with each other, going to the birthday parties of each other's kids, and spending their lives together looking after one another.

This concept gets repeated so many times at our church. There is Annette Silver-Betts and the hundreds of kids whose lives she has INCARNATED through musical theater camp. There are also people like Erma Spivey and Laverne Robinson who have INCARNATED in people's lives by a simple ministry of cooking an unexpected meal for a family. And, of course, there is a woman named Marge Hoffman who has the spiritual gifts of "HELPS" like no one I've ever seen. Marge INCARNATES into people's lives simply by listening and watching for people who need help. Then, Marge quietly and humbly steps up and says, "How can I help you?"

This is how we, in the Church, get into the lives of people to be able to share Christ. This is how we, in the Church, encourage and lift up one another. How especially important it is in a time when people often use technology to avoid contact with one another and, as a result, suffer significantly from loneliness. INCARNATION isn't easy. It takes time and investment of ourselves. In the process of INCARNATING into the lives of people, sometimes they may disappoint and hurt us. But just as God is so patient with us as He INCARNATES our lives, so we are to do the same with others.

INCARNATION, when you think about it, is really simple. It's not rocket science! It all begins when we find ways to meet people where they are, and then we INCARNATE their lives. From there, we wait and see opportunities God the Holy Spirit provides for us to connect with them. The goal we want to achieve is seasoning their lives with the "salt" of the Good News (Matthew 5:13) telling us that, in Christ, "God is for us" so "Who can stand against us?" (Romans 8:31)

89

STRONG ROCK or TRANSPARENT HUMAN? BOTH

I want to make the beginning of this essay a devotional time to marvel at Jesus. As the God-man, 100% human and 100% fully God, He is extraordinary to observe. He is at the same time so UNlike you and me and so LIKE you and me. Check out the following pictures of our Lord: Matthew 8:23–27 vs. Luke 22:41–46; Mark 9:20–29 (especially verse 23) vs. John 11:33–36.

I point you to these verses to make you think about your role as a pastor/ urban ministry leader. Is the correct role for us to be the STRONG ROCK who never shows fear about any situation? Whose faith never wavers? And who never shows our own hurt or struggle with sin? Or, as a leader of other Christ followers, am I supposed to be TRANSPARENT with parts of my life—showing my struggle with temptation, openly confessing when I was wrong and even letting people know when they've hurt me? Are we simply to take every painful word or evil action people launch against us? I think you know the answers. I think you've been feeling the literary set-up. Please receive this next point.

In the same way that Jesus, the Master Shepherd/Pastor, presented Himself, the answer for us is BOTH... BOTH STRONG ROCK and TRANSPARENT HUMAN.

We are to stand as a STRONG ROCK to our people. However, not by our own power, but rather by pointing our people to the source of our strength.

The writer of Psalm 121 put it so candidly in verse 2, "My help comes from the Lord, Who made heaven and earth." When the Lord is in our corner, we can handle anything. I like how Paul said it to the Philippians, "I can handle all things through Christ who strengthens me." (Philippians 4:13, Schmidtke translation)

At the same time, people in our churches today need to see the man under the clerical robe on Sunday morning is real. We need to "keep it totally 100" with them.

Why not let our church family members see how we hurt and weep when a loved one dies? Why not let people in the church family know we struggle with temptation and sin just like they do? Of course, prudence is necessary regarding what a pastor/church leader shares and to whom he shares anything. Why not be honest with people when what they have said and what they have done have hurt you? Can't those moments be wonderful, healthy occasions to confess to one another and share forgiveness in Jesus with each other? I think it's healthy to share with people in the ministry when we are going through hard times and are feeling a little discouraged. The words of 1 Thessalonians 5:11 don't have an exemption for pastors/ urban ministry leaders.

In everything, keep on pointing people to Jesus. He is our strength. He gives us permission to be transparent, knowing His grace can cover any and every hurt and failure of our lives!

90

MOMENTS OF AWE

I do believe in miracles and signs and wonders. I see God perform them all the time. No, I've never seen someone get out of their wheelchair on the spot and start running a 40-yard dash. No, I've never seen someone walk on water like Jesus did—except one time when it was a trick. My son, Nat, did that when he was about 10 years old on a lake by my parent's house. The picture looks like he was walking on the water when, in fact, he was taking steps on submerged cinder blocks in shallow water!

Yet, I've seen God do the impossible! Let me share some of what I've seen over the past 30 years:

- People (like JH) who had been an addict for 30 years of her life and had her chains broken by the Christ!

- Young men (like AB) had their lives turned around and then grew up into Godly Christian men through our church's outreach programs.

- A local politician (FBS) pushed aside a multi-million-dollar deal for his neighborhood (that would have also made himself some money) in favor of letting us build homes for families through Better Living Communities. This has changed our church community forever.

- Two days after Christmas in the first decade of the 21st century, I got a call from a dear Christian friend (K) saying that God had directed her to underwrite most of the cost for me and eight other Bethlehem ministry leaders to go to Africa for 10 days to minister with revival outreach services.

- A dear Christian couple (JNG) who, through their extraordinary giving, have empowered Bethlehem Church to be able to live fiscally well beyond the length of my pastorate, if we stay faithful to putting the Lord first in our own giving.

- Colleagues in ministry (GB & ASB) have turned down a variety of job opportunities that would have automatically doubled their salaries, for the sake of continuing the very important missional work of Bethlehem both in and beyond our community.

- When a *coup* d'état occurred in my second year of ministry at Bethlehem to immediately vote me out as pastor, a group of older ladies in our congregation rose up and defeated that uprising (you were one of them, AW).

- A network of sister churches, foundations, and private individuals give their dynamic support to our ministry in abundant financial ways, through volunteering to serve and encouraging me—year in and year out.

Because of friends God used, I have led prayer in the presence of a United States president, received an honorary doctorate degree, watched our ministry win local civil community awards, and seen 1,000 people gather for the first groundbreaking of our housing ministry. I can't explain any of this, except it is the undeniable work of our Lord through His people!

I share with you this very small sampling of all of the signs and wonders I've seen simply to say that God is working amazing happenings around us all the time. We need to take note of them, realize how blessed we are, and "forget not all of His benefits." (Psalm 103:2)

Chronicle what the Lord is doing for you on your ministry journey.

It is so useful and needed for the hard days of ministry when you feel forgotten or discouraged.

91

GRATEFUL & THIRSTING

Sometimes one name accurately identifies a person. Cherilyn Sarkisian goes only by "Cher," and everybody knows who she is. The same was true for Prince Rogers Nelson and his one-word name, "Prince." I don't think I even knew that he was Gordon Matthew Thomas Sumner, but I certainly know the name "Sting." And in our urban community, there's only one "Beyoncé."

At Bethlehem, some wouldn't know who Stafford Bradley Dilworth is, but everybody knows "Red," his nickname. Red has lived some kind of life. In his apartment, you'll see a picture of him as a paratrooper who used to jump out of planes while in the Service. His big, James Earl Jones kind of ominous voice was well-suited for him when he worked for the St. Louis Airport Police for many years. As Red himself would tell you, he came to our ministry not long after experiencing a hard divorce that left him somewhat bitter, a little frustrated with God, and impatient in the anger department. But the Gospel of our Lord Jesus Christ has worked in him in an abundant way at Bethlehem, especially through our Men's Ministry small group Bible study. God the Holy Spirit has recreated Red into a man who is now GRATEFUL and THIRSTING.

I find the combination of those two words to be a meaningful portrait of what I personally want to grow to be as a follower of Jesus. Those two words also seem to accurately describe the Apostle Paul. I think the blend of those words would be an important place for any urban ministry leader to be. Let me explain these two words.

Compare GRATEFUL vs. complaining or whining about what life

and ministry is not. I can tell you exactly what it's like to stand at the head of the complaining line. For example, "We don't have enough money," or "We don't have enough help," or "Why can't our ministry grow like that ministry?" or "It feels as if the Lord has forgotten me."

Whining is usually with the spotlight on ME. But grateful is different. It usually takes the emphasis off me and is about recognizing the impact, gifts, and blessings SOMEONE ELSE has placed in my life. That "someone else" is our LORD, even though He often does His blessing work through the movements of His people.

What comes naturally to all of us is whining and putting our eyes on ourselves. That's what John the Baptizer knew to be true about himself when he said to his followers in John 3:30, "HE (Jesus) must increase, but I must decrease." On the other hand, it takes faith and Godly wisdom to know the truth of James 1:17. I also love how the Apostle Paul started so many of his letters to churches. He started with a GRATEFUL HEART for the people God had made them to be and for the blessings God had given them—instead of only focusing on what was wrong or deficient. That's definitely a lesson for me, maybe for you as well.

But before the lesson comes home regarding my attitude toward my church, I need to take it to my own heart. Thanks, God, for grace and forgiveness and for continuing to accept me back when I've blown it! Thanks, God, for the people You've placed around me in both my family and my extended family of friends! Thanks, God, for perfect timing in my life, even though I have fought You on it and accused You of being late so many times! (My friend Red lived that truth as he waited for a new heart to be transplanted in him. I learned from him as I watched him wait with faith.) Thanks, God, for knowing what my portion is, as Proverbs 30:8–9 outlines. There's real joy in living a life of thankfulness and working in a ministry with a grateful spirit.

Add to that grace of gratitude the word, "THIRSTING."

For my friend, Red, his deep THIRSTING is for the Scriptures so that he can know Christ better. When I watch him in Bible study, I think about

Philippians 3:10. THIRSTING needs to start with each of us and our personal relationship with God.

Admittedly, when your life as an urban ministry leader is so full of writing and teaching Bible studies, producing sermons, and being the "spiritual answer man" for a congregation of people, it's easy to set aside the personal passion of Jeremiah 15:16 (please look it up) for another time because we're too busy right now. I've been there too many times myself. Paul knew the danger well, as he wrote in 1 Corinthians 9:27. Sometimes that is also a real danger to me. Help me Holy Spirit! I have to be John, the child of God, before I am John, the pastor.

There is another THIRSTING each of us needs as urban ministry leaders. Think with me about WHAT THIRST IS. Thirst is a strong desire for something to drink. Thirst only exists until it is satisfied. Thirst has an irritating quality about it—my thirst won't let me stay in my present thirsting state because it pushes me to action. I must drink in order to have my thirst satisfied. One other thing about thirst—except in the case of coming to Jesus (John 6:25)—this side of heaven, thirst always returns. Paul spoke about the thirst that every urban ministry leader needs in Romans 10:1 when he said, "Brethren, my heart's desire and my prayer to God for them (his Jewish brothers) is for their salvation." Did you get it? With each new person I meet, I need to "thirst" that they would come to know the Savior. With the person who has been in and out of our church, and now is in a significant life crisis, my hopeful thirst needs to be, "Could this be the moment they return to the Lord with their whole heart?"

Our THIRST for everybody to know Christ launches us into thinking about new ways to meet people with the Savior: trying different approaches, taking ministry risks, and continuing to ask the question, "Why not?" instead of remaining shackled in past ministry methods that have lost their effectiveness. As we have tasted the goodness of our Lord, the THIRST of mission moves us not to give up on anyone.

GRATEFUL and THIRSTING. In the end, we who work in the city need BOTH. We need to celebrate God's blessings to us with gratitude, or we'll burn out with discouragement. But we can't sit to ourselves, comfortable that we ourselves know the Good Shepherd. As Jesus Himself said, we "must work the works of Him" who has also sent us in His name to the entire world. (John 9:4) Chew on these two words. How is your life and ministry both GRATEFUL and THIRSTING?

92

MVP

Over the years during my ministry at Bethlehem, I've received a lot of accolades and recognition for ministry that has happened. I appreciate the kind words and encouragement from people. But I know the REAL MVP of my ministry life and my life in general is my wife, Sharon Schmidtke. MVP means Most VALUABLE Person. I have so much to say. It's hard to find a place to start. But let me begin with the following statement to those of you who are thinking about going into an inner-city ministry to work.

If you're married, and your wife isn't committed to your going to lead an urban ministry, DON'T GO! If you're thinking about getting married, make sure your future wife is committed to standing by you in an urban parish, BEFORE you get married or take the assignment to an urban parish. I know I'm getting into your business, and I hope I said that right. What I want you to know is that YOUR WIFE is AN ESSENTIAL PARTNER to this ministry endeavor!

It is such an asset to have a wife who loves Christ and is a child of God. It's vital. I honor my wife because she:

- prays for me
- encourages me and cheers me on in doing God's work
- listens when I need to vent or "bounce an idea off" of her

- understands that I can't tell her everything about my ministry (things confidential stay confidential)

- compliments me about the husband I am, encourages me in what I can be, but doesn't beat me down about who I am not, even when I fall short of being who I should be

- doesn't insist on worldly extravagances for her life but actually teaches me to be content and satisfied with what the Lord gives us

- is a student of God's Word and is gifted at understanding how the deep truths of God's Word operate in practical, daily living

- isn't full of the desire for accolades and status for herself—(don't *EVER* call my wife "First Lady of Bethlehem," or you might get smacked by her)

- has the spiritual gift of "helps" and is constantly willing to help me or anybody else in any way she can

- joins me and comes with me in much of the ministry work

- is full of unending forgiveness and patience

- has sometimes played both the roles of Mom and Dad to our children

- is probably the wisest person I know on this Earth

- is someone whom the Holy Spirit has formed to be the "face and voice of the Lord" every time I look to her

I mentioned earlier that my wife grew up in the Salvation Army. She is the daughter of the greatest mother-in-law ever, the late Ruth Heiss, who was also a minister in the Salvation Army church. Again, I think the Salvation Army has a valuable model of placing workers for ministry where they rarely ever put a full-time church worker in a place alone. As I mentioned earlier, they usually send teams of at least two people. That concept is sorely needed in urban ministry places. Being alone as the leader of an urban ministry can be really hard. Even brother pastors, while they understand the ministry, don't understand the unique context of an urban ministry where there is usually significant financial struggle, transiency with people, not enough leadership, and almost a constant flow of people with problems in your office (many with problems way beyond your spiritual training). However, most urban ministries don't have the funds to have two full-time paid workers. Thus, how valuable it is for an urban ministry worker to have a wife who is supportive and stands with him in ministry.

Sharon Schmidtke is a blessing from the Lord, not just as my wife but also as my partner in this ministry.

P.S. Twenty-five years ago, Concordia Seminary invited my wife and an experienced pastor's wife, Mrs. Ida Odom, to host an evening with other pastor wives and talk about what it's like to be a pastor's wife in an urban ministry. I heard later that it was a great and very useful evening. I'm not sure why it wasn't repeated. My wife would be a great person for others to contact when their spouse is considering a call to an urban ministry.

93

F-A-M-I-L-Y

Just as having a wife who is all in when it comes to serving with you in an urban ministry, having a family that is behind you is vital as well.

Let's be real. Preacher's Kids live in a life context that was *NOT their choice*. Life as a PK can often be like living in a glass house. People think PKs should always say and do the right things. They forget that PKs are kids just like other kids. Even though holding the bar of behavior higher for them isn't fair, that is what many people in our world still do.

I can only give unending thanks to the Lord for my sons, Dan, Mike, Nat, and my daughter, Tequila. I have great kids. I also have great daughters-in-law—Amber, Genese, and Paola. And terrific grandchildren: Taylar, Joseph, Asher, Jesus, José, and TBA (a granddaughter who is already alive, but she just hasn't been born yet). My kids have been behind me in ministry at Bethlehem every step of the way. I am so grateful they know the Lord and love Him and have participated in our ministry work at Bethlehem. They've had incredible patience with me and been so sacrificial in sharing their dad with the people of our Bethlehem family and the people we reach with our Bethlehem ministry. I am so proud of the Godly Christian adults they have now become. Please be patient with me as I briefly "brag" on them:

- Dan is a deacon in our church and wise beyond his years in the ways of the Lord. He is a young man with thoughtful counsel. He has truly made our basketball ministry an outreach *ministry* of bringing Christ into the lives of young men through basketball.

- Mike is among the most spiritually-balanced people I know. He was among the team of editors who read the manuscript of these essays. God has used Mike to stretch my ministry thinking in so many ways. He has the gift to speak truth in a way that is full of love and hope!

- Nat has followed me into a vocation of full-time ministry. As a Lutheran School teacher in the primary grades, he is using his infectious love for Christ, his passionate love for young people, and his inventive mind to keep challenging the Church to answer the question, "Why not?" Why can't we try ministry in a new way that may be especially meaningful to people? The same "Let's go!" attitude that was at the heart of his athletic career, he has now transitioned into his leadership in God's Kingdom!

- Tequila, though not my biological child, is in every way my daughter. God has knit her creativity in music, dance, and drama to be a kindred spirit to mine. She is already (and will continue to be) mightily used by the Lord.

Although the Apostle John wasn't talking about biological children, what God moved him to write in 3 John 4 is really spot on, "I have no greater joy than this, to hear of my children walking in the truth."

People often wonder whether an inner-city church and community is the right place to raise a family. I'd like to make five comments that answer that inquiry with a "Yes!"

Make Your Ministry a Quality Fit for Your Kids

When Sharon and I left Christ Lutheran Church in Peoria, Illinois, where I served the first two years of my ministry, my biggest concern was for my two young sons, Dan and Mike. (Tequila and Nat weren't here yet.) We left a congregation with a top-notch Sunday School program for kids. We were coming to a congregation where my kids would basically be the only young children in the entire church! Would my kids suffer in their Christian education? *Not in God's plans.* In the first place, He had prepared a Godly woman named Mildred Holland to embrace my kids in Sunday school and Wednesday Night Bible program with her flannel graph board. Second, the Lord put before me the task of constructing a Christian education program for children that would be excellent for my kids—as well as for the kids of the community. By God's grace, we did that, and my kids never suffered. Think about it in your context. Why not work on your church's kids programs to be at the same level you'd expect in a program you would feel comfortable putting your own children into? As you train workers in that program, train them to the high standard you would expect if they taught your own children.

Shelter Your Kids?

The fear some parents express about being in an inner-city ministry is something like, "My children will be exposed to unsavory things that I don't think they should be exposed to as a child." Let's paint a more detailed picture of what those "things" are: gun violence, people dying more frequently, evil talk, racism, sexual behavior displeasing to God, drugs, unimaginable poverty, abuse of all kinds, people who want nothing to do with God, etc. That's a pretty good initial list. Certainly, these life situations are serious and out of the will of God. They can be destructive, especially to children. At the same time, in the day in which we live, they are already easily accessible to very young children via the information superhighway. Even preschoolers are already exposed on the Internet to violence and other unsavory parts of real life, if not by the video games they themselves play, then certainly by games they watch older siblings and friends play. Today, it would be impossible to quarantine any child from that.

What I think is most important is this:

Let's not leave our children to grow up in this world on their own.

Let's be close to our children when they see graphic violence or sexuality to teach them that this isn't God's way.

Let's be by the side of our children to help them understand how suddenly life can end through gun violence, but then, also, how important is our eternal confidence of life beyond death through Christ, our Savior.

Let's talk about, and even show our kids, how drugs can destroy families; yet, also, let's show our kids Christ's power to break any addictive chain.

Let's teach our kids about the power of confession and forgiveness at an early age... that through Christ and His death for our sins, we can be forgiven of any failure and live forward to know that God, in Christ, is "not counting our sins against us." (2 Corinthians 5:19)

Thirty years ago, just after I came to Bethlehem, I recall a family member saying to me, "John, I know the work in the inner-city is important, but you have little kids. Don't you think it would be better for your family for you to take a call to a suburban church and get away from all the violence?" So where should we have gone? To Columbine, Colorado, or to Sandy Hook, New Jersey—both tragic sites of massive school shootings? To a more middle-class suburban community? Where experts tell us more drug dollars are exchanged (because there is more money there), even though it's not as public because drugs are dealt in houses, rather than on street corners? You've got the point.

Your Kids Don't Have to Miss Out

I wondered about another concern when we came to Bethlehem in 1989. Will my kids miss out on opportunities because I'm in a small inner-city church, and my salary isn't high enough to leave much disposable income? NOPE! GOD HAD THAT ALL PLANNED! My kids were able to go to a Lutheran grade school and high school, not because we could afford it, but because of others whom God sent to help us pay for it! In addition, my kids didn't miss out on opportunities to play sports or be involved with music or the other arts because we created some of those programs at Bethlehem (both for my own kids and for kids of the community). God set it up! My kids had good friends, both from church and from the parochial school they attended. We got to know their friends' parents. God worked it out! My kids saw almost all of the United States from St. Louis eastward when our Gospel Choir would go on the road and my family would come along. We got to see and experience so much WHILE we were doing ministry together.

The Opportunity to Pass on Your Faith

All four of my children know their faith in Jesus Christ and *know how to pass on their faith*. They learned this through the experience of growing up at Bethlehem. My kids saw us use basketball ministry as a way to reach out to young men. My kids have been a part of our outreach in the summer when we reach new community kids through our Taking Jesus to the Streets ministry. They know clearly that to reach people with the Gospel, the best approach is not to wait on people to come to us, but for us to go to people. While in some ministries you have to wait until you become an adult to really be involved in fully serving the Lord, at Bethlehem the kids serve, youth serve, and adults serve, regardless of age! If I were to die today, I know that my kids have been trained in the spiritual heritage of their parents to trust in Christ as their Savior.

Use Your Church Family to Help Raise Your Kids

People in our church family babysat our kids when they were young when we wanted to get a night away as a couple. People in our church family have brought us special meals to give us a night free from cooking. As our kids grew into their high school years, people in our church family became the needed voices to say the same things that Sharon and I were saying to our kids, but our children needed to hear those words from somebody else's voice! We trusted their voices because we had lived our lives together around the Savior and His Word. God has those people in your congregation/ministry to help you with your kids. The hard part for most of us is that we need to squash our own pride that often thinks we need to handle every part of raising our kids by ourselves!

My Mom & Dad—Bob & Marilyn Schmidtke

It's hard to see my computer screen right now as I write the last paragraphs of this book because tears keep flooding my eyes. I don't think we would have been able to be here at Bethlehem all this time had it not been for my mom and dad and their help to our family. From their perspective, while their help has come because I am their son, it goes deeper than that. Helping us has been an important piece of their service to the Lord Jesus.

There was a time in the first years of my ministry when I had a big problem with this. I was full of pride. I thought it was a badge of strength to be independent and do everything myself, including financing everything in the care of my family.

Life changed for me one day because of a very frank conversation my dad had with me. We had been faithful listeners to the preaching of Chuck Swindoll via his tape ministry and had just listened to a sermon series Chuck preached on "Spiritual Gifts." I pushed back at my dad's offer to help our family when our van was facing some overwhelming repair bills. My dad said, **"John, why do you get to use your gift of bringing Jesus to people in the inner-city, but you won't allow me to use my gift?** I can't do what you do. But the Lord has enabled me to make a good amount of money throughout my life. I have the gift of 'extraordinary giving.' I want to use my gift to help you do your work at Bethlehem. Let me use my gift." My dad was right. I accepted. I was blessed by the Lord through my dad. My dad was blessed even more as he used his gift.

That lesson about giving has had more generational ripples than my dad and mom would even know. God used it to pour a new kind of giving into Sharon and me. And now, 30 years later, guess what? Sharon and I have watched it ripple into the next generation of giving with Dan, Mike, Nat, and Tequila, as they give to help others know Christ. And to them, like to Sharon and me, like to my dad and mom, we absolutely know that we are merely the GLOVE of GOD'S HAND.

On a personal note, there is nothing more joyous and rewarding than this—to see in my own family and in my church family how "one generation shall praise Your works to another (generation), And shall declare Your mighty acts." (Psalm 145:4) This is **THE JOURNEY THE LORD HAS ME ON.**

EPILOGUE

This book was written prior to the tragic death of George Floyd in Minneapolis, Minnesota. Yet, I wanted to express that perhaps, more than ever in my lifetime, this is the time for the Lord's Church to be the Lord's Church.

This is a historical moment for us to listen compassionately, stand for what is right, and BE the Gospel of Jesus Christ to hurting people. It seems to me that it is a moment for us:

- To talk less and listen more
- To let His love be seen in us toward others before it comes from our lips
- To let ourselves decrease and our serving in Jesus' name to increase!

Only in Christ can we find hope and healing for the forgotten places and forgotten people, even in this season!

SCRIPTURE INDEX

For your convenience, each scripture is listed by the coordinating essay number available in the Table of Contents.

GENESIS

2:15–17	45
2:16–17	79
4:9	55
12:10–20	38
18:12	38
41:14–36	78

NUMBERS

22:28	29

DEUTERONOMY

8:3	17

JOSHUA

2	56
23:14	66
24:15	32

1 SAMUEL

20:12–34	22

2 SAMUEL

11	56

1 CHRONICLES

17:16	61
29:14	36

JOB

23:10	62, 79

PSALMS

4:8	79
27:1–3	16
27:10	20, 45, 88
32:1–7	20
32:3–5	55
33:3	26
34:8–10	78
40:1–3	26
40:3	26
96:1	26
98:1	26
100:2	9
103:2	69
118	20
119:67	45
119:93	17
121	70
127:1	20
144:9	26
145:4	77
146:3–6	42
147:1	75

PROVERBS

3:5	*81*
3:5–6	*17*
11:25	*81*
12:25	*63*
15:4	*63*
16:18	*63*
18:21	*63*
22:6	*75, 76*
27:17	*29*
28:5	*87*
29:23	*42*
30:8–9	*91*

ISAIAH

1:3–18	*87*
1:18	*20, 33*
41:10	*42*
43:25	*33*
48:10	*45*
53:5	*87*
55:10–11	*76*
58:10–11	*81*
64:6	*87*

JEREMIAH

15:16	*91*

LAMENTATIONS

3:22–23	*28*

EZEKIEL

3:1–3	*38*

37:1–14	*32*

DANIEL

3	*57*
3:25	*57*
3:27	*57*

JONAH

1:4	*79*

MICAH

6:8	*87*

HABAKKUK

3:17–19	*59*

HAGGAI

2:8	*70*

MATTHEW

1:23	*88*
4:18–22	*33*
4:19	*4*
5:13	*88*
6:33	*36, 38*
7:3–5	*20*
7:13–14	*75*
8:23–27	*89*
8:32	*73*
9:9–13	*56*
10:10	*31*
10:29–31	*17, 45*
14:28–29	*83*

16:21–23	*33*	15:4–6	*15*
16	*23*	15:11–32	*45*
19:13–15	*28*	15:28–30	*55*
19:16–26	*44, 55*	19:1–10	*20*
23:37	*35*	19:10	*75*
25:14–30	*50, 61*	19:8	*38*
25:34–40	*80*	19:41	*35*
26:68–75	*33*	19:42	*35*
27:54	*32*	22:41–46	*89*

MARK

JOHN

1:21–39	*19*	3:30	*91*
1:40–41	*88*	3:36	*75*
2:14–17	*65*	4:10, 14	*13*
3:31–35	*20*	4:16–19	*56*
4:3–9, 13–20	*38*	4:31–34	*17*
5:1–5	*73*	6	*5*
5:25–28	*55*	6:14	*58*
8:36	*80*	6:25	*91*
9:14–29	*70*	6:26–27	*30, 58, 80*
9:20–29	*89*	6:35	*13, 88*
16:15	*10, 19, 30, 36, 40, 45*	8	*33*
		8:7	*33*
16:16	*75*	8:3–11	*20*

LUKE

		9:4	*91*
4:16	*66*	10:14	*10*
6:36	*80*	11:20–35	*55*
8:2	*33*	11:25	*75*
10:7	*31, 84*	11:33–36	*89*
11:28	*17*	15:5	*33, 45*
12:15–21	*44, 55*	16:33	*38*
15:3–7	*76*	19:25–27	*20*

20:11–18	*33*
21:15–17	*33, 35*

ACTS

1:8	*68, 85*
2:38	*3*
4:7–13, 18–20	*33*
4:32	*20*
4:36–37	*81*
8:1	*3*
9	*33*
9:26–27	*22, 81*
13:1–12	*22*
13:13	*67*
15:36–41	*67, 82*
16:13	*22*
17:22–34	*8, 13*
18:3–4	*40*
18:24–28	*82*
20:23	*42*
22:3	*40*

ROMANS

1:16	*8, 13, 59*
1:26–28	*87*
3:10–12	*65*
3:23	*33*
4:16	*38*
5:8	*75*
7:18–19	*33*
8:31	*88*
10:1	*91*
10:9	*4*
10:17	*4, 20*

1 CORINTHIANS

3:6	*12, 34*
3:7	*61*
6:19–20	*87*
4:2	*50*
9:14	*31*
9:19–23	*4*
9:27	*91*
10:13	*62*
10:24	*36*
12	*42*
12:12–31	*35*
15:9–10	*20*
15:10	*33*
15:56–57	*75*
15:58	*23, 76*

2 CORINTHIANS

1:4	*17*
2:17	*40*
4:4	*81, 88*
5:14–15	*36*
5:15	*81*
5:17	*79*
5:19	*93*
5:20	*66*
5:21	*84*
6:18	*20*
8:1–3	*47*
9:7	*53*

GALATIANS

1:8	*73*
3:26–29	*36*
6:1	*20, 33, 65*
6:9	*42*
6:10	*30, 80*

EPHESIANS

2:8	*75*
2:19	*8*
2:19–22	*36*
3:20	*5*
3:20–21	*38*
4:7–16	*63*
4:31	*20*
4:32	*20*
6:11–12, 17	*65*
6:12	*16*
6:17	*73*

PHILIPPIANS

2:3ff.	*17*
2:3–4	*81*
2:4	*9*
2:5–11	*9*
2:13	*17*
3:4–6	*40*
3:10	*91*
3:20	*56, 79, 87*
4:13	*89*
4:19	*70*

COLOSSIANS

3:13–15	*73*
3:23	*49*

1 THESSALONIANS

5:4–11	*65*
5:11	*65*

1 TIMOTHY

1:2	*82*
1:12	*42*
1:12–16	*65*
1:15	*75*
1:18	*82*
2:4	*61*
4:7–8	*65*
5:18	*31, 84*
6:10	*44*

2 TIMOTHY

1:2	*82*
1:10	*16*
2:1	*82*
2:4 3	*8*
2:13	*42, 75*
2:15	*37, 64, 71*
3:10–17	*8*
3:15–17	*59*
4:11	*67*

HEBREWS

4:12–16	*18*
8:12	*33*

10:23–25	*22, 27*		4:10–11	*6*
11:11	*38*		5:2	*42*
12:2	*35*		5:8	*59*
12:3	*35*			
13:8	*58*		**2 PETER**	
			3:9	*33, 38*
JAMES				
1:17	*91*		**1 JOHN**	
2:14–18	*17*		1:7	*33, 65*
2:18	*22*		1:9	*10, 20*
3:1–12	*17*		4:4	*16, 73*
			4:11	*67*
1 PETER			4:19	*20*
3:5–6	*38*			
3:18	*75*		**3 JOHN**	
4:8	*37*		4	*93*

TOPICAL INDEX

For your convenience, each topic is listed by the coordinating essay number available in the Table of Contents.

ACCOUNTABILITY
    Ministry *10, 40, 60, 61, 66, 71, 78, 79, 80, 84, 86*
    Social Ministry *30*

BALANCE *11, 40, 72*

CALLING
    On people *4*

CHANGE *13*

CHILDREN'S MINISTRY *28, 32, 43, 66, 77*

CHURCH BUSINESS *84, 85, 86*

CHURCH FAMILY *22*

CONFLICT RESOLUTION *14*

CREATIVE THINKING *5, 7, 32, 41, 43, 76, 77, 78, 83*

DEVELOPING LEADERS *9, 17, 21, 23, 41, 42, 56, 59, 63, 64, 72, 76, 77, 82, 84, 85, 86*

DISCIPLINE *9*

ENCOURAGEMENT *1, 5, 8, 16, 20, 27, 42, 45, 62, 63, 67, 69, 70, 75, 76, 81, 89, 90, 91, 92, 93*

ENTREPRENEURISM *40, 54*

EVANGELISM *4, 19, 32, 64*

FELLOWSHIP *22*

FIXING PROBLEMS *2*

FUNDING *3, 40, 41, 47, 48, 49, 50, 51, 52, 53, 54*

GOALS
  Setting *10*

GOD
  Keeping us *16*

GOD, THE HOLY SPIRIT *32*

GOD'S WORD
  Growth in *42, 55, 59, 73*
  Power *18, 36, 38, 73, 75*

GRATITUDE *53, 62, 69, 90, 91, 92*

LONGEVITY *50, 60, 66*

LOW DAYS *1, 16, 45, 57, 62*

MEMORIZATION *24*

MINISTRY
  Bi-vocational *40*
  Context *2*
  Disappointment *20, 35, 39, 45, 57, 58*
  Disruption *23, 71*
  Evaluating *10, 40, 46, 47, 56, 60, 61, 66, 68, 71, 79, 86, 87*
  Focus *12*
  Holistic *2, 3*
  Longevity *50*
  Motive *1*
  Old vs. New *8, 46*
  Opportunity *3, 40, 46, 60*

Partnerships   *6, 49, 76*
Planning   *4*
Portions   *25, 26*
Priorities   *19*
Programming   *5, 56, 59, 60, 64, 78, 79, 88*
Social   *30*
Support   *6, 60*

MISSION   *33, 35, 68, 80, 85*

MUSIC MINISTRY   *24, 25, 26, 76*

PEOPLE
Connecting to   *13, 56, 70, 79, 86*
Stewardship   *7*
Transiency   *3, 56*
Understanding   *2, 44, 54, 55, 56, 57, 58, 63, 79, 81, 86*

PERSONAL LIFE   *11, 35, 39, 44, 50, 51, 65, 67, 69, 70, 72, 83, 87, 88, 90, 92, 93*

PRAYER   *35, 70*

PREACHING   *37, 73, 74, 75*

REALNESS   *10, 60, 61*

RECOVERY   *20, 33, 70*

RELATIONSHIPS   *15, 67*

SELF
Destructive power   *18*

SERVING   *17*

SHEPHERDING PEOPLE   *15, 34, 35, 38, 56, 58, 59, 63, 71, 76, 79, 86, 88, 89*

SOCIAL MINISTRY   *30, 77, 80*

SPIRITUAL GROWTH   *17, 22, 42, 55, 59, 65, 71, 73, 91*

STAFF
Compensation   *31*
Full-time vs. Part-time   *31*
Volunteer   *31, 41*

STEWARDSHIP   *40*

STRENGTH
In adversity   *8*

STUDYING
God's Word   *17*

SUNDAY WORSHIP   *13*

TEAMWORK   *42, 72*

TIME MANAGEMENT   *34, 37*

TRANSFORMATION
Congregation   *8, 36, 37, 43, 46, 78, 79*

URBAN
Context   *8, 40, 56, 66, 68, 81, 83, 84, 85, 87, 88*

VISION   *78, 79, 84*

WORDS
Care with   *14*

WORSHIP   *13, 24, 25, 26, 28, 43, 64, 73, 74, 75, 77*

Thanks for your purchase of *A Place Not Forgotten*.

Quantity Discounts are available for *A Place Not Forgotten* if you would like to purchase additional copies for your study group.

Groups are using a selection of the essays as discussion starters to improve the ministry effectiveness of their church.

The best way to save on multiple copies is by contacting us direct at schmidtkestuff@gmail.com

Information on Quantity Pricing and other resources, including the video presentation of the poem, "Fight For Me Before," can be seen at schmidtkestuff.com.